NONPROFIT MONEYBALL

Nonprofit Moneyball

How To Build And Future Proof Your Team For Big League Fundraising

RYAN GINARD, CFRE

CONTENTS

ACKNOWLEDGMENTS

The past two years have been relatively big for me and my family, with the cornerstone of this period being the move back to Australia after residing in the U.S. for over a decade (and this will be the first time living overseas for my wife and kids). In what was a very busy period of change, I'm glad I had my writing to continue to ground me in my values, understand the progress (and work to do) of the broader social sector, and most of all continue to provide me with a cathartic avenue in which to ideate what the future of our field could look like.

My work was boosted somewhat in size and scope because of the surprising success of my last book Future Philanthropy. But rather than that be an exclamation point, one where I could continue to push the themes and ideas in a variety of different ways, through different lenses, or piggyback on some recent reports or trending news topics, I decided to push on and continue to explore new aspects of what makes our field great.

I initially thought that this would be through the continued commentary and deconstructing of the tech 'that came next' given how fast it's evolving. The significant gains being seen by the social sector as a result of its adoption, but alas, people kept coming back to the talent pillar and the concept of 'Nonprofit Moneyball.' That thesis - which was just one chapter upon publication - has now spawned all sorts of conversations across a range of different mediums including keynote speeches, podcasts, and opinion pieces.

Given I'm one of those folks that have strong opinions, loosely held, I would have been ignoring the 'data' as it were and taking an uninformed lane for what my readers wanted to learn more about. So, I doubled down on exploring and understanding what the skills were (both hard, soft, and transferable) that made fundraisers good at their jobs, and then pushed back against traditional approaches to see whether there were ways we could tip the scales in their favor to ultimately help them become even better at their craft.

I have met many people as a result of my first book. They have expanded my thinking exponentially, and to be honest, my hope for this sector in a world where sometimes institutional readiness is an easier sell than institutional change.

Yet many people have been ready for a while now, and they are the ones that are genuinely changing the way we look at, understand, use, and improve the impact of philanthropy, tech for good, and all the ways they both intersect broader society. With that being said, I wanted to give a shout-out to folks that personify this and have ultimately impacted my approach to this new missive.

Pearl Hoeglund, Jack Alotto, Alex Pittman, Jared Aaker, Jim Dries, Mark Hobbs, Rachel Crosbie, Zak Richards, Jack Heath, Andrew Leigh, Louis Diez, Robert Foster, Simon Rycraft, and Mitch Stein. Y'all are doing amazing things in all corners of the sector.

A big thanks also to those who have recently written books that have influenced my thinking including Jason Lewis, Kris Putnam-Walkerly, Blair Sadler, Evan Wildstein, Nathan Chappell, and Beth Breeze.

To my colleagues at the Australian National University including Alex Furman and the other College Heads of Advancement, Eric Billman (and his wife Sandra), Arik Thormahlen, Brooke Disney, Andi Morris, and Kellie Takenaka. And those who have been with me in the trenches, teaching me more than I could teach them - Anthony Chan, Brigid Lacey, and Enrica Luo.

And finally, a heartfelt thank you to the Advisors at Fundraise for Australia who have helped me get this exciting organization up and running and guided an informed version of progress, deterring me from simply marauding across the country trying to pattern past approaches that could 'Americanize' our philanthropy. You are all fantastic and way too generous with your time. Heather Little, Nigel Harris, David Sloan, Rosheen Singh, Krystian Seibert, and Nicola Britton you are all a testament to our profession, and I look forward to working with you to drive some genuinely audacious goals as we contribute to the Australian Government's push to double giving by 2030.

I also want to acknowledge my dyslexia for the first time. I know that seems rather left field, but it's something I uncovered whilst writing my last book (at 39 no less) and became evident through some intentional values-based coaching with the brilliant Caroline Crawford. No big deal, it just meant I finally had some clarity around a few things that never really 'added up.' To then discover it was something a number of my family had too (which had been a taboo subject for decades) helped start dismantling the stigma of what it is and what it means for those that have it.

It's safe to say I now tackle things differently and with a newfound relief that some of my most significant weaknesses could be chipped away at with new strategies and approaches. Dyslexia also makes my writing unique in many ways as it's more a tapestry of ideas rather than writing in a traditional story arc. It also leads to more creativity in my thinking as I pretty much run out of focus when reading articles, so I read the first couple of paragraphs, skim the middle, and then read the conclusion, effectively reverse engineering in my head what might have contributed to the findings. I joke that I have never read my book, well not in the traditional way, and I guess that's what helps, not poring over every last word so I get caught in the perfect.

And that's where I'll end it, with my version of perfect, my little family of Diane, Roman, and Ruby. I appreciate all you are and thank you for letting me pick my pen up when you all fall asleep. Love you.

INTRODUCTION

Fundraising is a team sport.

While it might sometimes feel like a genuinely lonely endeavor, the playing field represents an ocean of opportunity full of big plays and tactics to move the chains. This book is dedicated to those wanting to learn more about the 'game' of fundraising and all the things that go into being successful at it from an organizational and individual perspective.

While littered with sporting analogies and puns, the goal of this book is to provide you with that playbook to win.

And, you know what? I want you to win, and I want your organizations to win because, at the end of the day, those you serve need you to win.

What exactly is winning in the nonprofit sector? Is it raising more funds? Is it serving more people? Or are they the cause and effect of success? If you strip down the mission and vision statements of organizations, is winning a case of putting yourself out of business? Because to me, that needs to be the motivator, because if we are simply in this field to keep ourselves in jobs or simply to play the role of civic triage, then we have ultimately lost before even lacing up our boots.

I first conceptualized Nonprofit Moneyball after, yes, you guessed it, watching the hit movie with Brad Pitt and Jonah Hill ("Moneyball," 2011). I re-watched it during the COVID lockdowns when I was midway through writing (the now international award-winning book) Future Philanthropy, ideating the jobs of tomorrow and how the sector might go about identifying the talent that would fill those integral roles.

The movie, which was released in 2010 was based on the Michael Lewis book Moneyball: The Art of Winning an Unfair Game which chronicled the Oakland Athletics 2002 season (Lewis, 2003). The book, and movie, showcased how Oakland was so successful while having one of the lowest payrolls in baseball.

The "Moneyball" thesis was simple: Using statistical analysis, small-market baseball teams like the A's could change their odds for success by accruing assets that are undervalued or overlooked by other teams (and selling over-valued ones). Through a fundraising lens, this thesis could be compared to a small organization regularly securing large donations traditionally captured by larger national entities and institutions such as medical research organizations, hospitals, global humanitarian organizations, and more.

But back to the inspiration for this book. The standard statistics used to judge Major League Baseball (MLB) players were traditionally - up until that point - batting average, stolen bases, and runs batted in. However, Billy Beane and his staff discovered these statistics were secondary to on-base and slugging percent-ages. It was cheaper for the A's therefore to find players that performed well in these categories, and it paid off in the wins column once the team gelled.

The "Moneyball" concept was heavily contested in the A's organization and around the league because the conventional scouting method was being over-thrown. That was never Beane's goal, and it has not occurred in the MLB today. Scouts are still prevalent, but the idea of enhanced statistical analysis has become a critical part of baseball.

"Moneyball" changed the game in countless ways, from the scouting depart-ment to the actual on-field play. Prioritizing on-base and slugging percentages led to more technology and enhanced statistics. It also helped pitchers figure out how to attack batters, leading to higher strikeout rates. Now a game has three actual outcomes (home run, walk, or strikeout) which occur approximately 35% of the time ("Three True Outcomes," n.d.).

It has also made coaches handle pitching differently. Starters do not throw as many innings because relievers often have a better statistical chance to get a batter out by the third time through the order.

Analytics have also caused managers to shift their defenses depending on the batter. If a defender overwhelmingly moves to the right or left side of the infield, you will often see a batter hit the ball directly into the shift. The shift is thanks to tools like dispersal maps for hitters.

This isn't a simple numbers game though, because in today's society, where nonprofit sector information is more accessible and transparent than ever, it's not just the mission or history of the more established organizations that yields more significant donations. There are considerable disparities at play, including the ability to secure the very best in fundraising talent and the systems and tech that support their continued success.

Fundraising for smaller organizations is challenging. You are more often than not wearing many hats. You are also inversely disadvantaged through your own success - through higher expectations, the need to raise more funds to keep up with service demand, and so on. And when there are lean spells, you are the first to feel the pressure from those previously singing your praises.

If you're raising money for a small nonprofit organization, what's compounding the issue is that your donor base and prospect pipelines are much shallower than more prominent organizations in your space. Most nonprofits traditionally have only enough liquidity to last three months if the funding dries up (Sanchez, 2021). Salaries from these nonprofits are also modest at best in a time when costs of living are far outpacing wage growth and regular Consumer Price Index (CPI) increases.

In short, if you're fundraising for an entity with an annual budget below $1 million, you face the constant threat of job insecurity and are (probably) underpaid. In addition, your chances of exceeding your fundraising expectations are stacked against you as you compete against large development teams. And that doesn't even include the marketing, event, and research support these teams have the luxury of tapping into organization-wide.

"Moneyball" is a defining storyline for the professionalization of sports. Statistical analysis has become a key driver for progress in professional major league franchises, with organizations looking for any edge as they chase sporting immortality. This also rings true in other sectors. For example, a financial analyst can use stats to help them find undervalued stocks and bonds. So why are nonprofits so slow to use additional data points to assist with talent identification in fundraising and the processes that underpin them?

This Moneyball thesis has been far and away the most remarked-on concept from Future Philanthropy. It has been the genesis for several keynote speeches, webinars, and articles. It gave me the data point to determine what our practitioners want to discuss, learn more about, and inject into their organizations.

I'm also a sports junkie at my core so it's easy to draw those all-important comparisons. It's also why I write about professional sports teams as trustworthy anchor institutions for the communities they represent. I'm strangely more a fan of the administration of teams than the actual gameplay, always looking beyond the game to the individual and team stats, the strengths and weaknesses of the players and the schedule, and most importantly what defines a winning team culture.

I also put theory into practice when I formed a brand-new soccer club that would go on to become a staple of the community, an inclusive organization that provided more than just a place to play soccer, but a place where people felt they belonged regardless of whether they were a player, volunteer, or supporter.

That team was Springfield United, which now is one of the biggest clubs, in one of the fastest-growing communities in Australia with over 1000 players and 80 teams (Springfield United, n.d.). Being the founder and founding president of this club is one of the proudest moments in my life. The fact that it has just celebrated its 15th anniversary and has its own craft beer shows that great things can happen with hard work and surrounding yourself with those who share your vision.

And yes, I apply those same principles to building teams in my role as a fundraiser too.

Good fundraisers are hard to find, difficult to retain, and expensive to replace. What if we took the time to identify the people with the right skills and complementary experiences and partnered them with the organizations that best represented their values and passions, gave them the training to hit the ground running, and supported them with the tech and tools to empower their own fundraising success?

Creating an innovative nonprofit is difficult, especially without the right talent. Hiring the right employees for the right roles at the right time is critical, and this requires good resource management. That's why we need to lean more on HR data and, in the future, look to new approaches and tools that can help with our decision-making.

Professional sports teams today are big businesses and have changed exponentially over the past 30 years from the days our parents used to remember. Nonprofit organizations would be wise to follow suit because in reality a 501 c 3 is a tax designation, not a business model, but not a model with ready-made solutions you can simply pull off the shelf. Growth comes with an ask in our game, and that ask is typically executed by a fundraiser.

Your development lead is ultimately your quarterback of fundraising. The plays are drawn up by leadership in the form of strategic planning and budgeting, but it is the quarterback's job to ensure the plays are executed. Touchdowns can be scored by running backs (CEOs), wide receivers (board members and volunteers), and sometimes even the quarterback themselves. It is about positioning yourselves in the best way possible to be successful and why, like a quarterback, they need the support of their coach and team.

Like quarterbacks, fundraisers are central to all fundraising efforts and expensive to replace. Nonetheless, the typical tenure for a Director of Development is 16 months. Is that enough time to develop a mature portfolio and build up the networks, infrastructure, and messaging to be successful? The answer is no. It is more often than not that results are seen in the following 16 months. And yet, according to Simply Benefits Marketing, the average cost of replacing mid-level staff members is approximately 150% of the position's salary (Simply Benefits, 2022). Considering the monetary cost, along with the effect on donor relationships and institutional knowledge, the cost of replacing a Director of Development is much higher. But it wouldn't be Nonprofit Moneyball if we just accepted these stats. Do you as an organization want a fundraiser to stay long term or the best fundraiser available who could come in for two years and help you level up in major gifts and pipeline building? Some quarterbacks are more successful in certain formations, so this is what you need to weigh up.

However, to ensure the coach and their team support a nonprofit's quarterback, they must be trained and have access to educational resources to improve their performance. Unlike quarterbacks, fundraisers do not often benefit from a positive perception within the sector, let alone their organizations. So, while a seismic shift in how they are viewed needs to occur, beginning by investing in your fundraisers is a step in the right direction.

Look, this is a book for fundraisers, with some extra love for those slogging it out on frontlines on behalf of small to medium nonprofit organizations. One's with small budgets but big hearts, big ideas, and most of all big determination. The ones that aren't necessarily looking outside the box but looking objectively from a totally different one. Those that are new to the field and eager to learn more, and those that might be looking for a guide or flash of inspiration to level up their work and career.

Each chapter is filled with stats and tips to ensure this book has both cause and effect and, in some way, gets your mind to think that you are always just one visit away from a million-dollar gift. And that visit isn't just a speculatory cliché either, we show that with good values, habits, and data, you can uncover those one-in-a-million gems.

So how do we build a strong, dynamic, championship-winning caliber team? In Nonprofit Moneyball we will talk about everything from identifying and recruiting talent, building up our support base, strengthening operations, and finally, discussing the advances in our field that will drive greater efficiencies and effectiveness from our staff and the processes that support them. We also share the stats that are helping inform better decision-making and will help you justify any changes you deem necessary as a result of reading this book.

I hope the pages ahead will give you everything you need to develop your own playbook, knowing that fundraising success can be driven by strategy and execution together with the grit, passion, and determination that separates good and great. Remember, fundraising need not be a hail mary into the end zone, that one big swing for the fences at the bottom of the 9th inning, or the buzzer beater from the halfway line. It is both an art and a science and something that can be learned and systematized.

So, what are you waiting for, grab your cleats and let's hit the field!

Disclaimer.

Moneyball is a 2011 film based on the non-fiction book of the same name by Michael Lewis, and while the film is based on actual events, some of the details have been altered for dramatic effect. In reality, Billy Beane did make several bold moves that helped the Oakland A's become a competitive team despite having one of the lowest payrolls in Major League Baseball. However, not all the moves shown at the movie's end were entirely accurate. Some of which I use as examples here in the book.

For example, the film portrays Beane as having saved his job by implementing his new strategy, but in reality, Beane had already been given a contract extension before the 2002 season.

Overall, while the film takes some liberties with the facts, it does accurately capture the essence of Beane's unconventional approach to building a winning team. The success of the 2002 Oakland A's and the impact of Beane's strategy can be seen in the team's continued competitiveness and the adoption of similar approaches by other baseball teams.

Pre-Season Training For Fundraisers

Pre-season for professional sports teams is a period of time before the regular season begins, during which the team participates in a series of practice games, also known as exhibition games, to prepare for the upcoming season.

During the pre-season, professional sports teams may train intensively to improve their skills, conditioning, and teamwork. The team may use these exhibition games to test new strategies and lineups, evaluate new players, and determine the team's strengths and weaknesses.

Pre-season games are often played against other professional sports teams or college teams, and they may take place in various locations, including the team's home stadium or other venues around the country or internationally.

Pre-season games are typically less important than regular season games, and the outcomes of these games do not affect the team's standing in the regular season. However, pre-season games can be a valuable opportunity for teams to fine-tune their skills and prepare for the challenges of the regular season.

You also get heightened pre-season expectations for teams via predictions or projections from fans, media, and analysts based on their pre-season performances and roster changes.

However, it is essential to note that pre-season expectations are not always accurate predictors of how well a team will perform during the regular season. Many factors can impact a team's performance during the regular season, and a team's success during the pre-season does not necessarily guarantee success in the regular season.

Pre-season from a fundraiser perspective is the time spent a few months from the start of a new fiscal or calendar year where annual goals and metrics are devised and woven into the larger organizational goals.

I wanted to tackle this theme more as a primer for the content ahead rather than capturing the essence of the book through a foreword. I also wanted to give some quick actionable steps for your day-to-day work as a way of getting your mind thinking about the future and what it could be, and the beauty of this is you don't even have to get out your chair to build that fundraising muscle for the games ahead!

VISION MAPPING & STRATEGIC PHASING - A NEW PLAN FOR NONPROFIT GROWTH AND IMPACT

Where is the bold & courageous leadership of yesteryear? The leadership that is awe-inspiring, engaging, and future-focused? The leadership that writes those timeless quote graphics we see shared virally on a daily basis?

Well, the last one goes to the crux of this deep angst of mine. The last one actually highlights the current issues of leadership. The quest for the perfect soundbite, an aspirational rhetoric that lacks any real policy substance because it's structured in a way that grants the speaker flexibility if they need to pivot from bad outcomes, and the populist pandering to an individual's base rather than sticking their neck out for something because they feel morally compelled to – because it's what's right, not what's right now.

For me, the absence of authentic civic leadership both individually and organizationally is because we seek to capture our strategic thinking in a strategic plan. Our big-picture thinking is literally confined to a 3-year time period. While it is aligned with our mission, vision, and values, it is ultimately just a document that captures the thinking at a specific point in time, to be revisited three years later with (more than likely) new board members, a new moderator (a critical role in setting the agenda and moving the conversation) and an appetite for significant changes rather than informed and/or compounding progress.

Strategic plans stifle nonprofit innovation. They are outdated relics of the corporate sector that we are told are necessary to guide our work yet are more symbolic gestures of what we might achieve if we 'stick to the plan.' That is hyperbole, but do you know one organization that revisited its strategic plan during COVID? Not really. How could they? Many were just fighting to try and keep the doors open and the lights on rather than focusing on seeing an increase of 10% across a range of operational metrics that seem pretty insignificant amid a global pandemic.

While researching this piece I found an article in the Harvard Business Review (Kaplan, 1994) that hit the nail on the head as to my thinking. That article was published in 1994 which only goes to show how wild it is that we still follow this practice as the gold standard for nonprofit planning.

When strategic planning arrived on the scene in the mid-1960s, corporate leaders embraced it as "the one best way" to devise and implement strategies that would enhance the competitiveness of each business unit. True to the scientific management pioneered by Frederick Taylor, this one best way involved separating thinking from doing and creating a new function staffed by specialists: strategic planners. Planning systems were expected to produce the best strategies and step-by-step instructions for carrying out those strategies so that the doers, the managers of businesses, could not get them wrong. As we now know, planning has not exactly worked out that way.

While certainly not dead, strategic planning has long since fallen from its pedestal. But even now, few people fully understand the reason: strategic planning is not strategic thinking. Indeed, strategic planning often spoils strategic thinking, causing managers to confuse real vision with manipulating numbers. And this confusion lies at the heart of the issue: the most successful strategies are based on visions, not plans.

Look, strategic plans were created to provide a step-by-step plan for organizational staff to execute the board's goals.

Tanya Prive in a recent Inc. article (Prive, 2016) states that while strategic planning is great, in theory, more often than not it fails. "It turns out, giving someone a plan is far less effective than aligning your team on a vision or endpoint — meaning, getting people clear on where they need to go as the starting point. That's the difference between strategic planning (analysis) and strategic thinking (synthesis)."

And why 3 years? Was this to ensure the avoidance of the abject failures of the 5-year plans that were a notorious part of the old Soviet regime?

I get it. It's much like the genesis for political cycles of 3 – 4 years. You need just enough time to execute your ideas and show results, but not so long that the playing field could significantly change or the data that has informed those plans becomes somewhat outdated.

I have been the lead staff member for two strategic plans now. I have challenged their importance and challenged those that ideated them to think bigger and through a future-focused lens of what could be. And for the most part, we created something better, revisited the vision and values, and in one instance updated the organization's mission based on the evolving nature of our organization, the members it served and the sector at large.

I learned a great deal from these processes.

My suggestion for change would be to lean more into the visioning parts of organizational planning (would you expect anything less from the continued optimism of a philanthropic futurist?) This would result more in 'strategic phases' becoming the short to medium-term norm/guide and the organization's mission, vision, and values being continuously seen as the north star.

The phases would not be as rigid as 3-year plans based on calendar or fiscal year dates, allowing for them to be extended if the strategy, projects, and outcomes are leading to sustained growth, and also to be wound up early if they are not working or the environment of which they were operating in has substantially shifted.

Think of it as chapters of a book. Not all of them are the same length, some share significant plotlines and reveals, while others set the tone and slowly build suspense. Some books also become a series, all built off of the progress or main characters' narrative arc established in the previous book.

Continuing the character's analogy, board terms don't have to align with traditional norms. There is no need to lose stellar board members because they have served for a certain number of years. Having them serve for phases allows them to stay as long as needed, help on board and train new members, and also have natural jump-off points to exit the organization than abruptly resigning mid-term because they 'don't have the time anymore.'

This approach can also help with seamless leadership changes and ensure they build on past successes rather than forge their own path. Some organizations have 3-year leadership cycles where there is an incoming chair, chair, and past chair that operate as a three-headed dragon to great success, and which would fit this phasing approach tremendously.

Key characters such as staff can also benefit from this strategic phasing approach. This includes talent pipelines, executive officer contracts (and their extensions), and professional training that will lift up the focused work of that period of growth.

Strategic phasing can also support both progress and provide a safety net should expectations not be met. Stretch goals can be factored in and triggered once milestones are hit, rather than patting ourselves on the back when we tick off a goal a year early. They can also provide the scaffolding for the next strategic phase. As I mentioned, if goals are not being met, that phase can be wound down and a new one started. COVID would have been a prime example of what might have caused a reassessment of goals in relation to the vision of an organization, whether a realignment based on a new virtual form of delivery or the added costs of service delivery vis a vis declining revenue.

At the end of the day, social sector organizations don't need to follow a traditional model for determining the actions that will help them achieve their goals. They don't answer to shareholders, and their models for scale just aren't comparable. If an organization is successful, they have to raise more funds and hire more staff, they don't benefit from the economies of scale that underpin business, they can't make things 'cheaper' as there are in some instances literally lives at stake.

The strategy ultimately describes how the ends (goals) will be achieved by the means (resources). A piece of paper that guides that process during a finite time period, which has more than likely been generated by the bureaucratic theater of a board retreat won't make it more successful. It's like providing grants – pulling funding if they don't hit certain milestones, rather than asking why they are not hitting them, can they use more money or can we provide more technical assistance to help them succeed.

So, let's rethink what strategic planning looks like and realize that the traditional outputs shouldn't be boxes to be ticked, but opportunities to excel.

'REFACTORING' YOUR NONPROFITS GOVERNANCE – A NEW CULTURE FOR PROACTIVE INTERNAL IMPROVEMENTS

The expression "cutting of red tape" is something that politicians and corporate CEOs alike have mainly reserved. More often than not they are referring to the reduction of bureaucratic largesse which can sometimes slow down action. Still, depending on the context, delivery, and ultimately influence of those making the calls, it can also be used as a cloaked rationale for the reduction or removal of protective standards or regulations.

At the end of the day, there is good red tape – the type that has checks, and balances and acts as a procedural watchdog. There are indeed good cases for the removal of unnecessary bureaucracy that has either become duplicated across jurisdictions or has become outdated or obsolete in an ever-evolving society. Laws and regulations can become dated and that's something that warrants review. Just take Florida Statute 876.12 (Florida Statutes, § 876.12) which prohibits wearing masks or hoods covering the face in public – something that seemed strange in 2019 and even more so when we entered a full-blown global pandemic.

When it comes to tech there is definitely a case for further regulation, yet that is more from a reactionary standpoint as tech advances are far outpacing the legislative branch's ability to make informed decisions on things that are continuing to create mass upheaval in industries all across our economy. I mean, since 2000 one of the fastest bills I could find that went from introduction to enactment was the National Do-Not-Call Registry (Federal Trade Commission, n.d.) back in 2003 which took 6 weeks to pass.

Take electric scooters for example. Just a couple of years ago they were just an expensive niche market, and then overnight there were hundreds adorning the streets of every major U.S. city (or littering depending on who you asked). Local laws have been pieced together as they began to understand this new mode of transportation, knowing that fully regulating them immediately might end up stifling something that could become an integral part of an urban active transport mix.

So what mechanisms might exist for society to move beyond band-aid policies and ordinances, and more importantly see more good red-tape moves that won't be unraveled or repealed when a new administration comes to power?

The solutions to how we deal with tech regulations that affect our communities might actually come from the methodologies that fuel the tech space itself. *Refactoring.*

In computer programming and software design, code refactoring is the process of restructuring existing computer code – changing the factoring – without changing its external behavior. Refactoring is intended to improve the design, structure, and/or implementation of the software while preserving its functionality.

The term was coined by Thoughtworks (a software delivery company) Chief Scientist Martin Fowler, who in 2003 sought to understand the origins of the word (Fowler, 2005) and then became the prominent voice on it, eventually culminating in the book 'Refactoring' which was released in 2018 (Fowler & Beck, 2018).

The critical point I want to make here is that there is scope here to identify and implement a disciplined technique for restructuring an existing body of service delivery, altering its internal structure without changing its external behavior. Improving existing laws without striking them down in their entirety (unless that approach is needed).

A refactoring of society as it were, and a process that might want to be adopted by the social sector in the first instance as a way to improve grantmaking and service delivery, be more risk tolerant and not beholden to 'well that's the way we have always done it' and 'if it's not broken why fix it?' *The latter of course being the most pessimistic thing one can say.*

Pessimists would also say that in principle, all regulations for which the expected social costs exceed their expected social benefits should be eliminated. Still, in practice, this economic viewpoint refuses to seek the context and nuance of our society. Pro-growth approaches are not necessarily nation-building processes in this instance.

From a non-profit standpoint, it would be great if your governance committees looked at the refactoring principle as a mechanism for internal improvements, reviewing programs and internal policies periodically to see if they hit their goals and broader organizational missions. Making recommendations for change could be moved more frequently in board and executive meetings to ensure seamless and proactive improvements to the vitality and effectiveness of the organization (and evidence-based decisions).

The annual board retreat just doesn't cut it. Reacting to an incident that exposes your outdated policies and leaves you liable certainly doesn't cut it. And if you are happy for your board to meet once a month and just have them perform bureaucratic theater, then you might want to consider cuts of a different nature.

These changes shouldn't be restricted to just policies and regulations either. Program delivery, staffing structure, and budget lines (from a cost-benefit perspective) should not be taken off the table either. Looking at these items however needs to come with the caveat that those trying to 'refactor' the organization are there to identify items for review through informed recommendation, not micromanage the day-to-day operations of the organization.

Fowler says it best, "When a software system is successful, there is always a need to keep enhancing it, to fix problems and add new features."

With this mindset, a refactoring approach to nonprofit governance might also see recommendations of tech and automation enhancements that will serve the 'back of the house' all while freeing up time to do the most critical work – serving your community.

And yes, this is something that might serve our legislative and executive branches well too, but that's a rabbit hole I'm advising myself not to go down, but happy to discuss it if you have any questions!

100 SMALL WAYS TO LIFT UP YOUR NONPROFIT CAREER THIS YEAR WITHOUT REALLY TRYING...

I wanted to provide a bit of solace (and hope!) and show that you can make progress towards your goals every day by sharing 100 small ways to enhance your skills, your career and fully espouse the values that make those that work in our industry so special, valuable, unique and vital to our communities – the very fabric of them and their vibrancy.

So, without further ado – here are 100 things to ponder, adopt or share in your quest to make this your most successful year yet regardless of the circumstances (or dollars you are earmarked to secure). I have bunched them up too if you want to double down on hard or soft skills!

Giving Back/Pay it Forward – espousing our values is the most important foundation.

1. Give back – we don't do enough of it.
2. Thank people – we should do more of it.
3. Gift in lieu – donations have a lower environmental footprint for those that have it all.
4. Volunteer – to learn, help others, and ground ourselves in good.
5. Volunteer with your kid/sibling/partner – build memories & shared values.
6. Volunteer on a campaign – fight for what you believe in & learn more about community needs.
7. Become a mentor – help people realize their potential.
8. Make a big fuss on social media about new staff and personal/career wins – celebrate your peers!
9. Set up a recurring donation – commit to a cause, be invested in something.
10. Donate to a silent auction – regifting that unused timeshare has never been so much fun!
11. Nominate someone for an award – highlight those doing good work.
12. Share opportunities – opening doors might help ignite a generational leader.
13. Donate to a political campaign – real change is in the hands of those we send to Congress & representation matters. Give to someone you believe in.
14. Enroll someone to vote – all of our voices matter.
15. Give a gift to your colleagues for the holidays – show how much you value their work & friendship.
16. Give a gift to your boss on National Boss's Day – October 16!
17. Give a gift to your staff on National Employee Appreciation Day – March 4th!
18. Acknowledge staff's family successes – because their family is our extended family & we should be proud of their wins too.

19. Donate air miles – we mainly accrue these through work travel anyways, so donate them and enable someone to attend a significant event they might not be able to.

20. Pay for someone's membership – donate $150 to a professional association and allow an emerging leader to benefit from the network and their opportunities – a real good ROI for our industry.

21. Bring donuts – the fancy ones. Send an all-staff email and hear the pleasing sounds of staff sprinting to the kitchen.

Career Building – run your own race (& it's something you can control)

22. Join an affinity/professional association/group – expand your network & get access to curated learning opportunities.

23. Apply for a leadership cohort – acquire some essential skills and join a cohort that I guarantee will contain folks that will be in your life forever.

24. Know your worth – ask for a raise. You can download apps like PepTalkHer and get help developing a narrative to justify it too!

25. Get yourself a mentor – seek one out, and embrace the wisdom.

26. Set a 3-year credentialing goal – want your Masters or CFRE. Book it in now, don't let indecision be a barrier because in three years you will still be dreaming the same thing.

27. Refresh your resume – be ready for opportunity and marvel at your own achievements.

28. Apply anyways… – Research shows that while men apply to jobs when they meet an average of 60% of the criteria, women and underrepresented/underestimated individuals only apply when they 'tick every box.' So, if you think you have what it takes, have transferable skills, and are quick to learn, but don't necessarily meet every single dot point on the job description, please apply.

29. Nominate yourself for an award – because you can & you know you deserve credit!

Fundraising – if you don't ask you don't get (& it's easier than it seems)

30. Make 3 asks per morning – you can't raise funds if you aren't taking meetings. Contact three folks in your database daily to move the conversation forward.

31. Ditch the electronic signature for ink – if you are mailing out something, take the extra time and use a blue ballpoint pen. It's those extra touches that are the most authentic.

32. Convene some fundraisers – get together some of your peers to talk shop, opportunities, trends & ideas. The pie isn't exclusive...

33. Send a voice note instead of a text – it generates extra buy-in and avoids confusion of context.

34. Send birthday cards – list all your portfolio's birthdays and put in a calendar reminder to write them a card a week prior.

35. Send children's books on the birth of their new child – insert a note inside the cover.

36. Write a thank you note to donors – because writing is better than email.

37. Get a digital business card – they cost $20, sit in your wallet & save the trees. I use Linq.

38. Wear merch – be proud of where you work, wear a lapel pin to get identified at a donor meeting & you get a real kick when a random person gives you a shout-out in public.

39. Join Calendly – make scheduling meetings easier & let donors pick the length of time to talk.

40. Count what doesn't necessarily count – a lot goes into an ask so celebrate & review the metrics that end up on the cutting room floor. Looking at them might identify new enhancements for the team's processes & approaches.

41. Pick up the phone – cold calling is not scary.

42. Be prepared – when you make that call, ensure you know who you are calling and be ready to build a real conversation if they pick up. Don't squander an opportunity.

43. Reverse engineer goals – goals can be daunting, break them down & win the year.

44. Add your top 10 donors to a Google alert – never miss a beat or circuit breaker to connect.

45. Add your top 50 donors to a Twitter group – monitor what folks are saying through the clutter of social media and comment promptly.

Organizational Excellence – because making our place of work better is also important!

46. Do quarterly goals check-ins – yearly goal reviews are a missed opportunity to pivot, reimagine and ground the team in current circumstances.

47. Increase the staff development budget – decrease the conference budget and encourage real investments in your team

48. Incentivize learning – identify opportunities and remove barriers to entry by making them pay upfront. Support them authentically.

49. Do a pay audit – review everyone's role annually. If people are receiving different pay for the same amount of work, change it and bring everyone up to the higher level.

50. Invite those you serve to your board – if you are an educational non-profit, invite one of your students to the board as a full voting member. They benefit from the experience, and you benefit from their voice, representation & experiences.

51. Once a quarter give the staff one afternoon off for discovery – go to a museum, watch a documentary, meet with an academic. Come back inspired and willing to share your learnings.

52. Give an hour or so of grace at the end of the day if it's raining – commutes suck & the rain just delays folks from returning to their families.

53. Give staff time to volunteer – it's often hard to find the time to give back amongst all the crazy.

54. Don't give up on an employee – invest in them, speak to them, don't just manage them out.

55. Give staff a company card – don't make them pay upfront and take forever to reimburse. You don't know their situation.

56. Invest in automation – onboard platforms that automate repetitive tasks, and give your staff back the time to advance the work, not just backfill it with more rudimentary ones.

57. Ensure there are no 'gotcha' moments – communicate bottlenecks, don't sweep them under the carpet.

58. Sign up for ChatGPT - save hours on your rudimentary administrative tasks.

59. Bring your dog to work day – there is no better morale booster!

60. Set up a Slack channel – if you have Slack or Teams to communicate (as many organizations have implemented during COVID), set up a fun channel where people can express themselves beyond work – sharing recipes, book recommendations, or pictures of their cats that were not welcome to the bring your dog to work day.

61. Do away with salary cloaking – share the salary range in all job ads.

62. Think beyond the 3-year strategic plan – strategic plans guide & progress the immediate work but also stifle long-term creativity. Leave space in staff/board retreats to think bigger.

63. Be future-focused – Once a month have some time in the staff meeting for new ideas and future thinking.

Balance – because we all need it!

64. Make your bed – watch the video by US Navy Admiral William H McRaven on YouTube & you'll understand why (Admiral McRaven, 2014).

65. Bring a plant to your desk – moving back to the office 'for reals' this year? Bring a friend, care for your friend, and grow with your friend.

66. Bring a water bottle to your desk – drink up, and schedule a reminder if need be.

67. Reality test – remain objective by seeing things as they really are. This capacity involves recognizing when emotions or personal biases can cause one to be less objective.

68. Be kind – treat others how you want to be treated

69. Congratulate others on their wins – follow the adage that there is no 'I' in team

70. Don't settle – we can & be more. Push others, push yourself. Dare to dream.

71. If possible, take the stairs – it helps lessen the impact of those donuts your colleague brought in.

72. Change your phone to grayscale – clicking the home button 3 times will change the color of your screen & will ensure you aren't checking it as often.

73. Always book an extra day off after a holiday – we never give ourselves enough time to decompress. We don't need a holiday after a holiday, just a break.

74. Write down quotes or ideas – curate things that inspire you & download all that clutters the mind.

75. Be curious – Ask questions and listen to the answers.

76. Keep a small pad/notebook on you at all times – jot down everything you see, hear, learn & do during the day & recap each night. I use the Field Notes books as they come in left-handed versions. Moleskin is another classic.

77. Ask your partner to come to a work event – let them see what you do firsthand, it makes the question "what did you do today" more authentic.

78. Take your kid to a gala – because they'll love the opportunity to dress up.

79. Call people in, don't call them out – cancel culture is a blight on our society and we are so quick to call folks out without context. Let's be more constructive and let's be more like point 68. Kind, but constructive.

80. Critical thinking – is what you are reading true? Is what you were taught a fair reflection of what happened? Is the messenger biased? Think for yourself, and make informed decisions.

Engineer a spark – create the good you want to see in the world...

81. Start or join a book club – explore new topics and/or dive deeper into your interests – challenge your assumptions with your peers to enhance your learning.

82. Write one blog piece – identify something you are interested in and write a 500-word article on it. Write it for yourself not for the clicks and post it out!

83. Expand that blog – cut the blog up into conversational pieces. Share on social media channels to keep the conversation going.

84. Partner with someone for another blog – write an article with a peer to enhance the viewpoint and networks you can be exposed to. Use the Op-Ed project to help!

85. Subscribe to Lumen5 – upload your article to this AI platform and like magic, it will create a professional 2-minute video you can upload to YouTube and share to your network.

86. Convert to a podcast – the Anchor plug-in on WordPress will turn your article into a podcast episode!

87. Comment – don't sit on the fence, if you have something constructive or insightful to say please share it. Don't second guess or worry about what others think, it adds to civil discourse and helps refine your own narrative.

88. Subscribe or buy membership to local news outlets – support local news & the stories that count in our neighborhoods. If local news continues to get swallowed up,

we lose our identity and don't see some of the hard, yet prevailing ills in our community that can be solved with our involvement.

89. If something in the world is frustrating you, write (politely) to your elected representative – the staff will read it at least and it's a step towards being an advocate for your community.

90. Join or set up a giving circle – pool your resources, learn about certain issues, and grant funds in a more informed and impactful way.

91. Invite people into the sector – your friend that is killing it in finance shares with you that they want more meaning from their work, so don't just ask them to volunteer, encourage them to become a CFO at a nonprofit.

92. Invite people into your group – most people don't join a group as they either don't know about it or feel they must be asked. Proactively identify & invite talent to our work and the professional associations that drive knowledge, opportunities, and advocacy.

Learning – continuous learning doesn't have to come from a textbook.

93. Subscribe to 3 new podcasts – there are so many great voices & stories out there, subscribe to a few new shows to learn more history, skills, information, whatever!

94. Drop in on chats – listen to other thought leaders & peers about interesting topics on platforms such as Clubhouse and the Twitter Spaces function. This is a great space to open your mind to new ideas, practice public speaking & test out narratives.

95. Focus on 3 hashtags – social media can be really useful if you drill down to certain subject areas. You'll identify the leading voices, ideas, and opportunities for you in these niches rather than be lost in all the hubris & toxicity of the platforms when left to the algorithms to dictate your main feeds. I normally meander through #philanthropy #nptech #tech4good…join me!

96. Go to a different conference session – look for a session that isn't in your wheelhouse or discipline, sit down and learn &/or be challenged.

97. Take a free community college or continuing education course – learn a new language or how to use Adobe InDesign…for free!

98. Subscribe to Canva – this is such a great platform. Terrific for those with a limited marketing budget & want to wean themselves off of Microsoft Paint & the Comic Sans font.

99. Ask some what-ifs… – what if I was on the school board, what would I do? What would I bring? What could I do better? It'll also help you learn more about things by taking more than just a surface-level look at how our community works.

100. Act on those what-ifs (& divide them by two) – what is stopping you from running for school board? And what's stopping you from doing it at the next election rather than in 6 years? If you have something to offer, put yourself forward.

This isn't an exhaustive list, heck, it's a list that will mean different things to different people. All I know is that progress compounds, we can all do & be more and from little things, big things grow.

If this list has inspired growth and you want to learn more about curating a better future, please feel free to visit my website (www.ryanginard.com) and download 'The Fifteen Rules of Philanthropic Futurism' an exclusive free chapter from my book 'Future Philanthropy – The Tech, Trends & Talent Defining New Civic Leadership'. The Fifteen Rules of Philanthropic Futurism have been developed to help you approach your work in the social sector through a lens of futurism.

FUNDRAISING IS A SUPERSKILL THAT WILL INCREASE YOUR LQ

All fundraisers are different, and we are all works in progress. The one common thread I have found from those I regard as the 'best in the game' however is that of an insatiable thirst for learning. Learning more about the trends, learning more about their donors, and learning more about those whose work they impact, and then trying to understand how they all connect. That's why I ended the top 100 list with learning because the best fundraisers have a high LQ, which stands for learnability quotient, or those playing at home with a certain level of intrigue, a person's ability, and a desire to keep picking up new skills.

LQ is one attribute of why those hall-of-fame sports stars can perform at the highest levels for over 10 years in their professional leagues, despite each sport's constant evolution. Whether it's learning about new superfoods and diets, the newest hyperbaric chamber to speed up recovery, or simply honing their golf swing, they are always seeking an edge, and an edge they look to tweak every pre-season.

The idea of LQ is that our ability to learn is a measurable skill and the higher the number, the better we are to adapt to new situations and challenges in our work lives. Personally, I see this as just a fancier term for skill stacking and its ability to strengthen your resolve through periods of change. This is a good thing as it lends a bit more credence to organizations seeing the potential of an employee to grow. I would also liken it to eventually finding a way to identify and understand a candidate's 'ceiling' through the lens of curiosity and adaptability.

It's not a truly qualitative model for performance or recruitment (yet), but one that should be at least on our radar. It's also an emerging term that has a bit of nuance to it too – I'm seeing a healthy dose of suggestions to improve your LQ through things like cooking classes, learning a new language, or playing an instrument as one of those work-life balance opportunities.

If you read this book as a board member, project officer, or another fundraising adjacent role, I would advocate for folks looking to increase their LQ by learning and understanding the key fundraising skills, practices, and processes.

You see, I have always seen the skill of fundraising as one of those super skills – the courage to ask for the support of something you believe in, the ability to deal with rejection, the art of telling a story, and so on. The skills are highly transferable and also drive stronger relationships both in the office and externally.

There are plenty of different takes here but a couple of learning opportunities and approaches that resonate with me that might be good for non-fundraising nonprofit and social sector workers include;

Fundraising 101. Like a core requisite at university, people interested in acquiring fundraising skills can undertake some sort of foundational course that will help build their confidence in negotiations and making an ask, skills that can move the needle just a little more for your school or sports team that are seeking funds and need more help than simply selling raffle tickets and a baseline knowledge of how to be a more effective Director or Board Member.

The ability to become more of a generalist in your field. Learn more about what your members and donors do in a professional setting – 'Knowing enough to be dangerous' as it were. Enough to converse with a savvy prospect and know when/where to connect the dots as a result. You don't have to have a Masters in AI to talk about the benefits of it, nor do you need to be a member of the bar to discuss funding for anti-recidivism programs.

LQ is something nonprofit workers have in abundance, they wear many hats, learn their roles on the job as it were, and that professional development budget is normally so minuscule that sometimes identifying online courses that are not directly applicable to our work but are definitely complementary or transferable are the key to continued growth. Fundraising is a team sport after all so maybe an organizational commitment to improving everyone's LQ is part of building that all-important internal culture.

1

IDENTIFYING, RECRUITING AND EMPOWERING A GENERATION OF NEW FUNDRAISING TALENT

It's about getting things down to one number. Using the stats the way we read them, we'll find value in players that no one else can see. People are overlooked for a variety of biased reasons and perceived flaws. Age, appearance, personality. Bill James and mathematics cut straight through that. Billy, of the 20,000 notable players for us to consider, I believe that there is a championship team of twenty-five people that we can afford, because everyone else in baseball undervalues them.

| 1 |

Understanding & Setting The Field

Understanding The Field

Challenges for the Nonprofit Sector

The nonprofit sector feels the pain of change more acutely than most. While it has the heads and hearts for change, it doesn't necessarily have the deep pockets and all that comes with the luxury of large revenues. Even if it did, it comes with a cost.

For example, when you sell lots of commercial products, you can benefit from creating more at a cheaper cost per unit. This will drive higher profit margins. When your programs grow at a nonprofit, you must raise more money to build them out and hire more staff to keep up with demand.

Sometimes it's just too much. Nonprofits fail for one, two, or all three of the same reasons for-profit businesses fail:

- A lack of capital (donations).

- A product (cause) that does not compel enough people to act.
- A faulty model for customer (donor) attraction and retention.

So how do we as a sector keep up with other industries whose business models are ultimately more flexible and incentivized? An embrace of the fundraising talent and tech available to us would be a terrific start.

Embracing the Role of Fundraisers

The sector is evolving at a breakneck pace. This is especially true for the way donors engage, the way donors think, and the way donors give. Understanding fundraising fundamentals and embracing fundraising as a core cultural value will ensure continued high-impact giving and strengthen donor-organizational relationships. It also leverages a trove of data to help make for more effective service delivery and those valuable success stories that showcase our work.

Nonprofits work with spoken and unspoken motivations that are often more emotionally charged than those in the for-profit world. It is the job of our fundraisers to identify those motivations. Then, it's a matter of connecting the motivations with their organization's cause, communicating the social return on investment, and developing lasting partnerships to sustain their organization.

And if we are to have an authentic fundraising culture that reshapes our nonprofit structures and adapts to the changes we are seeing, it's wise to focus on professionalism in fundraising in general.

The Challenges That Fundraisers Face

According to a Chronicle of Philanthropy survey, 51% of fundraisers planned to leave their jobs this year (Chronicle of Philanthropy, 2020). More alarmingly, three in ten respondents said they recently left or plan to leave the development field altogether in the next two years. The survey highlighted that the main issues included too much pressure to meet unrealistic fundraising goals, too little pay, and frustrating organizational cultures.

Fundraising goals can be challenging due to the uncertainty of revenues beyond endowments and multi-year grants. Due to outside forces and unforeseen events (global pandemic, anyone?), fundraising revenues can fluctuate much like the stock market. There will be up years and down years, but there should still be an ability to project out historical gains over time. To avoid any pitfalls, an organization should have multi-year goals which would bring more predictability, stability, and intentionality around fundraising. This would negate the temptation to overreach the year following a strong showing, allowing consolidation of the gains made and putting all excess funds into reserves (that good old rainy-day fund).

The Fundraiser Stigma

One of the biggest stumbling blocks to the professionalism of the fundraising sector, however, is the stigma associated with it.

Apart from the CEO role, there is perhaps no lonelier position than those operating in development. They deal with low budgets, sky-high expectations, and a unique pressure from leadership to identify the donors and funds that will not only help keep the lights on but expand services, fund a new building, and establish a seven-figure endowment from scratch. It's often a thankless task.

No wonder the typical tenure for a Development Director is 16 months (Philanthropy Daily, 2022). **Sixteen** months. Think about whether that's enough time to develop a mature portfolio and build up the networks, infrastructure, and messaging to be successful. The 16 months following is where you'll see actual dividends in this line of work.

A New Foundation for Fundraisers

While I'm not advocating for a complete pardon of responsibilities in year one, I am advocating for time, patience from management, and the baseline for frontline fundraising staff in this first year to simply make budget. If this target is surpassed, then the expectations are not to be raised exponentially—they should grow organically. This is about building a healthy foundation and long-lasting partnership with your lead development staff. Try to realize that investing in them can take your fundraising to the next level.

That investment should be front-loaded, too. There is currently no specific degree in fundraising. Instead, the principles and best practices are covered within degree programs focused on nonprofit management and philanthropy. Going to college because you want to be a fundraiser would definitely end the "I fell into this" saying.

Becoming great at anything is not a matter of blind luck. Formal education is essential in fundraising, as bad habits can manifest early in an individual's career without the right training. There is an abundance of donors out there, and with the proper education, even the newest development staff can make impactful asks for the benefit of their cause.

The Future for Fundraisers

Ultimately, education and re-education are needed to further an up-to-date understanding of a complex and evolving industry. New giving vehicles and platforms are bursting onto the scene almost daily. We must all continue to be students of giving.

In addition to our call for better pathways for fundraisers in the sector, we must also acknowledge that fit is imperative in workplace partnership. There needs to be a renewed focus on choosing your next staff members. Finding that sweet spot is difficult, but tools exist to measure a candidate's direct and indirect experience, communication skills, and values.

Setting The Field

Let's not confuse the key tenets of what Nonprofit Moneyball is. It's about building the team. The data element is important but should be used in informing recruiting decisions and the decisions made thereafter from an organizational perspective. I have seen several nonprofit tech companies try and coin this term which has lent itself to a sort of tech arrogance where companies say "we know how to fix it". In reality, some haven't truly spent any time on the frontlines of a nonprofit and our sector shakes out merely as another revenue vertical.

Talent is the main focal point of a professional sports team. The on-field 'product' determines that binary success of wins and losses, but as we all know, some clubs are successful across various metrics with championships just being that cherry on top.

Recruitment and retaining staff aren't all that different from a sports team from an anecdotal point of view. We see players come and go, we see players on the sidelines for a while through vacations and annual leave for example and we also see them seek 'bigger contracts' through promotions and pay rises.

So how do you go about building a true championship-winning team and how do we define winning as a small to medium nonprofit organization? There are a variety of different options available. We break them down over the following pages and also provide some food for thought for the sector at large as we potentially see millions of individuals moving to the services industries over the next decade, needing to upskill or pivot as many traditional jobs become obsolete through automation and AI which in effect are the same thing).

Creating an innovative nonprofit is difficult, especially without the right talent. Hiring the right employees for the right roles at the right time is critical, and this requires good resource management. That's why we need to lean more on HR data and, in the future, look to new approaches and tools that can help with our decision-making. Let's break down some simple approaches that nonprofits can use now to identify new talent and compete for a greater slice of that fundraising pie.

Look Beyond the Traditional Markers: With a deeper bench of skills, organizations can tackle the most complex social problems. But where does HR find this new generation of nonprofit game changers? And how does it attract those individuals? The great news is you don't have to look that far. Hundreds of those game changers are working in your communities seasonally. But who are they? Community organizers and political field staff are well-versed in the importance of metrics, with a strong sense of what the end goal is. These emerging leaders also work tirelessly around the clock on cause-based issues, exist in large numbers, and are readily available (especially post-campaign). They are well-connected, hardworking, and jacks of all trades. Many also specialize in fundraising, all understanding the importance of the "ask." Their challenge, however, is that they probably don't hit all the job prerequisites, and that's where the problem lies. How do we help nonprofit organizations identify these transferable skills via the application process and ultimately look outside the box to de-risk their candidacy?

Empower Your HR Team: Nonprofit benchmark reports have shown that nearly half of the human resource executive staff who were surveyed identified an increase in their overall organizational influence—predominantly through more recognition by top-level executives that HR plays an integral role in executing an organization's mission. This represents a big opportunity for nonprofits and both public and private foundations to increase their capacity, be more impactful, and achieve their goals through the identification and development of talented staff. As social justice moves away from transferring wealth and toward building social infrastructure to help all members of society reach their potential, the sector is also seeing a parallel shift from purely program-based philanthropy to a campaign-like approach where engaging and building nontraditional constituencies and developing cross-sector partnerships are key to delivering tangible outcomes to those they seek to serve. The study, undertaken by XpertHR, reveals a renewed acknowledgment of HR's role in achieving organizational success and, on further reflection, its ability to equip organizations with new talent that will adapt to the rapidly changing philanthropic sector.

Encourage Inclusive Recruiting: The rigidity of minimum qualifications is slowly shifting as the modern workforce evolves, with credentialing fast replacing the prestige of the college you attended and the specialization of your degree. However, plenty of research still shows bias in how job descriptions are drafted and reviewed. This has to be a focus of ongoing change to ensure equality of opportunity in the job market. Many folks read job descriptions and opt out of applying as they don't "see themselves" in that role or they discredit their chances before they even apply. This is a major factor in continuing unequal pay for women and people of color. The immediate medicine for this systematic issue is to review the language of the role and ensure things such as educational requirements reflect the bare minimum for the relevant career experience.

Look Beyond Your Network: Besides making job descriptions more inclusive, expanding your reach when advertising your job is paramount. Along with all of your local recruitment sites and specialized nonprofit job boards, start sharing your opportunities with Hispanic Chambers of Commerce, Black business society chapters, and workforce partnerships and alliances that provide job search and career development resources to all job seekers, regardless of income or background and at no cost to the candidates. These networks are not only dynamic in helping amplify talent, but their members are also the ones at the forefront of societal change. Your organization would be all the richer for their participation, whether applying to your roles or serving on your boards. So reach out authentically and build enduring partnerships that can help advance each other's missions.

Stop Salary Cloaking: While legislation has been passed in several states making it illegal for employers to ask for an employee's salary history, a subtle change to job advertisements could lead to savings in time and resources and play an important role in retainment levels and issues around pay parity. Salary cloaking is the practice of not posting a salary range for that role, arguably in the hope of attracting strong candidates without having them opt out of the opportunity at first glance. This is problematic in the nonprofit space as wages are notoriously low to begin with. Over the course of the recruiting process, it wastes people's time searching, applying, screening candidates, and interviewing, just for a candidate to say, "No thanks, I have a family to support." I cannot stress this enough:

When an employee takes a lower salary, it perpetuates wage gaps and affects their lifetime earnings and—to be frank—their sustained satisfaction in the position. Most fundraisers move on for better pay and with the high turnover costs, this can be addressed on the front end by adding the simple detail of what you are willing to pay.

Upgrade Your Systems and Adopt Automation: So, you are excited about the diverse talent pool you have sourced for your next open position. That's great! The last thing you want is for your internal systems to let this potential finalist fall through the cracks or be snapped up by another organization because you took your time. (If they applied for your job opening, there is a high probability they are applying elsewhere too.) By analyzing and reassessing your organization's hiring process, you can ensure everyone who interviews with you has a great experience (thus improving your brand and standing in the sector) and that candidates feel supported through the onboarding process, ultimately setting them up for success.

Today's hiring process should have elements of standardization for consistency, tools that capture all of the information gathered on candidates, and automated components to ensure that the time taken from posting the role to that hire's eventual orientation hits established benchmarks. A great tool for this is Smartsheet, a platform that can be tailor-made for your internal needs and has the capacity to generate action items when candidates move along to additional stages of the process. Coupled with weekly reports to managers to ensure transparency and identify bottlenecks, tools like this can give your organization best-in-class processes at a fraction of the time and cost of a large acquisition team.

Expect significant strides over the coming years for numerous HR offerings and applications. Google has been redefining the sector with its early research into data-driven HR focused on the optimal length of the hiring process, leading to Google's "Rule of Four" for interviews (Schneider, 2018). Data collected from Google's 2016 interviews indicated that 95 percent of the time, panels of just four interviewers made the same hiring decision as panels of more than four interviewers, a decision that saved both time and money. So be rigorous and patient in your hiring process, as the return on investment for getting the right fundraiser on your team can be a game changer for building capacity toward your organizational goals.

Use Assessment Tools: What do you do when you can't decide between two finalists for a role? Let's say that one of those candidates comes from a traditional fundraising background and is credentialed as a Certified Fund Raising Executive (CFRE). The other has limited experience but has been more successful in raising funds over a smaller period of time. More often than not, organizations take the safer option, which is the one with more years of experience and professional qualifications. Yet what if there was one more data set that could help make a more informed decision?

Cultural fit is just as important as an employee's skills and experience. By using behavioral assessments at the front end of the interviewing process, leaders can measure future indicators around performance and motivation, with the end goal of designing and building high-performing teams. Tools like the Predictive Index (PI) allow you to run your job description through its platform, develop a desired range for an employee's behavioral and cognitive fit, and gather further input from team members who will regularly interact with that individual to refine the key indicators of success and help develop particular interview questions based on the candidate's profile.

This, however, might be reserved for larger organizations, given that the average candidate would not like to have their resume (or cognitive skills for that matter) screened by an algorithm. A study conducted by the Pew Research Center found 76 percent of US workers would not want to apply for a job that screened their resume in this way, with most who were surveyed thinking the algorithm would do a worse job than a human (Perrin, 2017).

The path to innovation is seldom a smooth one. The good news, though, is that innovation doesn't have to be new. It just needs to be new to you—and why wouldn't you explore the hiring practices and rationale of larger organizations and their HR practices? Data-driven HR also helps to remove a certain level of human bias from recruitment efforts and opens the door to undervalued talent just as long as nuance is applied to ensure particular groups aren't being overlooked at the beginning of the process.

The compounding crises of the past couple of years have been felt deeply throughout the nonprofit sector even though, according to Giving USA's 2022 report, giving by individuals in 2021 increased by 4.9% over the previous year. An additional finding in the Dorothy A. Johnson Center's annual trends in philanthropy found that while individual total giving was rising, the number of individuals giving was decreasing. This has put fundraisers in a difficult and evolving context.

According to a report from the UK-based Institute of Sustainable Philanthropy (ISP) and Revolutionise International, 46 percent of nonprofit fundraisers in the United States and the United Kingdom plan to leave their current employer within the next two years due to growing workplace frustrations, while 9 percent intend to leave the field entirely. The report, titled "What Makes Fundraisers Tick? A Study of Identity, Motivation, and Well-being," is based on survey responses from 2,700 development professionals, 82 percent female, completed in May and June of 2022. The report identifies a lack of professional growth, autonomy, and board support as primary factors contributing to rising dissatisfaction and reduced commitment to fundraising work. The report emphasizes that losing talented fundraisers is unsustainable, particularly for smaller nonprofits struggling with chronic vacancies and high turnover rates.

Consider taking calculated risks in your recruitment processes because, at the end of the day, it's a simple equation. There is a lot of talent out there with relevant and transferable skills. People who can motivate others to vote and donate to support critical community issues can replicate this process (with a bit of fine-tuning) to turn supporters into donors and community volunteers into civic leaders. So, whether you're swinging for the fences or just trying to get your operations to first base, it's worth looking at.

The sector is evolving at a breakneck pace - the way donors engage, the way donors think, and the way donors give. Ultimately, professional education and re-education are needed to continue an up-to-date understanding of a complex and evolving industry. New giving vehicles and platforms are bursting onto the scene almost daily (including a free learning portal from the Fundraising Academy). With a continuing tinkering of tax policy occurring with every new Congress sworn in, we must all continue to be students of giving—this will keep us motivated in one of the most critical positions in any successful fundraising team.

While Moneyball didn't win the Oakland A's a World Series championship, the methodology was successfully applied at the Boston Red Sox organization through Theo Epstein. It eventually helped them end an 86-year drought to win the World Series. And then when he went on to the Chicago Cubs, it helped them end their own 108-year curse. What fundraising campaign will be your World Series? And what team will you assemble to achieve your most audacious goals? Let's break it down further, position by position.

| 2 |

Building A Winning Team

Free Agency

Free agency is a term used in professional sports to describe the status of a player who is not currently under contract with a team and is thus free to sign with any team that offers them a contract.

In most professional sports leagues, players are typically bound to their team through a contract that specifies the length of their stay and the compensation they will receive. However, once a player's contract has expired or been terminated, they become a free agent and can sign with any team that offers them a contract.

Free agency can take several forms, depending on the specific league and the rules governing player movement. In some cases, free agents are subject to a "salary cap" that limits the amount of money a team can offer them, to prevent wealthy teams from simply buying up all the best players. In other cases, free agents may be subject to a "draft pick compensation" system, in which teams that sign high-profile free agents must give up a certain number of draft picks to the team that initially owned the player's rights.

Overall, free agency is a vital part of professional sports, as it allows players to move between teams and seek out the best possible opportunities while promoting competitiveness and parity within the league.

Free agency is most closely related to your standard recruitment processes of which you need to ask yourselves, "Are we getting the best candidate pools we can, and if not why not?"

1 LINK, 1 PARAGRAPH & 2 NUMBERS. 3 FRONT-END ADDITIONS TO DIVERSIFY YOUR CANDIDATE POOL

So you've made a conscious effort to make your job description more inclusive. You have even distributed the opportunity to new networks including your Black and Hispanic chambers of commerce. Yet by the time the application deadline rolls around, the candidate pool looks unsurprisingly similar to every other opening you have had.

There is no doubt your organization is passionate about hiring the right people because we understand what's at stake for those our clients serve, and that's why we are continually looking to diversify talent to ensure our applicant pool is the most dynamic, yet robust one available to us when a hiring need arises.

There are three simple things you can do to achieve this.

Invite candidates in rather than having them rule themselves out: I specifically mention inviting candidates in because we need to be open to non-traditional candidates and encourage them to see themselves in the role which I think can be achieved by simply adding the following sentence to job postings;

Research shows that while men apply to jobs when they meet an average of 60% of the criteria, women and underrepresented/underestimated individuals only apply when they 'tick every box.' So, if you think you have what it takes, have transferable skills, and are quick to learn, but don't necessarily meet every single dot point on the job description, please apply.

Share your salary range: You should also be sharing your salary range. While legislation has been passed in several U.S. states making it illegal for employers to ask for an employee's salary history, a subtle change to job advertisements could lead to savings in time and resources and play an important role in retention levels and issues around pay parity. Salary cloaking is the practice of not posting a salary range for that role, arguably in the hope of attracting strong candidates and not having them opt out of the opportunity at first glance. This is of course problematic. In the nonprofit space, wages are notoriously low to begin with, and over the course of the recruiting process, it wastes people's time searching, applying, screening candidates, and interviewing, just for a candidate to say no thanks, I have a family to support. I cannot stress this part enough. When an employee takes a lower salary, it perpetuates wage gaps and affects the employee's lifetime earnings and—to be frank—their sustained satisfaction in the position.

The Chronicle of Philanthropy reported on the fact that critical nonprofit roles such as fundraisers only last 16 months in their role and then move on for better pay. There is always a high cost of turnover, and this can be addressed on the front end by adding the simple detail of what you are willing to give.

Encourage candidates to connect: We don't keep donors at arm's length so why prospective candidates? Invite candidates to

NONPROFIT MONEYBALL - 33

learn more about the role and the organization by including the lead recruiter or hiring manager's email address or LinkedIn profile.

Trust, transparency, and authenticity are important traits and values of the nonprofit sector so why not open a dialogue with prospective applicants as soon as possible? Not only will it help applicants decide on their application or not, but you are also showcasing your values too.

Creating an innovative nonprofit is difficult, especially without the right talent. Hiring the right employees for the right roles at the right time is critical, especially for a nonprofit: Annual turnover in the U.S. (in 2017) was 26.3%, based on data from the Bureau of Labor Statistics. The cost of replacing an individual employee can range from one-half to two times the employee's annual salary – with that comes the caveat of it being a conservative estimate (Altman, 2017). So, a 10-person organization with an average salary of $50,000 could have turnover and replacement costs of approximately $66,000 to $260,000 per year.

So let's be upfront, honest, and authentic in our hiring. Let's pay people what they are worth and show them how to move up the ladder, seeing themselves in the organization long term. Ultimately it leads to more job security and, as a result, lower turnover and a generationally segmented workforce.

The social sector is changing and will need new voices, experiences, education, training, and expertise in supporting programs and projects looking to deliver real impact for those they serve. And if adding one 1 link, 1 paragraph, and 2 numbers to our job ads can support this shift then obviously we would be all the better for it.

The Draft

A professional sports draft is a process used by professional sports leagues to allocate new players to their teams. Typically, the draft involves eligible players being selected in a predetermined order by teams in the league, with the order of selection being determined by the teams' performance in the previous season. The draft is designed to promote parity among teams by giving weaker teams the first opportunity to select new talent, and by limiting the ability of stronger teams to simply buy up all of the available talent.

In a typical draft, eligible players will have declared their availability for selection and will have been evaluated by scouts and coaches from the different teams. The draft can take place over several rounds, with each team selecting one or more players in each round. Once a team has selected a player, they will be offered a contract to join and compete in the league.

The most well-known professional sports drafts are those held by the National Football League (NFL), the National Basketball Association (NBA), and Major League Baseball (MLB). Still, many other sports leagues also use a draft system to allocate new talent to their teams.

A nonprofit draft can be likened to recruiting a referral, a volunteer, or a student joining a nonprofit directly upon graduation from high school or university.

I'm bullish on the latter especially if in time there is a concerted push by the sector and government to help lift up fundraising as a strong career option. We are already seeing this in Australia with the National Skills Commission identifying Fundraising as one of the fastest-growing and best-paid jobs in the country. Once we turn the corner as it were, guidance counselors will recommend it to high school leavers, community and technical colleges will have study options to fast-track careers, and ultimately universities will offer undergraduate degrees in it.

I would also like to see a mechanism built into all crowdfunding platforms that if they reach a certain number (say $5,000), they receive an email inviting them to think about a fundraising career, noting that it was the authentic stories, the strategy to secure funds and the tenacity to reach their goals being essential skills of fundraisers we should be seeking and sourcing for roles.

Alas, we aren't there yet so what are a few options to secure new talent beyond the traditional avenues we have available?

Internal hiring: There are several ways to leverage internal candidates for fundraising jobs:

Identify potential candidates: Review your organization's current employees to identify those who have skills and experience relevant to fundraising. Look for individuals with experience in sales, marketing, event planning, or other related fields.

Provide training and development opportunities: Offer training and development opportunities for employees who are interested in fundraising. This could include workshops, conferences, or online courses on topics such as grant writing, donor cultivation, and major gifts.

Encourage internal mobility: Encourage employees to explore career paths within the organization. This could involve offering job shadowing opportunities or mentorship programs to help employees gain exposure to different areas of the organization, including fundraising.

Create a culture of philanthropy: Foster a culture of philanthropy within your organization by educating employees on the importance of fundraising and its impact on your mission. Encourage employees to participate in fundraising activities, such as donating or volunteering at a fundraising event.

Offer incentives: Consider offering incentives for employees who successfully transition into fundraising roles, such as bonuses, promotions, or other recognition. This can help motivate employees to pursue fundraising careers and reward those who excel in their new roles.

Converting volunteers. To encourage your best volunteers to become full-time fundraisers:

- Identify volunteers with an interest in fundraising and the required skills.
- Offer training and development opportunities, and provide hands-on experience.
- Provide competitive compensation packages, and recognize and reward those transitioning to full-time fundraising roles.

Building pipelines

Professional sports teams build talent pipelines by identifying and recruiting players with potential, developing their skills and experience, and making strategic moves to acquire the best players available. This helps teams build strong rosters and stay competitive over time.

Building a nonprofit talent pipeline is essential for several reasons:

Ensuring a steady supply of skilled fundraisers: By building a talent pipeline, organizations can proactively identify and cultivate candidates who have the skills and experience needed to fill key roles within the organization. This helps to ensure that there is a steady supply of talent available to meet current and future fundraising and operational needs.

Reducing hiring time and costs: Having a talent pipeline in place can reduce the time and cost associated with the recruitment process. Since the organization has already identified and nurtured potential candidates, they can quickly fill open roles with qualified candidates without conducting an extensive search.

Improving workforce diversity: By building a diverse talent pipeline, organizations can ensure they have access to a broad range of candidates with different backgrounds, perspectives, and experiences. This can lead to a more inclusive and innovative workforce.

Enhancing reputation: A strong talent pipeline can enhance an organization's reputation by demonstrating a commitment to investing in and developing employees. This can help to attract and retain top talent.

Developing future leaders: By cultivating talent within the organization, organizations can develop a pipeline of future leaders who have the skills and experience needed to take on leadership roles within the organization.

Overall, building a talent pipeline is an essential strategy for organizations looking to build a strong, sustainable workforce and maintain a competitive advantage in today's rapidly changing social sector.

The nonprofit sector is the third largest employer in the U.S. economy and that workforce has been one of the hardest hit through the pandemic. Before the onset of COVID-19, nonprofit organizations accounted for at least 12.5 million total jobs. In Australia, it's 10% of the total country's workforce. As reported in data from the Center for Civil Society Studies (CCSS) at Johns Hopkins University and its 2020 Nonprofit Employment Report, during the first three months of the pandemic (i.e., March, April, and May 2020), nonprofits lost a conservatively estimated 1.64 million of those jobs, reducing the nonprofit workforce by 13.2% as of May 2020.

Following a few months of gains, by mid-year in 2022 we saw a significant slowing in the recovery of nonprofit jobs during that period. We even saw a slight reversal in recent positive growth, representing an additional loss of 0.4% over the 557,000 jobs lost since it was tracked last year.

That's why it's important to look at the effects of the 'great resignation' phenomena by taking a proactive look at our current social-sector talent and how we can start building a better foundation for change; looking at those new voices, approaches, and partners; and putting them in a position to be successful. This shouldn't be about resignations, it should be about reprioritizations.

So how can nonprofits establish real leadership pipelines instead of leaking a golden generation of talent?

Firstly we need to support them in their professional development to ensure they reach their full potential, all the while looking at opportunities to step into leadership roles and become those powerful voices, complete with lived experience, that our sector is crying out for.

It should be a fluid process rather than a forced outcome—an intentional, strategic step forward rather than a byproduct of fortune. We need to take control of our futures, not just take a reactive approach to change that is determined by outside forces. Black Lives Matter is a movement, it wasn't a moment. All the companies and organizations that diversified their staff, diversified their boards, and changed their narrative must be motivated by a shared vision of the future and not the fear of being left behind or overtaken.

Diversity is not just a box to be ticked; it is a commitment to change for the better, a change in which fairness is key and justice is at its core.

People, not processes drive change, and as part of our commitment to forging an equitable and socially just future, we must invest in our emerging leaders, their lived experiences, and their ideas for the future.

Ultimately, we need to be more aware of what is required to attract, keep, and elevate nonprofit talent. We need to understand how to challenge current narratives of what our workforce looks like, how it acts, and the environment it operates in. We collectively must chart a path to what steps we can take now and over the next decade to ensure that our sector is the most dynamic and impactful it can be—a place where workers' identity can have both legacy and currency, rather than being made to choose by the pressures of an outdated view of success and those leaders that have perpetuated that view for the majority of their careers.

Taxi Squads

A taxi squad in professional sports refers to a group of players who are signed to a team but are not part of the team's active roster. The purpose of a taxi squad is to provide teams with additional depth and flexibility, allowing them to quickly bring in players in case of injury, illness, or other unexpected events.

The specific rules and regulations governing taxi squads can vary depending on the sport and the league. In some cases, taxi squads are limited to a certain number of players, while in others they may be open-ended. Similarly, some leagues require teams to make formal transactions to move players on and off the taxi squad, while others allow teams to make changes on a more ad hoc basis.

Generally, players on a taxi squad are paid a lower salary than those on the active roster and may be required to practice separately from the main team. However, they remain under contract with the team and can be called up to the active roster anytime.

Taxi squads can be particularly useful in sports such as hockey or football, where injuries are common and can quickly deplete a team's roster. By having a group of extra players on hand, teams can avoid being caught shorthanded, and can quickly bring in replacement players without having to rely on expensive or risky trades.

Talent pools can come from anywhere. Qualify them and reach back out when other opportunities exist or for other roles where their skills might be good. The industry should do this better. It should be a talent clearinghouse given all the people that apply for roles with recruitment firms etc.

If you have identified individuals who were good for a role but were not the preferred candidate, there are several steps you can take to continue cultivating their potential and keep them engaged:

Provide feedback: Let the individual know what impressed you about their skills and experience. Share areas where they can improve and offer guidance on developing their skills. Giving feedback can demonstrate that you value their potential and want to help them grow.

Communicate regularly: Stay in touch with the individual and communicate regularly about their progress and potential opportunities. Let them know that you are keeping them in mind for future roles and projects, and offer guidance on how they can continue to develop their skills.

By leveraging internal candidates for fundraising jobs, you can tap into the talent and knowledge that already exists within your organization, while also creating opportunities for career growth and development for your employees.

The sector would also be wise to think about talent more holistically too. This includes strategies to capture interested candidates that either don't make it to the interview stage and more importantly those who do and while qualified, were not the selected candidate. I'm talking about the candidates that made the final phase that were just passed over for a candidate that was a better fit for that organization at that point in time. I'm sure small nonprofits that struggle to identify suitable candidates would jump at the chance at some of the talent that are looking for new challenges but are unaware of other opportunities due to their network or ability to market the roles more broadly. Maybe there is scope to have an organization that looks at this issue and becomes somewhat of a clearinghouse of fundraising talent.

Trialists

Trialists are athletes who are invited to participate in a trial or try out with a professional sports team to showcase their skills and potentially earn a spot on the team's roster. These tryouts are often held in the preseason or offseason and allow the team's coaching staff and management to evaluate the player's abilities and determine if they would be a good fit for the team. In some cases, trialists may be signed to short-term contracts or invited to participate in further training with the team, while others may not be offered a contract and are free to pursue other opportunities. We see this in several ways in our sector and acknowledge that some self-promotion and marketing might be needed to separate you from the crowd.

Internships: Internships offer opportunities for individuals to develop fundraising skills in a real-world setting. This hands-on experience can help individuals build a strong foundation of knowledge and skills that can be transferred to a full-time fundraising role.

Internships can serve as a pipeline for recruiting top talent to full-time fundraising roles. By offering internships, nonprofits can identify promising individuals and provide them with opportunities to gain experience and skills that will make them strong candidates for future positions.

Secondments: Secondments can be highly beneficial for developing fundraisers in nonprofits in the following ways:

Exposure to new skills and experiences: Secondments offer opportunities for fundraisers to gain exposure to new skills and experiences that they may not have been exposed to in their current roles. This can help broaden their skill sets and prepare them for future career opportunities.

Increased collaboration and innovation: Secondments encourage collaboration and knowledge-sharing between different departments or organizations. This can lead to innovative approaches to fundraising and new insights into donor behavior. This should be more prevalent in our sector, especially with shared credit for securing gifts.

Retention and career development: By offering secondments, nonprofits can demonstrate their commitment to employee development and career advancement. This can increase employee satisfaction and retention, as well as attract top talent to the organization.

As I mentioned, trials are also a way to market yourself. Traditional fundraising approaches are changing. The vehicles through which funds are being invested are changing. Philanthropy is transitioning from funding as a charitable transaction to one with a social justice lens at its core. To adapt to this paradigm shift, the sector is going to need new voices, experiences, education, training, and expertise when it comes to executing these dynamic new takes on how we support programs and projects looking to deliver real impact for those they serve.

And it's not just the type of staff that must change. So how can you crack into the fundraising field with purpose rather than "accidentally" find their way there?

I receive many questions on how to get a job in fundraising, and I'm aware that much of the advice you can find on the web is to focus on "following your passions" and working on your soft skills. What I'm here to tell you is that there are far more practical approaches that will get you closer to your dream job and help you thrive when you get there.

Use Power Mapping: This is a visual tool and process that social justice organizers often use to identify people of influence to build a comprehensive lobbying strategy and effect change through groups and individuals. This methodology can be readily applied by those seeking to break into the philanthropic sector. Just list all the leaders who are driving change and innovation and align with your values or where you want to be career-wise and then create a sub-tier listing of emerging leaders with whom you want to connect. Follow and connect with them on social media, learn which groups they align with, and then begin tracing back the dots. These lines will then lead to those top-tier leaders (given the common two degrees of separation we see through the sector), and you will have a warm lead who can connect you.

Network: Many opportunities exist within the philanthropy sector that are geared solely toward engaging new and diverse voices in the field. Keep an eye out for conference scholarships that give you full program access, including the pre-conference networking events, and link up with the professional groups that can help expand your knowledge and understanding of the sector's nuances within your region. Your local chapters of the Association of Fundraising Professionals (AFP), Emerging Practitioners in Philanthropy (EPIP), and the Young Nonprofit Professionals Network (YNPN) are great organizations to connect with. Join a committee and then progress to the board. It's a great experience, and you learn quickly about programming, fundraising, and governance with a focus on your own professional development.

Build Your Own Informal Groups: Create an informal group of your peers (which can be organized through a simple Facebook group) and meet regularly to discuss opportunities and sector trends and to work through ideas and pain points to advance your respective careers. This approach has been applied in several ways: roundtables where prominent community leaders are invited to speak, book clubs and happy hours that layer in local viewpoints, and the more intentional and intellectually enriching 8-3-1 events championed by fellow futurist Trista Harris in her book Future Good. The overall premise for that type of event is to gather eight individuals for three hours to discuss one major issue affecting their community.

Become a Funder: What better way to learn about organized philanthropy, grantmaking, and your community than by joining or starting a giving circle? Many giving circles let members give at a level that is meaningful to them, and there are plenty of platforms (such as Amplifier and Growfund) that help you receive and distribute funds to make the process as simple as possible so you can focus on the giving part. Other options include opening a donor-advised fund (DAF), which is very much like a charitable bank account. It is more expensive to open this kind of account, with the lower-end establishment fees needing an initial contribution of between

$2,500 and $5,000. However, DAFs may become exponentially more affordable in the near future, which will be discussed later in this book.

You can also consider pitching to your parents or extended family the benefits of establishing a family fund as a way to give back to your community, espouse your values, and invest in your professional development. It will bring your family closer together while bringing you closer to a possible career move.

Pursue Your Credentials: While degrees and master's programs are questionably still prerequisites for senior-level and executive positions, the institution you receive them is becoming far less important in the greater scheme of things. The core lessons from an MBA and MPA (master's in public administration) are what are of the most value. Many private nonprofit universities now have month-long courses, meaning you can graduate in just over a year. Together with the availability of additional professional accreditations such as the Certified Fundraising Executive (CFRE) and Certified Nonprofit Professional (CNP), there are plenty of options to build out your resume while building up your own experiences. Don't let a year go by waiting for the right time or trying to be flexible for the right position. Get back to school, get credentialed, and you will get ahead in the long term. It's a lot more affordable than you think.

Join Learning Groups: There are many new niche leadership organizations—progressive, identity-focused, city- and sector-specific cohorts—spreading out nationwide, providing participants with core skills across organizing, strategy, and PR. The best part of these groups is the strong bonds you make with sector-wide peers and the alumni network to which you now belong, one where numerous jobs and other unique opportunities are made available.

Take a Leadership Role on a Nonprofit's Board or Committee: Join a nonprofit board to learn about governance and the real needs of a social-sector organization. Understanding the difficulties of fundraising, sustainability, and capacity will give you a greater appreciation of the main beneficiaries of philanthropic funds and give you a unique lens for enhancing the process and impact of a funder's investment. This is also where you will be at the same table as funders—with many major donors of those organizations (both corporate and individual) traditionally playing leadership roles. One pitfall to be aware of is that people who are at the beginning of their career feel they have to be asked to join a board or shy away from service due to "give and get" requirements. This is not necessarily the case. Seek out organizations where mission and values align, volunteer or serve on a committee to get a feel for that organization, and then state your case to join that board and manage their expectations. You will be surprised at how accommodating organizations will be for the right skills, ideas, and energy.

Don't Mistake Skills for Experience: I firmly believe that generalists—those who have applied their talents to a multitude of different roles and sectors over their career—have strong transferable skills and know enough to hit the ground running (and in several cases have a higher ceiling in terms of their potential). Don't be deterred from applying for that dream job due to those elusive "preferred experiences and qualifications." You never know what the hiring manager is looking for or which candidates have built out that particular talent pool. Remember, you have to be in it to win it!

Apply for a Fellowship: This is technically a one-year paid internship and a position you will still need to apply and interview for, but one that more often than not results in becoming a full-time employee. The added benefit here is twofold—the position is often endowed or named by the donor who has made this capacity-building position possible, which provides that extra bit of prestige, and the role is normally created to help drive a particular issue or emerging trend in the sector. This is a great opportunity to make yourself indispensable to the organization.

Work with a Mentor: Plenty of articles out there discuss the benefits of identifying a mentor. Given that the philanthropy sector is quite niche and narrow, receiving wise counsel and feedback on navigating a career in the sector is extremely important. There are also other benefits such as being taken to significant events as their guest, leveraging their networks to recommend you for potential roles, and acting as a reference. But remember, mentoring is more than just coaching, it's a much deeper relationship and investment in turn.

Volunteer: Can't afford that $1,000 ticket to SXSW EDU? Heck, most professional half-day summits are $100 or more these days too. However, there is a way in if you miss out on conference scholarships, and that's by volunteering. Reach out to organizations hosting exciting conferences in the field and volunteer to help out at registration or to be a note-taker in breakout sessions. This will probably result in a shift from two to five hours (with the bonus of meeting and greeting guests and VIPs who you probably power mapped by now), and then you'll have the opportunity to check out the rest of the conference for that day.

Hot tip: Get involved with the conferences of Regional Associations of Grantmakers and the prominent National Philanthropy Day functions. National associations that will need local support may also come to your city. And here's the kicker: you'll likely get a complimentary lunch too, and executives these days aren't just eating the rubber chicken.

If you want a job in philanthropy, it's important that you understand that identifying and acquiring the skills, experience, and leadership required to deliver real impact through an evolving philanthropic landscape is paramount. And with many recent changes and emerging trends in the sector—and the possibility of many more over the next decade—more opportunities and entry points now exist for you to approach this career shift or promotion in an intentional way.

Scouting

Scouts in professional sports are individuals teams or organizations employ to evaluate players and assess their potential for success at the professional level. Scouts are typically responsible for identifying and analyzing amateur and professional players, and for providing recommendations to team management regarding which players to draft, sign, or trade for.

The specific duties of a scout may vary depending on the sport and the organization, but typically involve a combination of the following:

Player Evaluation: Scouts evaluate players by attending games, watching videos, and analyzing statistics to assess their strengths, weaknesses, and overall potential. This can involve evaluating physical attributes such as speed, strength, and agility, as well as mental attributes such as intelligence, attitude, and work ethic.

Talent Identification: Scouts are responsible for identifying potential prospects, and for developing an understanding of the market for players in the league. This may involve scouting at amateur events or tracking players who are already playing professionally.

Reporting: Scouts report their findings to team management, typically through written reports or verbal presentations. These reports will often include detailed assessments of players' strengths and weaknesses, as well as recommendations for whether or not the team should draft, sign, or trade for a particular player.

Networking: Scouts often attend events and engage with other scouts, coaches, and players to develop relationships and build networks within the industry. This can help them to stay informed about emerging trends and opportunities in the sport and to build a reputation as a trusted evaluator of talent.

Overall, the role of a scout is crucial in professional sports, as they play a key role in helping teams to identify and acquire the best possible talent. Scouts must have a deep understanding of the sport they work in, as well as strong analytical skills and the ability to work well under pressure.

Empowering your HR team here to act as scouts and build a talent pipeline is paramount.

People are your most important asset. There is no dispute around that. Yet how can we identify those values-aligned people, who will help drive your organization to new heights, and who will remain happy and productive in both the good times and the bad? And how will technology ensure these folks are identified and elevated to your attention in the most competitive job markets?

Consider what's best for your organization. Is it having someone come in for two years and help your organization level up and then move on? Or having someone who will stay for at least five years to build and grow a program over time methodically?

Here are two other questions that may be keeping hiring managers up at night:

1. How do we know what we are getting—or, most importantly, who?
2. How do we use tech to help ensure our candidate pools are as diverse as they are dynamic?

Recruitment has historically been a minefield of inconsistency. It is full of biases that have spawned jaw-dropping research around the percentage of interview callbacks for white- or Black-sounding candidates. It sees folks benefit from either directly or indirectly knowing someone at an organization who has managed to get them noticed or—for the sake of interpersonal politics—screened by HR. And you have hiring managers skimming hundreds of emails and making decisions based on a hunch and not by any sort of science except thinking "he/she looks like they are worth talking to."

The end goal for recruitment is always to fill the job vacancy. It's the process's most binary function (and I would encourage you to understand your vacancy rates from a budgetary standpoint). But it's time we went beyond that to find the best fit, both for the position and for the culture of the organization. It's about scouting those opportunities ahead of a position becoming available so that your fundraising plans aren't affected by gaps in capacity.

In my past hiring roles, whether overseeing the process or as the hiring manager, I have approached it seriously and with growth in mind—for myself, the employee, and the organization as a whole. I would take the time to think about the candidates rather than rush through my immediate feedback, pondering what weaknesses of ours this person can cover, what the ceiling could be for our team with this missing piece in place, and how the candidate might challenge us to be better.

I wanted to present my case both qualitatively and quantitatively, and for a while, I became fascinated with finding useful ranges of data sets to help me make more informed choices. I created a reporting structure and policies to elevate these additional insights, so they also informed others who were asked to participate in panel interviews. This also gave employees the tools and training to enhance the process for them and the candidate.

This standard is what is commonly referred to as talent optimization, something I am a big proponent of. It is a way to layer in more scientific methods when building candidate pools and lowering the risk of a bad or underwhelming hire. This can be a very expensive mistake, especially for a nonprofit organization.

We must continually seek better ways to evaluate candidates. I bet that in a few years, tech that screens behavioral traits and cognitive abilities will become the norm, not just a tool used by large tech firms. I also mention that I'm a certified Predictive Index (PI) practitioner. PI is an award-winning talent optimization platform that aligns business strategy with people strategy for optimal business results. It helps groups design great teams and cultures, make objective hiring decisions, and foster effective employee engagement.

More than 8,000 clients and 350 partners use PI—Nissan, DocuSign, and Subway, to name just a few—across more than 140 countries. It was the platform I felt could best help me succeed in my hiring hypothesis. It not only helped me review my position descriptions (both current and future) but also took into account the expectations of this role from other members of staff through pattern analysis, providing me with a 360-degree viewpoint of who might best succeed in a particular job by understanding the team's traits, tendencies, and cognitive abilities. How might this new person fit now and in the long term was what we hoped to derive.

After these initial internal surveys, a job target was generated, which would then be used to highlight those that aligned best with the skills, capacity for critical thinking, and defining behaviors. Candidates at different stages of the hiring process would then take both cognitive and behavioral tests, with those whose results fit within the identified ranges being elevated to the top of the list.

The main stumbling block for the scaling of talent optimization software is the fact that there is a disconnect between what the testing means and how it is used. This isn't a pass-or-fail scenario; it's just another data point. It shouldn't be a way to disqualify candidates early in the process and is probably best used to screen your finalists if you are struggling to choose between them. Note: If they are like-for-like candidates, always go with the diverse hire.

Talent optimization isn't just about the hiring process, either. I am still finding new ways to help empower managers to build high-performing teams, analyze employee engagement and take customized action, uncover and grow leadership potential, increase productivity, and ensure a great job fit for employees and candidates despite all the day-to-day challenges thrown our way.

Talent optimization, if used to strengthen a talent pool rather than try to engineer the perfect candidate, will help make amazing things happen and with AI sure to accelerate and scale these capabilities over the coming years, the ability to identify and recruit the very best talent for nonprofit organizations will eventually be just a few clicks away.

But this is a Rolls Royce approach, so what can small teams do to level up? I believe that lies in platforms like LinkedIn rather than larger groups like Indeed or Zip Recruiter.

LinkedIn is a professional networking platform that is used by millions of professionals across the globe. However, I find that it is still a very underutilized tool by the nonprofit industry.

For example, our HR teams may not be using advanced search filters, creating compelling job postings, or utilizing LinkedIn's messaging and outreach features to connect with potential candidates.

So, while LinkedIn is a powerful recruitment tool, it's important to use it effectively to get the most out of it.

For example, have you ever performed a Boolean search when proactively searching for candidates on the platform? A Boolean search is a technique used in databases and search engines that allows you to combine keywords with operators such as "AND," "OR," and "NOT" to produce more accurate and targeted results.

For example, if you were looking for candidates with experience in fundraising and were indigenous, you could use a Boolean search and enter "fundraising AND indigenous" as your search query. This would return results that contain both the words and help you identify candidates in the field and then encourage them to apply.

Similarly, if you wanted to exclude specific results from your search, you could use the "NOT" operator. For example, if you were looking for major gift fundraisers but wanted to exclude results for entry-level positions, you could use the search query "major giving and NOT entry level."

Boolean searches allow you to refine your search and get more specific results, which can be helpful in recruitment when you are looking for highly qualified and specific candidates.

So back to LinkedIn. It can be an effective tool for identifying new candidates because it has:

1. Large user base: LinkedIn has a massive user base with over 900 million members across 200 countries. This makes it an excellent platform to search for candidates.
2. Detailed profiles: LinkedIn profiles provide lots of information about a candidate's skills, experience, and education. This makes it easier for recruiters to find candidates with the right skills and qualifications.
3. Search filters: As mentioned, LinkedIn provides various search filters that can be used to narrow down the candidate

pool based on factors such as location, industry, job title, and experience level.

4. Networking: LinkedIn allows users to connect with professionals in their industry and join groups related to their profession. This makes it easier to find and connect with potential candidates.

5. Messaging: LinkedIn also allows recruiters to send messages to potential candidates directly, which can be a great way to start a conversation and gauge interest in a position.

The path to finding your next job has taken many different turns over the past few decades. Back in the day you either found it in the newspaper classifieds, took the time to visit a job center and peruse the boards, or dropped your resume off to several companies you located in the Yellow Pages.

Fast forward a decade or so and then most of this has gone digital. Job boards went online, and social media has captured some of the passing interest of job seekers. But now even those static job boards aren't doing the 'job'. With demand for fundraisers at an all-time high, being proactive in your talent sourcing is essential and platforms like LinkedIn can help you also look at transferable skills where a simple message asking them if they have considered a role in the sector could secure you hungry talent with a high ceiling for excellence in the craft.

Recruiting Outside The Box

Professional sports teams recruit overseas players for a variety of reasons, including:

Skill level: Overseas players may bring a high level of skill and talent to a team, making them more competitive and increasing their chances of success. Some countries have a strong tradition and history in specific sports, such as soccer in Europe or basketball in the United States, which can lead to a deep pool of talented players.

Marketability: Overseas players can also increase the marketability of a team, especially if they come from a country with a large fan base or a significant media presence. Teams may also look to expand their global reach by signing popular international players.

Cost: In some cases, overseas players may be less expensive to recruit than domestic players due to differences in salary expectations, taxes, or other factors. This can be especially attractive to teams that are operating under salary caps or other financial restrictions. *I believe in paying someone their worth but acknowledge the business side of professional sports.*

Diversity: Recruiting overseas players can also bring a level of diversity and cultural exchange to a team, which can enhance team chemistry and help players learn from different styles of play and coaching.

Overall, recruiting overseas players can provide professional sports teams with a competitive advantage, increase their marketability, reduce costs, and enhance team diversity and cultural exchange.

This is akin to securing talent from either outside of the sector or outside of town. I recently read a terrific opinion piece in the Wall St Journal titled 'Innovation Moves to Middle America – Migration of entrepreneurs may yield fewer photo-sharing apps and more practical solutions' where I was captivated by the following paragraph;

Many have noted that talent and capital are starting to move out of the nation's three major tech hubs and into various more affordable cities like Phoenix, Salt Lake City and Tulsa, Oklahoma. But most are missing the more important point: The nation's tech workers likely won't work on the same kinds of projects that dominated their time when they were ensconced in their hubs. Entrepreneurs who previously worked in tech bubbles—places that have produced far too many photo-sharing apps—will suddenly be exposed to a wider range of real-world challenges that they likely would never have encountered without the pandemic.

What sparked my interest here was the mention of Tulsa, Oklahoma. Tulsa is the original home of Black Wall Street and has seen a coalition of leaders in government, business, philanthropy, and education come together to jump-start its startup ecosystem. Though the history of Black entrepreneurship in Tulsa is one of triumph and tragedy, the city is embracing collaborative solutions to develop resources for Black founders and using unique programs to attract new diverse talent to the community. For the better part of the 20th century, Tulsa was known as the "Oil Capital of the World," but today its economy is fueled by telecommunications, aviation, technology, and finance.

I have been watching the emergence of this city and its civic tech slant since I saw G.T. Bynum, the Mayor of Tulsa, speak on a panel at the first Upswell conference in Los Angeles. He discussed his strategies for data-driven economic mobility and that by using data, he could identify the local skills shortages and then target young folks who were not currently working or going to school to get the credentials to fill that need. It's also an approach that could be replicated for a range of other local indicators and outcomes.

He also spoke about a complementary approach to filling the talent gaps through Tulsa Remote, a program founded by the

George Kaiser Family Foundation, which offered 250 people the opportunity to relocate to Tulsa by providing individuals with a grant spread out over the course of the year. This was to help with moving expenses, a monthly stipend to help them navigate (and be supported financially in) the early stages of their transition, and the remainder as a welcome gift at the end of their first twelve months in their new city. Recipients of these grants were also given space at a co-working facility, which helped new residents to plug in quickly to a new collaborative community.

I like Tulsa Remote not only through the obvious talent identification and workforce development angles but also that philanthropy initially seeded its success. The George Kaiser Family Foundation was motivated to underwrite this program as a way to enhance the current local workforce by attracting diverse new talent to a forward-focused municipal administration. The program has now had multiple cycles and has added an upfront payment option for new residents buying a home.

So that leads me to introducing Mandi Ford Argo who recently moved to Tulsa to head up Venture for America's presence in the city. Born and raised in the great state of Texas, Mandi moved to Tulsa during the pandemic and immediately fell in love with the city and its people. She joined VFA after spending 8 years working at The University of Texas at Austin where she supported students and faculty in their career, research, and entrepreneurial endeavors. Most recently Mandi supported the UT College of Natural Science's fundraising efforts by overseeing relationships with companies and foundations that support research and development and student programs.

Mandi earned her bachelor's in philosophy and Executive master's in public leadership, both from The University of Texas. She loves motorcycles, exploring new restaurants, and her family- the main driver for her move to Tulsa.

As the Director for Tulsa for Venture For America, Mandi launched the organization's operations in Tulsa, the newest VFA city. Her goal is to support the entrepreneurial ecosystem in Tulsa by providing a pipeline of incredible talent for startups in the region. Her goal is to ultimately have VFA alums and Fellows launch their businesses in Tulsa and see Tulsa as a place to put down roots and grow.

Mandi is personally driven by the need to tackle inequity in access to entrepreneurship and is well-positioned to work on this issue every day. "I think we've all heard the statistics around how much VC funding goes to white male founders vs. everyone else, how many startup founders are white men, and how few people of color or women make it to a leadership role in any company- startup or otherwise. I believe entrepreneurship is a great economic development driver and an amazing path to financial success."

Like my ode to Tulsa above, Mandi recognizes that there is a lot of focus on Tulsa right now (and the issues she outlined), and is buoyed by the fact that philanthropic organizations are actively collaborating with. Funding organizations like Atento Capital, Build In Tulsa, and Venture For America to create access and provide resources that support founders from underrepresented communities.

"Philanthropy has the power to be a partner to advance equity and opportunity, uplifting underrepresented communities and giving a voice to those that are often overlooked."

The Schusterman Family Foundation is an example of philanthropy doing good in Mandi's eyes. "Their focus on DEI initiatives, especially in entrepreneurship and education, has been amazing. I'm also really impressed by the Lobeck Taylor Family Foundation. Their support of entrepreneurship in food and beverage, CPG, and retail space has led to a vibrant up-and-coming restaurant scene in Tulsa, making Tulsa a really attractive place to live and/or launch a restaurant (interested in doing this? Then check out their

Kitchen66 program). I'm also really excited to see the results of their investment in the market district on Historic Route 66. This is another great example of a public/private partnership that so far is a success."

But Mandi is quick to point out that the most successful actors in philanthropy are those that understand clearly defined roles and responsibilities in the broader ecosystem and are fully leveraging the benefits of being in their lanes and areas of expertise.

"The government is designed with certain restrictions and regulations for many reasons, including ensuring equity among all its citizens. That said, philanthropic organizations have a unique opportunity to leverage their power and influence to uplift the voices of underrepresented communities when governments fail in this regard."

"I believe that Martin Luther King Jr. was right when he said, 'the arc of the moral universe is long, but it bends toward justice.' The work happening in Tulsa right now – the commemoration of the Tulsa Race Massacre, the resources being poured into Tulsa to support BIPOC and underrepresented business founders, and the launch of programs to create access to education and resources – is profound. I'm excited to see a city take an active approach by collaborating with philanthropic organizations here to build a truly inclusive foundation for entrepreneurship and launch economic development initiatives that will create solutions that will long out-live its own founders."

And we are excited to see Mandi's influence here as she re-cruits, trains, connects, and supports a new generation of social sector leaders that will help drive a new economic and community vibrancy for Tulsa that has long been promised, but until now, not entirely realized. It's funny what can be done with new energy and ideas in our community, right?

Every candidate who lived in a different city than where our offices were and made it through the initial screening process was put forward to me as the hiring manager with caveats I had not asked for, nor was thinking about.

- "What are their motivations for the move?"
- "Why would they want to move from [insert name of current employer/city] to come here for this salary?"
- "There is no doubt that they are just trying to get to [insert city] and we will be used as a stopgap until they find something better."

This line of thinking needs to stop. Both in terms of physical location and also career pivots. Who are we to make assumptions about someone's motivations to apply for a position?

The nonprofit sector should be actively courting talent to move into our sector. If business is actively recruiting folks regardless of location and also providing them with relocation packages, then we need to get with the times and realize this as a viable strategy.

It's just another nonprofit stigma that needs to be overcome. If we are looking for a stellar candidate, one who we see as a key to improving our impact, culture, and bottom line, and we find that person in another state, then why is it so hard to justify a further $2,500 to subsidize their move, especially when you can add contractual clauses that will protect your investment and ultimately de-risk looking at someone from outside your network and the city you operate in?

Remember that talent is just as important as tech and that the right people can help you achieve your future goals. If we have learned anything from 2020, it's that location is just a place you log on to your computer and that working remotely can increase options for us to attract the best talent to our organizations.

It's also the same foundational argument for those coming from the corporate world including sales and marketing. Nonprofits should also be open to remote employees and those who wish to relocate out of the local area, as they should with those looking for a mid-career pivot (which is much more the norm with Generation Z).

During the COVID-19 pandemic, I had many random conversations with folks (mainly people we were buying furniture for our new house from) who shared that they were letting their leases run out or selling up and either traveling the country, moving to a more affordable city, or moving back to their hometown while still remaining employed with their current company. Workplace flexibility will become more of a deciding factor than ever regarding who people work for. If your organization isn't solely place-based, you seek to benefit from this as talent becomes more accessible and mobile than ever before.

Contract Negotiation

A contract extension in professional sports refers to an agreement between a team and a player to extend the duration of the player's existing contract beyond its original term. This is typically done to provide the player with additional years of guaranteed income and job security, while also ensuring that the team retains the player's services for a longer period of time.

In a contract extension, the terms of the player's existing contract are typically renegotiated to reflect the additional years of service. This may involve changes to the player's salary, bonuses, and other incentives, as well as modifications to the terms of the contract such as performance clauses and trade restrictions.

Contract extensions can benefit both the team and the player, as they allow the team to retain a valuable player for a longer period of time, while also providing the player with additional financial security and the opportunity to stay with a team they may have grown to love. In some cases, a contract extension may also help to avoid potential conflicts and distractions, such as when a player's contract is set to expire at the end of a season and the player becomes the subject of trade rumors or negotiations with other teams.

Overall, contract extensions are a common and important aspect of professional sports, and can play a key role in helping teams to build successful, long-term rosters. Nonprofits should look at this in one of two ways, either in terms of management on fixed terms contracts or as an important retention strategy, because if you don't secure your people long term others will snap them up as part of free agency, especially with lots of boutique nonprofit recruitment firms beginning to pop up. An experienced fundraiser in this market will get one or two emails from recruiters looking to fill roles and often ignore them, whereas someone in their first few years of fundraising will probably have their heads turned due to that outreach.

NOW IS THE TIME TO COMMIT TO LONG-TERM INVESTMENTS IN NONPROFIT STAFF

The Johns Hopkins Center for Civil Society Studies analysis on nonprofit job growth continues to be something to track post-COVID and folks, the stats aren't great.

Many jobs were lost in healthcare organizations, human services, arts, and recreation. If it weren't for an influx of jobs added by educational nonprofits at the time of writing, we would've been looking at a significant net loss rather than a modest gain.

Now for that big jaw-dropping number. Again, at the time of writing, the total nonprofit workforce was still 958,000 jobs down from when the pandemic took such a devastating hold on society back in February 2020. That's a 7.7% decline for the third largest sector employer and these numbers show that it will be a further two years until we get back to pre-pandemic levels.

The cuts could've been worse if there were sustained delays to the Covid-19 vaccine being available, ensuring that the critical mass of vaccinated citizens needed to start moving out of the fog of the pandemic would be achieved.

When that announcement came it was almost 18 months since we all grabbed our valuables from our offices and took up residence in temporary office space in our spare bedrooms, kitchen tables, and whether we put down the ironing board for the day. It was quite the ordeal, and no doubt one felt acutely by nonprofit staff nationwide, and one that can still continue to have reverberations across the social sector through the coming years.

During natural disasters, many of our societies' systems and infrastructure are exposed. Exposed for their neglect and under-investment. Exposed for lack of planning and mitigation and exposed for lack of foresight. Organizations can be eerily similar in certain aspects and nonprofit leaders need to understand that the possible next test of their organizational resolve is the exposure of their talent pipelines.

This forecast is coming more and more into focus. When jobholders were asked about their motivations for staying in their current role, 74% cited some variant of "sheltering in job," according to LinkedIn's Workforce Confidence Index.

Those responses included collecting a steady paycheck (59%), enjoying a company's perks and benefits (30%), waiting for a more favorable job market (15%), and having no time or energy to make a switch (14%).

My simple message is this. Having to let staff go because of decreased revenues is difficult. Losing staff shortly after the pandemic ended (to the degree we understood back then) – after you had fought so hard to keep over that period, tinkering with budgets, being more flexible with working conditions and expectations and other measures – that was no doubt a big blow to your organization in regards to bouncing back quickly when society and the economy got moving again.

So now is the time to start investing in your staff. Not just for your organization, but for the broader region you serve.

Working in the social sector is hard, but it's a palace where you can make a real difference in people's lives and help advance positive change for the causes you are most passionate about. The noblest motive is the public good and is best served by a commitment to fairness, equality, and creating systems that lead to opportunities for all.

Working in the social sector is hard, yes, but life is hardly easy.

I speak often about what I call the 'professional cliff face.' I feel that by not engaging emerging leaders and putting them on a pathway to leadership to which they can see, contribute to, and in a small way control, then we risk losing them as a true civic asset to our communities in the future. And by 'civic asset' I mean someone who is actively participating in the progress of their community in a multitude of ways, helping move money for good, leading on boards and committees, volunteering, and leveraging all of their skills and influence to make their region an even better place to live and work.

The 'cliff face' in this instance is that we are constantly built up earlier in our career, fast-tracked to middle management by our late 20s, and very active in our local community (mainly because of fewer responsibilities and a larger disposable income). There are a vast array of emerging leadership programs available to help build up and sharpen our talents, knowledge, and networks.

Then come our 30s. Life happens, we get into more serious relationships, we get married, we have kids, yet more importantly, we find ourselves still in middle management. Those that sit above us in senior leadership roles have been there for what seems like an eternity, waiting for their own chances to lead (they were effectively in the same position as us a decade or so ago).

So, we drift. We find more connection and purpose in family life. We get a mortgage, we care for our elderly family members, and we coach our kid's soccer team. We continue to work hard and try to block out other distractions to ensure we get that promotion, because then that will make our lives more complete, or so the story goes.

The reality of the matter is that once you fall into a different routine, it is more difficult to re-engage with your community in the ways that most excite you about it. Justifying knocking on doors for a few hours on a Saturday morning for a ballot measure over your kid's dance recital is a difficult ask. And when you add the compounding effects of stress, fatigue, and frustration, it's much easier to reach for a glass of wine and the remote in the evening than it is to hop in your car to city hall and speak to why a dog park in your neighborhood is a positive thing.

I hear about it way too often and excruciatingly more so, see it way too often. People in my eyes who have all the traits and tenacity to lead our community to greatness, slip through our grasp because of the log jam of leadership. They move to a bigger city with more opportunity, and they move out of the social sector to the corporate world saying they will be back, more enthusiastic than ever to help make that change we always discussed—and they never do. Because life happens and we default to newer talent because they have more time to support campaigns in various ways and be ready for populist fights in real-time, not waiting a few hours to get back to you as they renegotiate who is cooking dinner that evening.

It's a vicious cycle. And you know what? When that person above you or that long-serving CEO leaves, they rarely hire from within, citing the need to change gears and bring in new ideas and experience. Most of the time this comes in the form of someone from another city or state entirely. Sometimes you just can't win.

I'll be blunt: The social sector is the worst at pipeline management, and we might be about to find out how much so.

But we can do something about it. We need to look beyond those rose-colored glasses to ensure that everything is back to normal post-COVID. You see, the world has changed, work has changed. People have reflected on what they want and will be geared up to chase their dreams.

We need to do something about it or risk losing a huge amount of talent in the coming year.

I encourage social sector leaders to sit down with staff and begin a formal process that allows their employees to advance their careers to higher levels of salary, responsibility, or authority or risk losing them in what will be the biggest nonprofit talent-free agency in a generation. And if you lose them, there is no doubt our communities will lose them to a certain degree, and with the current state of our country, it's something we can ill-afford to do.

So, what strategies could exist to help keep our best and brightest on that upward trajectory with momentum and the support of their organizations?

Contract Limits: Much like term limits in politics, four- or five-year contracts for leaders that can only be renewed once might help yield several benefits for public entities, including a more focused commitment to results, more transparency and account-ability to the community, and an opportunity for periodic change and the ability to manage the organization's evolution and tran-sition. However, we would be naive as a sector to have a periodic drain of institutional knowledge. A nationally supported "golden gurus" program—which was initially pioneered in Australia—for philanthropy in which a CEO, during the last one to three years of their term, would be available for mentoring and/or consultant work with other foundations would be invaluable.

Cross-Training: Future leadership talent should be identified early and supported by the organization. This could be developed internally in several ways. Still, it makes sense to expose those em-ployees to different functions of the organization and lift up their skills in areas they are lacking. For example, a program director could be trained in nonprofit finance, or a development director could be asked to lead a new place-making project.

Professional Training: It can be awkward to ask for financial support for professional training. Yet I find it strange that the main opportunity to ask about it comes during the budgeting process or an annual review. It's like open enrollment for benefits where only a major qualifying event can drive any flexibility in the budget. Like-wise, it's much easier to ask for $1,500 to travel to San Francisco for a conference than to pay for your Certified Fundraising Executive (CFRE) accreditation or join your local leadership cohort.

Why is that? Is it because they feel you benefit personally and may leave shortly thereafter? If so, that's shortsightedness and insecurity from management who can't see the inherent benefits. Conferences are low-level learning opportunities; they're great for networking and sparking ideas, but hardly add to your skills and expertise in the field. Most employees don't want to ask for things for fear of rocking the boat against the strong current of power dynamics. Leaders should actively look to plug their shining stars into opportunity and reap the benefits of skilling their team up, keeping them engaged, and ultimately keeping them focused on the mission and loyal and energetic to the cause.

Special Teams

Special teams in football refer to a unit of players who are responsible for the various kicking and return aspects of the game. This includes kickoffs, punts, field goals, extra points, and kick and punt returns.

The special teams unit is typically composed of players who may not be starters on offense or defense but possess specific skills such as speed, agility, and tackling ability. Special teams players must also have a strong understanding of game strategy and be able to make split-second decisions in high-pressure situations.

The importance of special teams cannot be overstated as they can have a significant impact on the outcome of a game. A well-executed kickoff or punt return can give a team excellent field position, while a blocked kick or a missed field goal can also swing the game's momentum.

Here are 3 quick tips I have picked up along the way to help alleviate the pressure we all face in recruiting talent. I follow the internal processes and policies but sitting there waiting for candidates to find you will leave you disappointed.

Go beyond job boards: Don't pay $500 to sit on a static job board. Post on the freemium platforms like Indeed and Seek but don't pay a national association lots of money because they don't do any work for you. Avoid the same old candidates and have your investment yield some returns by hiring a candidate sourcer. You deserve quality candidates to choose from to help advance your mission, not a pool of mediocre ones.

Candidate packets: Recruitment is evolving too, and you must market roles in new and professional ways. A comprehensive candidate packet that addresses the role, the organization, and the culture can be the difference between a candidate applying or not. Candidates can see through a cut-and-pasted job description like glass.

Speed of recruitment: Fundraisers are always in demand, so don't miss out on your preferred candidates by having too many rounds of interviewing, having too much time in between rounds of interviewing, and having final checks delay the time between your choice and the time it takes to get out an offer. Even if you get a verbal acceptance, don't take it for granted. Also, check in every now and then between contracts being signed and them starting their first day, things can change in an instant, and making new employees feel valued and wanted before they even start is becoming increasingly more important.

Follow these tips and change the field in your favor.

| 3 |

Crafting A New Narrative For Success

I just wanted to end this part of the book with a call to arms. I have been reading up on narrative therapy after an article on LinkedIn recently piqued my interest. Not only from a personal point of view – after all, understanding our experiences are our experiences and that our past has to be seen as a window rather than as a mirror – but, also how it might relate to a recent conundrum I have been trying to unpack, that being how we perceive ourselves as fundraisers in the sector.

I once posted on LinkedIn about the term falling into fundraising. The conversation came with an equal amount of support, but also some significant pushback due to my choice of words. For those that didn't catch it, here it is:

Urgh – I saw it again. Another great profile piece on an accomplished fundraiser titled "Falling into Fundraising". Look, the most self-degrading thing a fundraiser can say is that they stumbled into the world of fundraising and it needs to change. We as fundraisers, need to change it.

It makes me sad when I hear that when talking to my peers. Building resources to enable organizations to do mission-based work to improve the lives of others and lift up society is something that should be admired rather than admonished.

Apart from the role of CEO, there is no lonelier position than those operating in grassroots nonprofit development – low budgets, sky-high expectations, and a unique pressure exerted by them from leadership to identify the donors and funds that will not only help keep the lights on but expand services, fund a new building and establish a seven-figure endowment from scratch.

Remember, fundraising is the process, not the job title. Just as a 501c3 is just a tax designation, not a business model. It's time to change the narrative. Our shared narrative on what we do and how we do it. Because it's all positive my friends – make no excuses for that.

As you might see, I feel so strongly about the need to change the external perceptions of charity work and better pathways into the profession that it elicited such a strong response and caused me to use the term 'self-degrading'.

Someone pointed out to me that they disagreed that it's self-degrading; and thought it was just a way of saying 'I hadn't realized it could be a career. I discovered it, loved it, and now that's what I do'. They went further in sharing that people who 'fall into fundraising' aren't ashamed, they're proud to do something they love that helps others.

And I fundamentally agree, I guess external perceptions are ultimately changed (and forged) in this instance through a more positive narrative, but how do we create one where the majority of fundraisers see themselves in it because, at the end of the day, they will be the ones that share their work, both the inputs, the outputs and the very real stories of impact which they played a fundamental role in?

I feel that narrative therapy, or the principles of it at least might help us move the conversation forward (Narrative Therapy, 2021).

Narrative therapy is a style of therapy that helps people become—and embrace being—an expert in their own lives. In narrative therapy, there is an emphasis on the stories that you develop and carry with you through your life.

As you experience events and interactions, you give meaning to those experiences and they, in turn, influence how you see yourself and the world. You can carry multiple stories at once, such as those related to your self-esteem, abilities, relationships, and work.

But how do we approach this respectfully to those that play key roles in helping build the resources needed to help build an even more dynamic & vibrant society – tackling the defining issues of our time and catalyzing the research that drives real societal progress?

It's funny because we actually have (and readily utilize) all the things we need to make this process a success. We are storytellers, we are connectors, we are knowledge brokers, we are advisors, and we ultimately play a key role in securing the resources that enable our organizations to carry out our important mission-driven work.

We build cases for support for all of our work, campaigns, and priorities so why don't we apply the same skills and energy to help lift up our profession – how we see ourselves in it and share that passion with the broader community? Fundraisers are equipped to help change the narrative, but it's not that easy, is it?

Or is it?

I think a lot of this tension (or angst) within the sector will be solved through further professionalization of the sector, which in turn will lead to better pipelines for staff wanting to become fund-raisers. And further professionalization of our field will also go a long way in changing the sometimes-transient nature of what is a critical position in our social sector.

It's important to have in mind the issues that lead to folks leaving fundraising including too much pressure to meet unrealistic fundraising goals, coupled with too little pay and frustrating orga-nizational cultures. I disagree with the pay concerns – in many instances,organizations with small budgets sometimes overpay to secure talent and inadvertently warp the career trajectory for fund-raisers – it's just that it's hard for individuals to uncouple the fact that when raising hundreds of thousands of dollars, we look at the money raised first and not the full responsibilities of the role we were employed for.

Now getting back to the crux of this little missive. This post was largely influenced by a recent post by EverTrue Founder & CEO Brent Grinna who shared the company's new mission statement after the recent merger of his company and ThankView.

"Our mission is to build relationships, inspire generosity and im-prove lives.

Our refreshed mission statement was recently crafted with input from our entire leadership team. Going through the process and being reminded of how much our team genuinely cares was inspiring.

And every single day, we see both anecdotes and data that demonstrate our mission in action. Relationships are built through a combination of data and software that leads to human connection. An authentic connec-tion between fundraiser and donor, student and donor, academic leader and donor can be the difference-maker in inspiring generosity. And that generosity creates access to education and non-profit services that improve lives. I know, because my life has been radically improved by way of the philanthropic support from Brown University that sparked my entrepreneurial journey."

This is a great narrative. It's simple, authentic, and relatable. Folks can see where the company is going, who it serves and ultimately see themselves in their future impact. I mentioned to Brent that frontline fundraisers could also use it as their own personal mission statement, and I guess that's why EverTrue is killing it right now – relatability to the work & building solutions in tandem with the needs & demands of the sector, but I digress.

While this mission statement was hardly developed overnight, there is no doubt all the pieces were uncovered by listening to their staff (and the field). To that end, and with that obvious segue, I believe that there are a few things we can do now to start changing the narrative for fundraisers and the work they do, right now;

A comprehensive sector review: I would love for our professional associations & networks AFP, PEAK Grantmaking, YNPN, Community Centric Fundraising, etc. to come together and talk with the frontline fundraisers they represent to talk about their role, how they see it, and their career aspirations. Just a salary review and an annual survey saying 'how can we better serve you' just doesn't cut it.

Another good practice & approach might be looking at what the skills & industries of these fundraisers were before they became fundraising professionals – whether it was from business, politics, or just a shift from nonprofit programs or marketing to fundraising. That will help us identify and build strong pipelines for further recruitment.

Finally, talking to nonprofit managers, recruiters, academics in this space and other relevant stakeholders on how they are seeing the industry trend will provide the data needed to sift through and inform how the sector moves forward. Even speaking with folks that have ultimately left the sector might give us inspired insight into how to retain & support those looking to make fundraising a career rather than a chapter within it.

A shared narrative on who we are and how we are seen: I would love for the sector to come to some sort of agreement on titles. I have written about how we can be creative about titles but fundamentally what do we do, are we philanthropic advisors, development professionals, advancement staff, or fundraisers? At a time when the sector has itself questioned what philanthropy means, we need to align our lingo so that there is no confusion with donors, organizations, and the community at large as to who we are and what we do.

A sector-wide campaign to recruit folks: We can be as creative as we need to be here, but why are we not attending job fairs, building links with chambers of commerce, and sharing flyers with workforce development & broader community groups? Again, a big problem is folks not even knowing fundraising is a career option and an extremely rewarding one at that. It would be amazing to see a billboard in every major metro city encouraging people to become fundraisers!

More celebration of our successes: Is it just me, or are the major awards for Philanthropy all geared towards the donors, campaigns, and volunteers? I agree that these are all key people & roles within our profession but why don't we celebrate fundraising excellence more, especially at the individual level? Why do we just give our fundraisers a pat on the back for raising a major gift, when ultimately it was their research, outreach, stewardship, and trust that helped facilitate the gift? I am not taking away the generosity of donors, all I am saying is that we don't exactly help ourselves in lessening the power dynamics by just talking about the gift. I would love to see our fundraisers interviewed in organization's blog posts, magazines that go out to alumni & members, and perhaps even interviews that discuss the gift with both the donor and the fundraiser talking about the process, not just the outcome. These stories of generosity can be all the more impactful if we show how good philanthropy is done, not just putting a line at the end of the article saying 'for more information contact our advancement team on...'

I guarantee if we did this we would see an uptick in the tenure of development staff from the reported 16 months to ones of 3, 4, 5+ years. All timeframes that can maximize impact and the return on a strong, authentic relationship with a donor.

I also recently re-read the AFP Code of Ethical Standards (Association of Fundraising Professionals, 2018). Personally, I don't see anything saying that fundraisers can't celebrate their wins. Lawyers do it all the time...'we secured $xx million on behalf of our clients', so why don't we. I have seen some friends and peers raise some big 8 figure gifts and simply reshared the big front-page story on LinkedIn with a simple – "I was excited to be a part of this donation". Look, if I raised $250 million for revolutionary new research into cancer treatment, I would want to share that. Those stories will inspire new people into the field and reaffirm to our sector why we do it.

Board and leadership training: Everyone in leadership roles should understand the importance of fundraising and their role in it. Period.

Education and training: There is currently no specific degree in fundraising, with the principles and best practices enshrined within programs focused on nonprofit management, philanthropy, and specialized certificate courses.

This is crazy, especially given the rising demand for trained fundraising professionals. So, what are the current options?

At the time of writing, one of the biggest learning platforms LinkedIn Learning had a grand total of 9 minutes of relevant fundraising content (and an hour on how to make a fundraising video) from the over 5,000 courses on its platform, while Coursera had just one free course from UC Davis which looks into annual campaigns, major & principal gifts and planned giving.

Look, education is important as fundraising can be a very amateur endeavor indeed, with bad habits occurring and manifesting early on in their careers without the right guidance and training. I cringe every time an organization asks for my advice and when I ask who their top 10 current prospects are, they just rattle off the top philanthropists they found in a Google search.

I previously worked for a Regional Association of Grantmakers. The most common question we fielded was what grants do you have available? It's had a confusing name, I get it, but come on, do your research.

There is an abundance of donors out there and with a bit of polish, even the greenest of development staff can be making impactful asks for the benefit of their cause.

That is why I continue to discuss groups looking to professionalize the sector and provide timely and relevant training that can lift up the sector and not use their tenure to push new products, books, or paid webinars. Candid, Nonprofit Hub, AFP, and the like, understand this and are to be commended for their efforts.

Talking about the future of work: AI and the automation of work are going to make several traditional jobs obsolete in the near future. Economic research reports are predicting much of this talent will be moving over to the service industry which is a terrific opportunity to recruit transferable talent into fundraising roles.

Look, at the end of the day we have work to do in selling our importance and worth in the sector (one that has its own problems with public perception), and while I know that there is a real energy to improve and elevate our work, it can't be at the cost of those that do that work.

From The Clubhouse: Fundraise for Australia

Moving back to Australia was a big decision for my family and me. My wife and two kids were all born and raised in San Diego, California, with my wife living there for 44 years before we moved to Austin, Texas, and the opportunity to grow in our careers and potentially own our first home.

While we achieved all this, it was at the expense of us laying roots in our new city, because in one of those strange twists of fate, we moved to Austin a couple of weeks before COVID shut everything down.

COVID, as it was for everyone, was a time of reflection, a somewhat forced chance to assess where we wanted to be, where we wanted to go, and what life we wanted our children to have. COVID was also a collective bubble that heightened our frustrations with the country's direction at the time.

So, we decided to return, and our decision was reaffirmed in just the first few days of our touching down. You see, when my son started his first day of school news broke of the shooting in Uvalde, Texas where 19 children and two teachers were gunned down.

I'm glad to live in a country where my kids can go to school and not worry about a maniac walking the halls with an AR-15 rifle, but I digress.

My main concern moving back was twofold, the first being the possibility of a cultural snapback after being out of the country for over a decade and the second was the state of the fundraising sector, especially after getting a taste of the gold standard across all facets of advancement services while at the University of Texas.

Some would say Australia is a good decade behind, but as Liesl Elder, the Chief Development Officer at Oxford University said to me, "Australia is not ten years behind; it is where it is'" a statement that has really helped me remain both grounded, patient but still wildly optimistic about the country's opportunity to weave generosity and giving into the very fabric of society.

I spent the first 7 months of my role working remotely in the U.S. meeting with several alumni across the country and trying to build a brand-new team from scratch. Getting the right mix of talent was imperative as they would need to hit the ground running in my absence, but as I quickly found, the narrative of a skill shortfall in fundraising rang true.

While Australia is a generous nation - currently ranked fourth in the World Giving Index, which considers three measures of generosity: financial, time, and acts of service - its rates of giving in relation to GDP are low in comparison to similar societies worldwide (0.81 percent), but with a new commitment from the current government to double philanthropic giving by 2030, there is a real opportunity to develop a new culture of giving within the country and to develop the infrastructure to ensure this goal is realized.

A critical part of that infrastructure will be frontline fundraisers - those who build cases of support and will need to make these additional 'asks' to grow and secure a larger share of funding - but they are often missing from the conversation and have been ultimately missing from the policies informing the governments 2030 goal.

My experience during the hiring process (of which I was definitely using Nonprofit Moneyball approaches), showed me that there was a two-speed challenge with the fundraising profession in Australia. The first is that the demand for fundraisers continues to outstrip supply (especially in more regional areas) and that this has been the case for a long time. The second is that there is a real need to see further professionalization of fundraising to ensure that we can continue to achieve new levels of industry excellence and best practice, and ensure we have the ability to support and retain our best and brightest fundraising talent.

So, I did what I couldn't do during COVID: lean into my community and do something about it, whether simply connecting with some folks that shared the same frustrations or starting something that could tackle the issues head-on. Of course, we went with the latter, which was informed by those conversations across the sector.

Fundraise for Australia (F4A) was launched after a year of conversations with that community. The initial goal was to have F4A become a fiscal partner of an established entity. Still, most organizations were focused on retaining fundraising numbers and advocating for other regulatory changes in the sector rather than recruiting. They encouraged our group to explore this space through a pilot program successfully launched at the end of 2022.

Fundraising for Australia aims to identify, recruit, develop, mobilize, and advocate for, as many of our nation's most promising fundraisers to help build a diverse and robust social sector that can raise the resources needed to support and strengthen our society.

F4A is unique to the Australian market and is the only fundraising-focused entity that identifies, recruits, and empowers new people in the field. We provide the course for free which is also new to a sector where affordable, localized, and accessible training is scarce. Comparative professional development courses from the Association of Fundraising Professionals (AFP), Council for Advancement and Support of Education (CASE), and Fundraising Institute of Australia (FIA) cost anywhere from $1750 up to $5500, with these educational costs often seen as a barrier for entry for new fundraisers and acutely felt by small to medium not for profit organizations with razor-thin margins and a limited budget for professional development.

We also support diversity, equity, and inclusion - because representation matters. We aim to recruit individuals in the knowledge that our profession more and more needs to reflect the communities they represent and fundraise for, and on behalf of.

The timing is also significant due to the aforementioned Government's goals to double philanthropy including cutting red tape across state lines, and the potential introduction of new giving vehicles and incentives. It has since opened a Productivity Commission inquiry into the sector. The National Skills Commission has also identified fundraising as one of Australia's fastest-growing – and also one of the best-paid – occupations.

We decided to take a cohort approach to F4A through discussions with chapter leaders in the U.S. from Teach for America, Code for America, and Venture for America. I was always impressed with my previous meetings with these organizations and learning how they work, how they successfully diversify and impact their fields, and on a visit to the Code for America HQ in San Francisco, how they scale and demonstrate success through a robust measurement framework.

A misunderstood part of creating an organization like F4A is what you actually do. Do we offer education or are we a job creator that delivers training? Wanting to be a complement to the ecosystem it was determined that it was indeed the latter so for the pilot we partnered with National University's Fundraising Academy to deliver a digestible curriculum. The Online Accelerate participants took was a live virtual fundraising certificate program. Through the cohort-based training model, participants will connect and collaborate with their peers to: discover effective lead qualification strategies; redefine donor objections; practice their Ask; explore different social styles; understand their ethical responsibilities; and more.

It was an incredible milestone for the program to kick off our inaugural Fellowship cohort in May 2023. 20 new and emerging fundraisers nationwide were selected to participate in our new training program. Participants received over 50 hours of training and be connected with the tools & opportunities that will help them supercharge their careers and deliver transformative change for their communities.

I'm excited about this program's future and its impact on our sector and fundraising nationwide. We are already discussing the benefits of scaling this program with the government and critical funders through our proposed 'Fundraising Futures' program - a 3-year project focused on inner rural communities with some of the highest youth unemployment rates in the country. These week-long in-person trainings will be the culmination of partnerships with local government, educators, and nonprofits to inform them of the benefits of these well-paid, and values-based jobs to the community, and ensure jobs are available to graduates immediately following the completion of this course.

If Fundraiser for Australia is successful we will see the following impact by 2030.

- Train 250 new fundraisers over the next three years in the communities they seek to serve and build resources on behalf of. These cohorts should also reflect the communities they come from and work within.
- Train 500 new fundraisers in the next three years across the country in a virtual format to give them the skills and knowledge needed to secure employment in this field.
- See an additional $117m in funds raised for communities by the 750 people we seek to train (using no compounding measures of career progression or principal gifts raised).
- Diversify the fundraising profession to see more people of color and first nations peoples as frontline fundraisers
- Annually surveying our fundraisers to see if the training and approach to keeping them engaged and connected through an alumni network, helps tackle sector issues of tenure, confidence, and other key metrics such as career growth, portfolio penetration, and the amount it takes to raise a dollar.

- Ensure the curriculum currently delivered by an international partner is tailored to the Australian fundraising landscape. This will include the drafting of a culturally and regulatory relevant text and teaching.
- Deliver this program at scale. Currently, the program is focused on one virtual cohort per year and a maximum of 50 individuals per year. By developing our own curriculum and training our own trainers we will be able to drop the cost per participant from $800 as it stands now to below $200.
- Raise an extra $1.8m in matched funds for salaried positions in the ten targeted communities through public philanthropic partnerships
- Create a compelling narrative for further investment in the field through the success of our trained fundraisers and the organizations they serve. This includes helping identify and recruit new and diverse volunteer leaders to their boards
- An evaluation study of individuals who show a propensity for this kind of work to help drive further identification and recruitment of Australian fundraisers at scale.
- Survey organizational leadership to see how fundraising staff have helped the organization grow beyond the binary outputs of dollars raised. How have they built culture, freed up time for program innovation etc.
- Secure several strategic partnerships with national associations and place-based grantmaking organizations to provide additional training and practical professional networking opportunities. This could be through scholarships for conferences, and memberships to the Fundraising Institute of Australia.

To take advantage of these opportunities and overcome these challenges, we need inspired and engaged individuals who bring energy, creativity, and new perspectives to the sector. Consider that many of us are about to be part of the most significant intergenerational transfer of wealth in Australian history – $3.5 trillion over the next two decades, according to the Productivity Commission - now is the time to invest in frontline fundraisers.

I genuinely hope that Fundraise for Australia can become a template for recruiting new talent to our field and a successful representation of what Nonprofit Moneyball can do for our society. If you are interested in this program and want to learn more about its goals, approaches, and fellowships please visit www.FundraiseForAustralia.com.

2

ORGANIZATIONAL
ARCHITECTURE

For forty-one million, you built a playoff team. You lost Damon, Giambi, Isringhausen, Pena and you won more games without them than you did with them. You won the exact same number of games that the Yankees won, but the Yankees spent one point four million per win and you paid two hundred and sixty thousand. I know you've taken it in the teeth out there, but the first guy through the wall. It always gets bloody, always. It's the threat of not just the way of doing business, but in their minds it's threatening the game. But really what it's threatening is their livelihoods, it's threatening their jobs, it's threatening the way that they do things. And every time that happens, whether it's the government or a way of doing business or whatever it is, the people are holding the reins, have their hands on the switch. They go bat shit crazy. I mean, anybody who's not building a team right and rebuilding it using your model, they're dinosaurs. They'll be sitting on their ass on the sofa in October, watching the Boston Red Sox win the World Series.

| 4 |

Front Office Culture

So, you've built the team, but that team can't be successful without a stellar back office and bold and courageous leadership to drive you to glory. It's the backbone of all successful sporting franchises and is responsible for the administrative and operational functions that support the team's on-field or on-court activities. This includes roles such as human resources, public relations, community relations, technology management, marketing and sales, facilities management, finance, and legal compliance. It is also underpinned by leadership. The owners, President, and coaches.

Ultimately, the goal of the back office is to ensure that the team operates smoothly and efficiently, both on and off the field. If operations are not managed well then players will leave, performances will falter, and revenues and support will drop as a result. Again, all things that nonprofits also fear - the possibility of losing staff and not meeting budget.

The front office is extremely important to a fundraiser too, with leadership setting the organization's goals and strategies. The advancement resources team provides critical support for the fundraising activities such as donor research, database management, gift processing, and reporting. It is designed to help fundraisers identify, cultivate, and steward donors more effectively.

Here are a few reasons why advancement services are so important for fundraisers:

Donor Research: Advancement services provide fundraisers valuable information about donors, including their giving history, interests, and preferences. This information can help fundraisers tailor their approach to individual donors and develop more effective fundraising strategies.

Database Management: Advancement services help fundraisers maintain accurate and up-to-date donor information in a centralized database. This makes it easier to track donor activity, analyze trends, and identify new opportunities for engagement and giving.

Gift Processing: Advancement services ensure that gifts are processed accurately and efficiently, which is critical for maintaining donor trust and satisfaction. This includes tasks such as gift entry, acknowledgment, and receipt.

Reporting: Advancement services provide fundraisers with the data and analytics they need to evaluate the success of their fundraising efforts and make data-driven decisions about future strategies.

So, let's take a quick look at some of the key issues and emerging best practices to ensure that the back office is both bold and efficient.

CEO (& Board)

The President/CEO of a professional sports team is the highest-ranking executive responsible for the overall management and operations of the organization. Their role is to provide leadership, vision, and strategy to ensure the team's success on and off the field.

Some of the key responsibilities of a President/CEO of a professional sports team include:

- Developing and implementing a strategic plan to achieve the team's goals and objectives.
- Managing the team's budget and finances, including overseeing revenue generation, expenses, and investments.
- Hiring and managing the executive team, coaches, and key personnel.
- Overseeing player personnel decisions, including drafting, trades, and free agency.
- Building (and maintaining) relationships with sponsors, media outlets, and the community.
- Representing the team in league meetings and negotiations.
- Ensuring that the team operates within legal and ethical guidelines.

Overall, the President/CEO is responsible for setting the tone and direction of the organization, and for ensuring that the team is successful both on and off the field. Their decisions and actions have a significant impact on the team's performance, reputation, and financial success.

For clarity's sake, I note that CEOs at small to medium non-profits typically interact with their board in a more hands-on manner than their counterparts in larger organizations. Therefore, I don't go into great detail about board makeup and working with volunteers even though I acknowledge their important role in setting and help meeting fundraising goals more broadly. I specifically wanted to discuss the fundraising culture as a foundational element to broader organizational success in fundraising.

Building a fundraising culture within a nonprofit organization means creating an environment where fundraising is recognized as an essential and ongoing aspect of the organization's operations and mission. It fosters a shared sense of responsibility and commitment to fundraising among staff, board members, volunteers, and other stakeholders.

A fundraising culture includes:

Shared values: A nonprofit's mission and values should be reflected in its fundraising efforts, clearly focusing on how fundraising supports its goals.

Clear communication: All staff, board members, and volunteers should understand the organization's fundraising goals and how they contribute to achieving its mission. They should also be able to communicate this information to donors and supporters.

Ongoing training: Fundraising skills and knowledge should be continually developed through training and mentorship opportunities.

Supportive leadership: Senior leaders should model a commitment to fundraising and provide resources and support for staff and volunteers to be successful in their fundraising efforts.

Recognition and celebration: Fundraising achievements should be recognized and celebrated within the organization, which can help to build morale and motivate staff and volunteers.

A fundraising culture is reinforced by recruiting new team members who share the same values and attitudes toward these goals. In Nonprofit Moneyball, each team member understands their role in achieving fundraising success and is accountable for their performance.

My key marker for setting up board members for a win/win situation with the organizations they are interested in is ensuring they sign an agreement before the start which outlines their obligations as a board member both legally and within the organization. One of those is a baseline 'give' which can be a recurring donation set up through the year (not a give or get - keep it clean), the second is an agreement that they are put to work in ways that tap into their expertise or passions and not being asked 'who they know'. We take the time to know our donors yet use our board members like a sure thing. It's a real travesty.

One of the best techniques I know is to include board members in your fundraising process is to invite them to come and learn more about the moves management process. Bring them to the office and show what goes into the strategy and how it aligns with organizational priorities and mission. By the end of the meeting, they will want to feel part of the process and will contribute leads they know might have a deeper connection to the work. Better yet, you can weave them into the cultivation by making them a secondary plan manager and hold their actions and next steps to account!

Also, you should be actively seeking a fundraiser for your board. That voice to back up your CEO and fundraiser when speaking to revenues etcetera is paramount to your success. They are also handy to help you develop campaign plans which seem to be becoming more regular than previous triggers such as milestone anniversaries or capital campaigns for something of need that needs sustained energy.

I'm also a fan of term limits which there are several benefits including:

Promoting fresh perspectives and new ideas: When a CEO has been in their position for a long time, they may become complacent and resistant to change. Term limits ensure that new leaders with fresh perspectives and innovative ideas can take the helm and drive the company forward.

Increasing accountability: With term limits, CEOs know they have a limited amount of time to achieve their goals and meet performance targets. This can increase their sense of urgency and accountability, ultimately benefiting the company and its stakeholders.

Improving succession planning: Term limits encourage companies to develop and implement succession plans for their CEO position. This ensures a smooth transition when the CEO's term ends and reduces the risk of disruptions or uncertainty for the company and its stakeholders.

Enhancing diversity: Term limits can help increase diversity at the top of the organization, by providing opportunities for new leaders with different backgrounds, experiences, and perspectives to take on leadership roles. This can ultimately benefit the company by promoting innovation and creativity, and by reflecting the diversity of its customers and stakeholders.

Reducing the risk of network transfers: Long-serving CEOs may have personal relationships with other executives, board members, or investors, potentially leading to those relationships ceasing after that CEO finishes or following them to their next gig. This is not in the best interests of the organization and sometimes when there is a lengthy period between their announcement to step down. When they do, term limits can help reduce the risk of other conflicts of interest.

Coaches (AKA Your Unit Managers)

A coach in professional sports is responsible for leading and directing a team of athletes in their training, game strategy, and overall performance. The coach is an essential figure who helps to guide the team toward achieving their goals and objectives.

Some of the key responsibilities of a coach in professional sports include:

- Developing a training program for the team and individual players to enhance their skills and overall performance.
- Creating game strategies and tactics to maximize the team's chances of winning.
- Providing motivation and inspiration to players to boost their confidence and encourage them to perform at their best.
- Evaluating the strengths and weaknesses of the team and individual players and making necessary adjustments to improve performance.
- Making in-game adjustments and substitutions based on the team's performance and the opponent's tactics.
- Collaborating with the team's management, including the general manager and president, to make personnel decisions, such as drafting, trades, and free agency.
- Building and maintaining positive relationships with players, coaching staff, and other members of the organization, such as medical staff and trainers.

- Representing the team in league meetings and media interviews.

Overall, a coach plays a vital role in the success of a professional sports team by providing guidance, leadership, and motivation to the players, and by implementing game strategies and tactics to help the team win.

In fundraising though it is quite easy to critique a manager of a frontline fundraiser and lay the blame for issues around staff retention and success squarely on their shoulders but that's want I want to clear up and a conversation that warrants much more debate in our industry. In reality, front-line fundraisers' managers mainly focus on their own portfolio, resulting in a lack of attention to other fundraisers. This is due to their evaluation criteria, which doesn't value management, leading to managers overloaded with a full caseload and unmotivated to manage the team effectively.

This isn't the case across the board. To be fair many of my managers over the past few roles have been some of the absolute best, with a genuine interest in my development, an understanding of what often counts but is not captured, and at the end of the day, leading in a way that inspires confidence, the space to bring your whole self to work and an openness to try new things, but challenging you to bring social proof to shift those broader leadership perspectives.

There is not too much you can do if you land with a bad manager, but there are things you can control in the process like doing your own due diligence around their leadership style (fundraising is a profession where everyone knows everyone, especially if you are in management), seeking your next role via referral, or networking through fundraising associations with a similar intention.

If you are currently in a situation with a bad manager, instead of trying to manage up or wait for change, just shift jobs. Fundraisers are in demand, and I would still hire a good fundraiser after 6 months in their current role if the reasoning was sound and it wasn't a pattern. Don't settle and know your value, life is too short to suffer the compounding anguish of a toxic work environment.

Sports Agents

Sports agents are professionals who represent and manage the business interests of athletes. They act as intermediaries between athletes and teams, helping clients secure contracts, negotiate deals, and manage their finances.

While you don't need an agent, in today's market those who get ahead, normally don't get ahead themselves, they have certain people in their corner advising them. The most common advice will be to ask your manager or to seek mentors, but let's be honest, these are very hard to find, and very hard to sustain. So why don't we just do what athletes do and pay for what we need to go from good to great.

You can hire amazing career coaches, EQ coaches, and even major gift coaches to provide professional and objective advice based on your goals, values, and situation. While screaming "Show me the money!" might be wide of the mark, having an awareness of your weaknesses and seeking expert opinions and guidance in them might be that circuit breaker you needed to get a more senior role or simply to understand your own fundraising persona better when it comes to interacting with prospects and organizational leadership.

I would also encourage you to develop relationships on LinkedIn with key leaders from executive search firms who are always looking to build talent pipelines. When it comes to that time when you are actively looking on the market, they will be the first to knock on your door when a great role comes across their desk, and let's be honest, most of them get a figure close to 20% of your salary, so they will be knocking on your door whether active or not!

| 5 |

Cultivating Your Fanbase

Donors

The supporters of a professional sports team are the fans who follow and support the team, attend games, buy merchandise, and create a community around the team. Supporters can also include sponsors and partners who financially support the team and benefit from the team's exposure and association. Additionally, supporters can include local businesses and government entities that benefit from the economic impact and cultural value that the team brings to the community.

In Moneyball, the Oakland A's faced a challenge when they lost several key players, including Jason Giambi and Johnny Damon, who were popular with fans. To keep fans excited about the team despite losing these big names, the A's had to focus on a new strategy and approach to the game. Here are some lessons that can be applied to engaging donors in your organization's work:

Communicate your strategy: The A's communicated their new strategy to fans and the media by emphasizing their focus on data-driven decision-making and undervalued players. For example, in the movie, the A's general manager Billy Beane met with reporters to explain the team's approach and how they used statistical analysis to find undervalued players. By communicating their strategy and approach, the A's generated excitement and interest among fans.

Highlight successes: Despite losing some popular players, the A's continued to win games and succeed in other areas. For example, in the movie, the A's went on a 20-game winning streak, a record in the American League. By highlighting their successes, the A's were able to keep fans engaged and excited about the team's performance.

Emphasize the impact: The A's emphasized the impact of their strategy on the game and how data-driven decision-making could lead to wins. For example, in the movie, Billy Beane explained to his team how traditional baseball statistics were flawed and how they could use new data to find undervalued players. By emphasizing the impact of their strategy, the A's were able to build support for their approach among fans and players.

Involve fans in the process: The A's involved fans in the process, such as through online polls to help select players. For example, in the movie, the A's held an online poll to ask fans to select the team's new song. By involving fans in the process, the A's were able to build a sense of community and engagement around the team.

Be transparent: The A's were transparent about their strategy and decision-making process. For example, in the movie, Billy Beane was open about his strategy and approach, even when it was unpopular with fans and other teams. By being transparent, the A's were able to build trust and credibility with their fans and stakeholders.

Overall, by communicating their strategy, highlighting successes, emphasizing the impact of their work, involving fans in the process, and being transparent, the A's were able to keep fans engaged and excited about the team's performance, even during times of change and challenge.

Lapsed Donors

Moneyball portrays the Oakland A's as facing initial resistance and skepticism from fans when they traded away some of their popular star players to pursue a new data-driven approach to building a competitive team. However, the movie also suggests that the team's success on the field and the overall excitement generated by their new approach helped to win back fans and build a new fanbase.

In reality, it's difficult to say how many fans the Oakland A's may have lost during their transition to the Moneyball era, as fan loyalty and engagement can be influenced by various factors beyond just the team's performance or roster changes. However, it's worth noting that the A's were able to maintain a competitive record on the field during this time, including making the playoffs in multiple seasons, which likely helped to keep some fans engaged and interested in the team's success. Additionally, the A's innovative approach to team building and focus on underdog players may have attracted new fans who were drawn to the team's unique identity and approach to the game.

All nonprofits are at risk of donors and members leaving the organization. Whether it is something we do, say, or don't do. Being a mission-focused organization demands a level of consistency across the things that determine whether a supporter is happy with our performance and impact, but it can never be the determining factor. You see we can't be everything to everyone, and we can't bend towards the personal feelings and thinking of individuals. If an organization decides to come out and support a particular legislative change that advances their work and helps those they represent then that decision should be made without fear of reprisal.

I have seen several organizations come out and make public statements about equity in the past five or so years. This is something that should be commended and has come with little pushback in terms of members lost. These decisions were not made lightly and the fear of losing influential benefactors factored into the conversations. I then saw a telling data point in the 2018 Fundraising Effectiveness report that said that for every 100 donors gained in the year previously, 99 donors were lost.

For these reasons, I have strong reservations about lapsed donors as a metric.

Lapsed donors as you may know are donors who have contributed but haven't donated within a corresponding amount of time (usually 12 months). It has long been a number that we have disproportionately looked at as a way to judge fundraiser performance around retention when it's just another negative label that the profession has had to carry.

I have spoken about phasing as a new approach to strategy and monitoring success and below will discuss building pipelines over 3-year prospect timeframes. But to make a point here, I would hope to see more focus on the costs per dollar raised which is similar to user acquisition costs in business.

Cost per dollar raised (CPDR) is a metric commonly used in fundraising to evaluate the efficiency of a nonprofit organization's fundraising efforts. It measures how much a nonprofit spends on fundraising to generate each dollar of donations.

A good industry benchmark for CPDR varies depending on the type of nonprofit organization and its fundraising methods. However, a commonly cited benchmark is that an organization should aim for a CPDR of $0.20 or less. This means that for every dollar raised, no more than $0.20 should be spent on fundraising efforts.

This benchmark is based on the guidelines provided by the Better Business Bureau Wise Giving Alliance, which is a charity watchdog organization that evaluates nonprofits based on their adherence to a set of standards for charity accountability. According to their standards, a nonprofit organization's fundraising expenses should not exceed 35% of its total expenses, and the CPDR should be $0.20 or less.

It's important to note that while the $0.20 benchmark is a commonly cited goal, it may not be realistic or appropriate for all organizations, as factors such as the organization's size, the fundraising methods used, and the cause being supported can all affect CPDR. Additionally, the goal of fundraising is to raise as much money as possible for the organization's mission, and sometimes higher CPDR may be necessary to achieve this goal.

So, as you can see, numbers will be different for small fundraising shops but at least you will have a more realistic measure to show progress against. I would also recommend you change the internal narrative around this work too, noting that each new fiscal year you are essentially starting from scratch, and inform your fundraising goal around past years' donations, the expected larger gifts from the previous year of cultivation, and any other 'knowns' for the year including campaigns, organizational anniversaries, etc. That way you will have a more realistic target for the year ahead rather than your leadership just adding 10 - 20% on top (please don't get me started on that!).

Donor retention however is something that shouldn't be overlooked and is a reflection of the work being done and your stewardship approach. Beyond the 'policy' and the unique touch points that come from a fundraiser based on their experience, relationship, and creativity (think sending birthday cards, a baby onesie for a donor about to have a child, etc.), there are ways you can monitor the engagement of supporters and know when they may be at risk of not giving another annual gift or renewing their membership and that's through donor scoring.

There is no best practice with donor scoring and many of the organizations that utilize this have simply activated some of the add-ons that come through with their CRM, marketing automation platform, and/or email marketing service.

Donor scoring simply attributes a score to each 'action' they take with your organization. These could be as simple as opening a newsletter or liking a post on your social media channels (lower scores) up to hours volunteered (higher scores). These points totals would then act as a snapshot of engagement and highlight those that should be getting more attention.

Seeing that one of your biggest corporate supporters has had a big swing in terms of their previous engagement might tell you a story you couldn't see from pulling simple reports, for example, they may have had a change in staff, and you may need to change the point of contact and begin to build a new relationship with them.

Donor scores provide nuance to the old spreadsheets that show your supporters and their 'year anniversary'. Gone should be the invoice sent a month or so ahead of that date and gone should be the transactional approach of simply retaining them at that level of previous giving. Moneyball fundraisers should look at upgrading donors based on donor scores and see renewals not as another metric to hit, but as an evolution of world-class donor stewardship.

Member Acquisition & Prospect Pipelines

A membership director at a professional sports team is responsible for managing the team's membership programs. These programs are designed to engage with fans and supporters of the team and offer various benefits and exclusive experiences to members.

The membership director is responsible for developing and implementing the team's membership strategy, including setting membership goals, creating membership packages, and determining pricing. They work closely with other departments, such as marketing and sales, to promote and sell memberships to fans and supporters.

Once members have joined, the membership director is responsible for managing their accounts, ensuring they receive all the benefits and perks associated with their membership. They may also work on creating and managing events that are exclusive to members, such as meet and greets with players, exclusive stadium tours, and access to team facilities.

Overall, the membership director plays a crucial role in building and maintaining relationships with fans and supporters of the team, creating a sense of community and loyalty that helps to drive ticket sales and overall team success.

Moneyball (the original book by Michael Lewis) emphasizes the importance of data analysis and statistics in sports. Similarly, a fundraising team can benefit from data analysis to identify new donors. Here are a few steps that a fundraising team can take to identify new donors using the principles of Moneyball:

Define your objective: The first step is to define what you are trying to achieve. Are you looking to increase the number of donors or the total amount of money raised? Be specific about your goals so that you can measure progress.

Analyze existing data: Look at your existing donor data to identify patterns and trends. This data can include donation history, demographics, and communication preferences. Use this data to identify the characteristics of your most valuable donors.

Identify potential donor pools: Once you have analyzed your existing donor data, identify potential donor pools based on characteristics that match your most valuable donors. These pools can include individuals with similar demographics, interests, or giving histories.

Create a prospect list: Use your gathered data to create a list of potential donors. This list should include individuals who have not yet donated to your organization but have the potential to do so based on their characteristics.

Develop a targeted outreach strategy: Based on the characteristics of your potential donors, develop a targeted outreach strategy that speaks to their interests and motivations. This strategy can include personalized messaging, tailored events, and targeted communications.

Use data to track progress: Finally, use data to track progress and refine your strategy. Measure the success of your outreach efforts, and adjust your strategy based on what works and what doesn't.

Moving past cognitive biases around who donors are and developing a theory-based strategy for prospecting requires a more comprehensive approach to data analysis and a shift in the way fundraising teams think about donors. Here are some steps that can help you develop a more theory-based strategy for prospecting:

Define your theory of change: Start by defining your theory of change, which is a clear and specific statement of the change you want to create in the world and the steps you need to take to achieve it. Your theory of change should be rooted in evidence and data and help you identify the types of donors you need to target.

Conduct research: Gather data on the characteristics of donors most likely to support your organization's theory of change. This research can include quantitative and qualitative data, such as surveys, interviews, and focus groups.

Develop personas: Based on your research, develop personas representing the types of donors you want to target. These personas should include demographic information, interests, values, and motivations.

Use data analytics: Use data analytics to identify patterns and trends in donor behavior, beyond simple wealth ratings and past giving history. This can include analyzing online behavior, social media activity, and other engagement indicators.

Test and iterate: Use a test-and-learn approach to prospecting, testing different messages, channels, and tactics to identify what works best for each persona. Continuously iterate your strategy based on what you learn from your data.

Use a collaborative approach: Finally, use a collaborative approach to prospecting, involving stakeholders from across your organization, including program staff, board members, and volunteers. By involving a diverse set of perspectives, you can develop a more nuanced and effective strategy.

By taking a more theory-based approach to prospecting, you can move past cognitive biases and develop a more targeted and effective strategy for identifying new donors.

Pinch Hitting For Prospects

Pinch hitting is a term used in baseball to describe a player who comes off the bench to bat in place of another player in the lineup. This usually occurs when the team needs a hit in a crucial situation, such as when they are trailing late in the game or when they need to score a run to tie or win the game.

In the movie, the Oakland Athletics recruited a player named Scott Hatteberg to be their pinch hitter. Hatteberg was a former catcher who had suffered an elbow injury that prevented him from playing that position anymore.

Oakland General Manager Billy Beane openly admitted how the team had pursued Hatteberg because of his high on-base percentage, which Athletics' management had determined was most often correlated with runs scored. According to Beane, it was one of the most affordable skills at that time for small-market clubs like the A's. Infield coach Ron Washington worked with Hatteberg to teach him the new position. The fictionalized version of Hatteberg played by Chris Pratt is a key character in the film.

A career highlight for Hatteberg came on September 4, 2002. The A's had won 19 straight games to tie the American League record. With their next game, against the Kansas City Royals, tied at 11 after the A's had blown an 11–0 lead, Hatteberg pinch-hit with one out and the bases empty in the bottom of the ninth inning. He drove a walk-off home run to give the A's a 12–11 win and a then-American League record 20-game winning streak.

I will play that role of pinch hitter right now and help you swing for the fences with a few high-percentage plays I use to move the needle with prospects.

Quantity leads to quality.

In Moneyball, it was determined that the best way of scoring a run was to first get on base. For *Nonprofit Moneyball* that comes by increasing the volume of potential donors or prospects by casting a wider net and reaching out to more people. You can increase the likelihood of identifying high-quality donors who are genuinely interested in the organization's cause and have the capacity to make significant contributions by doing this simple task.

You aren't going to identify more donors by sitting at your desk. You aren't going to cultivate transformational gifts through a simple back-and-forth with a prospect over email. So get out on the field, talk to people, and see good things start to happen.

However, it's important to note that simply increasing the number of prospects or potential donors is not enough on its own. To effectively leverage the "quantity leads to quality" approach, a nonprofit must also have strong systems in place for identifying and cultivating high-quality donors, such as targeted marketing campaigns, personalized outreach, and effective donor stewardship practices.

No.

Great fundraisers distinguish themselves by their approach to rejection.

Confidence in your work will change your thinking on donor objections from a negative response to a welcomed one as a sign of interest. As a fundraiser, you should be prepared to encounter different objections and know how to overcome them. The reasons for a prospect's hesitation to give should be examined more closely, providing an opportunity to ask more questions and identify the driving force that will inspire them to give.

Facing rejection is a universal drawback in professional fund-raising. Great fundraisers have the ability to separate their own worth from their work and push on until they find the next prospective donor who is ready to say yes. The ability to persevere in the face of rejection sets them apart.

You should remember that rejection is not directed toward you personally, and it should not discourage you. This is a rare and precious opportunity to champion something that should fulfill you and benefit others, and a few closed doors should not stop you from pursuing it.

Portfolio construction.

This isn't one for the fundraisers per se, but one that anyone who sets the goals should be aware of. Don't just give a fundraiser a portfolio of 50 - 100 prospects or a mish-mash of inherited prospects from other fundraisers. Give them a 60% full portfolio of 30 warm leads and let them build up the rest of the portfolio over the next twelve months as part of their goals. Having a fundraiser help craft their portfolio provides extra buy-in and will ultimately benefit their fundraising 'persona'. Give them a chance to be successful and yield the benefits of this early trust-building tactic.

Rule of 3.

Here's my top tip for prospect outreach/pipeline building. I do this RELIGIOUSLY. It's why my pipeline is always healthy and I take 115+ intro/qualification meetings a year.

The first thing I do when I get to my desk in the morning, before ANYTHING...is to send three messages seeking to connect. (email/text/InMail/carrier pigeon)

It's a healthy habit and it COMPOUNDS. 3 messages per work day are 15 messages a week. Across 46 weeks (taking into account 6 weeks of holidays) that relates to 690 unique outreach emails.

Why 3? To me, it's manageable. Too many meetings spreads you too thin and becomes somewhat transactional. The best part of my job is meeting people, hearing about their stories and success, and helping them think about their legacy and what impact they can have. That takes time and the time to listen.

What's your morning routine? Does it move the needle?

No trojan horses.

Be proud of your role as a fundraiser! When you reach out to a prospect for the first time don't shy away from why you are engaging with them. Say who you are, because there is nothing worse than getting a meeting with someone and not setting the expectations of that meeting. It's damaging to the organization's reputation if you ask for them to meet over one thing and then start asking them for money.

Yes, you will more often than not get ghosted or turned down with your outreach (that's just the nature of our jobs), but if they say yes, then be prepared to move the conversation forward constructively. Below is the email I regularly use and has served me well over the years - noting that it's now taken quite the Australian tone!

Dear [insert name here],

G'day from the [insert university here]!

My name is Ryan Ginard and I am the [insert position here]. My job is to work with alumni who might want to become more involved with the [insert university or college here] as donors, volunteers, or simply as better-informed advocates for the University.

I just wanted to reach out to you ahead of my trip to [insert city or region here] in the next few weeks [specify dates if needed here]. We are looking to reconnect with several esteemed alumni in the area and If you are open to it, I would love to schedule a brief meeting together to discuss your experience at [insert university here] and your career to date. I make no assumption about the kind of relationship you might want to have with [insert university here], but I'm confident our conversation would help to clarify that.

Please let me know if you are available to meet in person at a location convenient to you.

I'll plan to follow up in a few days unless I hear from you before then.

Sincerely,

[insert signature here]

As you can see, there are elements of clarity in the outreach, urgency around timing and response, and of course what the next steps are. It is important to also frame the language in a way that acknowledges their success and opens the door for them to recall their time at university through this lens which will help the prospect rebuild affinity with the institution in the lead-up to the meeting. It also reaffirms that while there is no obligation in meeting, they know your role and where the conversation may go.

Time horizons.

Fundraisers should have a portfolio that maps out several major gifts over three years. By aligning fundraising portfolios with this timeframe, fundraisers and their organizational leadership can make informed decisions about future revenues and expenses.

Additionally, a three-year timeframe allows for the evaluation of the effectiveness of various fundraising strategies and the identification of trends in donor behavior. By analyzing data over a longer period, fundraisers can identify patterns and adjust their strategies accordingly.

Make the ask.

You should be confident in making an ask in your first meeting if it makes sense and the conversation moves in that direction. Always be prepared for this! However, when securing a major gift, we know it may take some time, but don't let this be a deterrent from closing a gift within 3 meetings.

You shouldn't overthink the process and put all the burden on your shoulders to build trust and rapport with the prospect. The reality is that their relationship is with the organization and not with you. Don't waste time getting to know their story when this has already been conveyed to your nonprofit and has been captured in the CRM. Pick up from where the last gift officer left off.

Your first meeting should be to qualify or requalify the prospect by ascertaining their philanthropic interests, affinity, situation, and whether they would be open to learning more as a donor. I like to close a meeting by asking for permission to put forward a proposal in the future and establish expectations around the next steps.

Walk them through the numbers.

Always include in proposals the donor math. Provide break-downs of how funding will be spent over a specified timeframe, what the annual yield will be from a proposed endowment, and how much matching can be activated (especially not forgetting what might be leveraged from their organizations - check out the company 'Double the Donation' for insights here). The most important one is sharing the tax implications of their gifts and the actual dollar costs once the deductions have been realized.

Don't perfect. Play the averages with proposals.

That future proposal should also be submitted in the immediate future too. Another outcome affected by a lack of fundraiser confidence is waiting until there is a 95-99% chance the gift will be secured. For example, not putting a gift plan into the CRM until a gift deed has been submitted to the donor for signature.

I recommend delivering a proposal to a prospect when there is a greater than 60% chance the gift might be realized. There are many positives in doing this including moving the gift conversation to a conclusion quicker and also having a substantive document of which to work with. Potential donors might become more invested by seeing their name on a building rendering and suggest ways to make their gift more impactful (and potentially bigger).

Don't worry, there are checks and balances for those leaders concerned with fundraisers falling into the habit of putting forward proposals too quickly. That is penetration rates (the number of successful gifts closed as a percentage of proposals submitted). Don't just have a goal of proposals submitted as this is a number that can see multiple proposals rushed just to meet annual metrics.

Keep the pipeline healthy. All engagements with prospects need to be less than 90 days.

Finally, keep that portfolio healthy. All prospects should have had at least one substantive contact (or attempt to contact them) made every 90 days. Momentum is important in gift conversations but so is awareness. If someone comes into a substantial windfall, you want them to be thinking of you whenever they have a capital gains issue!

| 6 |

The Back Office

HR and Organizational Influence: Striking The Balance

HR departments in professional sports teams play a crucial role in supporting their players beyond the traditional functions of HR. They can help ensure that players have the resources and support they need to be successful on and off the field.

Some ways that HR departments in sports teams can help players beyond the traditional functions include:

Mental health support: Many sports teams have mental health professionals on staff or provide access to mental health resources for their players. HR can help connect players with these resources and ensure they have the support they need to address mental health challenges.

Career development: Professional sports careers are often short-lived, so HR departments may help players plan for their post-playing careers. This may include connecting players with job opportunities or offering career development resources and training programs.

Personal finance management: HR departments can help players manage their finances, including budgeting and investing. This is especially important for young players who may suddenly come into a lot of money and need guidance on managing it responsibly.

Community engagement: Many sports teams have programs encouraging players to engage with the local community and give back. HR can help players identify volunteer opportunities and coordinate their participation in community outreach programs.

Diversity, equity, and inclusion initiatives: HR departments in sports teams can lead efforts to promote diversity, equity, and inclusion within the organization and in the broader community. This may include providing training on cultural competency, developing diversity recruitment programs, and supporting employee resource groups.

I truly believe the HR functions within nonprofits will become more important and thus more influential in supporting organizational success. They will be key in identifying the skills and talent that will define *Nonprofit Moneyball* in the future and ensuring their development is supported through intentional development tracks that will drive team satisfaction and retention rates. As for development tracks may I suggest you track down a most excellent resource from The Council for Advancement and Support of Education (CASE) on recognizing a need for a pedagogical framework for professional development programming and their eight competency clusters which are composed of both the hard and soft skills that result in fundraising success.

HR can also be a champion for diversity, equity, and inclusion and for innovating approaches for work-life balance, new benefits and leave provisions and potentially catalyze fairer work conditions through unionization.

According to a recent study in the Chronicle on Philanthropy, The Nonprofit Professional Employees Union has grown from 300 workers at 12 organizations in 2018 to 1,500 workers at nearly 50 organizations today. Since 2019 the Nonprofit Employees United has unionized workers at 68 organizations. The News Guild-Communications Workers of America went from having five unions recognized in 2019 to 44 today.

The Chronicle also shared that the increase in nonprofit unions comes at a time when unions have been rising in popularity among all Americans. Approval of unions, at 71%, is at its highest since 1965, according to Gallup. While the number of unionizing non-profits is increasing, they likely make up a small part of the overall workforce. The government does not break out statistics for non-profit unionization. Still, union members make up about 10% of the total workforce — about half of what it was in 1983, according to the U.S. Bureau of Labor Statistics.

The article said nonprofit employees may be more predisposed to unionizing than other workers. They tend to be younger, well educated, and altruistic — a perfect blend of characteristics that tip people toward interest in unions, said David Zonderman, a history professor at North Carolina State University who teaches labor and nonprofit history and provided comment for the story.

It concluded that nonprofits come from a tradition of charity and sacrifice, and most pay their employees less than private companies and the government. As a result, many unionizing workers are looking for livable wages and opportunities to advance, all the more important as housing costs and inflation have shot up. Others see unions as a way to press for greater racial equity.

Rebel Talent

"Rebel talent" refers to individuals who possess unconventional or nontraditional qualities, skills, or approaches that set them apart from the mainstream or traditional norms within a particular context, such as a workplace or a creative field. These individuals tend to challenge established conventions and bring fresh perspectives to the table.

These individuals are great to level up an organization for the period of time they remain with you (as I alluded to in the scouting section), as they understand that the most dangerous thing for your organization and the social sector at large, is to remain loyal to - and not question - the status quo.

Nonprofit Moneyball, and the film for that matter, lean into the benefits (and drawbacks) of this approach and there was no better lightning rod for the conversation than that of Jeremy Giambi. Jeremy was brought in at a time when Beane was trying to fill the OBP gap after losing his brother Jason (Giambi) and Johnny Damon in free agency. Giambi had a .404 OBP in 2002 at that time.

In the movie, after the A's lose a game, Billy Beane hears funk music coming from the players' locker room. Irritated, he walks in to see Jeremy Giambi dancing on a table and other players having a good time. Billy takes a baseball bat and smashes the stereo playing music, startling the players and stopping the music]

Billy Beane: [to Giambi] Get down. Is losing fun?
[no answer]
Billy Beane: Is losing fun?

Jeremy Giambi: No.

Billy Beane: Then what are you having fun for?

[Billy throws the baseball bat where it hits a set of weights making a long, loud crashing noise]

Billy Beane: [points to that area] That is what losing sounds like.

Hiring for rebel talent is tricky. How many times have you been in an interview and been excited for the opportunity to work with that candidate, only to retreat from that opportunity by questioning whether they will 'go within two years'?

You should hire the best available talent through the lens of culture. Will they be a culture add or a culture drain? The questions in an interview need to be geared towards fit, not just behavioral questions to bring color and context to the candidate's resume. Inviting them to interview underlines that they have the skills and experience (or potential to succeed in the role), so why waste your time reaffirming your initial instincts?

Giambi was a culture drain in the end so was moved on shortly ahead of the A's record-winning streak. Managing rebel talent can sometimes present challenges, as their nonconformity can clash with established structures and norms. My point is that rebel talent though, if embraced, can get your organization where you dream of it being, and on an accelerated timeline.

Finding ways to harness their creativity and perspective while ensuring alignment with organizational goals is often a delicate balance. Still, overall, it represents a form of diversity in thought and approach, which can lead to exciting breakthroughs and advancements in various domains.

I strongly relate to this and believe I have been successful in my career due to being that 'rebel talent' in previous roles. I also hire similar folks, looking specifically for the following qualities;

Creative Thinking: Rebel talents often excel at thinking outside the box, developing innovative solutions, and pushing boundaries.

Risk-taking: They are more likely to take calculated risks, which can lead to breakthroughs and new ways of doing things.

Independence: Rebel talents often exhibit a strong sense of independence (self-starters) and are willing to pursue their own paths, even if they go against the norm.

Courage: Challenging established norms requires courage, and rebel talents are often unafraid to voice their dissent or challenge authority.

Adaptability: They can adapt quickly to changing situations and are often open to experimenting with new approaches.

Disruption: Rebel talents can disrupt established patterns, sparking change and innovation within their environments.

Curiosity: They strongly desire to learn, explore, and understand different perspectives, leading to a broader range of influences on their thinking.

Rebel talent in the nonprofit space is more often folks that are very driven and passionate about the potential of organizations to move the social needle. You don't need to give them the keys to the car, but they will be every bit as effective in the passenger seat giving directions. Think rally car partnerships for that essential sporting anecdote.

For leaders, you can foster culture through new innovation as long as you create a safe and supportive environment for ideas. Let rebel talent flow, don't disrupt it, don't be afraid of it, and encourage curiosity.

You should naturally evolve with rebel talent, so reaffirm that you are in their corner and will support them in their growth, whether in or outside the organization (including being a professional reference). They will inevitably move on after a period of 18 months or so but will have no doubt moved the organization forward toward its goals.

We are seeing more individuals look towards a career portfolio (many roles and experiences that are largely complementary to the sector and their values) rather than a career path and that's a good thing especially as the nonprofit sector has thrived with an army of generalists rather than subject matter experts.

Jeremy Giambi: [knocking on door] You wanted to see me?

Billy Beane: Yeah, Jeremy, grab a seat.

[Jeremy sits down]

Billy Beane: Jeremy, you've been traded to the Phillies. This is Ed Wade's number. He's a good guy, he's the GM. He's expecting your call. Buddy will help you with the plane flight. You're a good ballplayer, Jeremy, and we wish you the best.

[Jeremy sighs and exits].

THE SOCIAL SECTOR AS A CHAMPION FOR A NEW 35 HOUR WORK WEEK

Much of the current discussion around the future of work has been through the lens of COVID which is wholly understandable. The global pandemic effectively tore up the playbook of service delivery, rendered many a strategic plan obsolete, and confined plenty of fiscal year budget papers to the shredder. It has also hauled plenty of organizations back in from the tech shadows by accelerating the adoption of digital services, products, and trends in remote work.

All of these changes represent a paradigm shift for major industries in our society, but rather than merely trying to balance the old and new – for example introducing flexible work agreements and having meetings and events occurring both in-person with virtual options this is ultimately an opportunity to prime our society for the inevitable transformations in our workplaces that will result from the rapid onset and evolution of the fourth industrial revolution.

What I'm saying is the pre-pandemic way of doing things is now in our rearview mirror and holding on to them as an ode to the 'good old days ideating around the water cooler' shouldn't be something we romanticize about. At the end of the day, it's about the work, it's about the mission. If the work is getting done, why does it exclusively need to be confined to the four walls of an office? And with the rapid adoption of automotive processes do we still need to have our results, outputs, production, and ourselves defined by 40 hours of it?

I was fascinated to read the recent results of the recent report by UK think tank Autonomy, which for four years, tracked 2,500 employees in Iceland who had reduced their working hours from 35 to 36 hours per week.

Researchers found that "worker wellbeing dramatically increased across a range of indicators, from perceived stress and burnout to health and work-life balance."

At the same time, productivity remained the same or improved for the majority of workplaces, the study said. Participants worked at various places such as hospitals, offices, playschools, and social service offices.

In Iceland on average, most employees work 40 hours per week, and it is illegal to work more than 13 hours a day. When the trial started, the employees worked 40-hour weeks and later shortened it to 35 to 36 hours. Participants said the reduced hours allowed them to focus on exercising and socializing, which enhanced their work performance.

"By the time of this report's publication in June 2021, 86% of Iceland's working population are now on contracts that have either moved them to shorter working hours or give them the right to do so in the future," the study noted. "These trials are therefore an incredible success story of working time reduction, of interest to campaigners and workers worldwide."

The recent pandemic has already shifted the landscape in relation to where we work and how we work. Could it also catalyze a new conversation on how long we work?

If anything, the past 18 months have shown us, it's what matters most, and to many that have been friends, family, and quality of life. With millions of people losing their jobs or being furloughed, and the fact many had to rapidly adjust to working from home as offices closed along with schools and other childcare options, we have to acknowledge that we are a resilient species, yet one whose circumstances are inherently fragile. You can lose everything in an instant.

There is a solid case to be made for a four-day workweek. It's a case argued previously by Anthony Veal, an Adjunct Professor at the University of Technology Sydney's Business School in his book *Whatever Happened to the Leisure Society?*

Veal states that there is no reason why the long-term march towards reduced working hours should stop at the arbitrary "standard" figure of five days and 40 hours established in the post-World War II period. He doesn't believe widespread adoption of the four-day week will come quickly or all in one go. Instead, it's going to have to come incrementally.

It took half of the 20th century and a great deal of campaigning against concerted employer opposition for workers in Western industrial societies to reduce their standard working week from 60 hours over six days to 40 hours over five days, so where might this new momentum come from?

My recommendation would be the social sector for several reasons. It's the third-largest employer in the country and one that is going to be disproportionately affected by automation and the further digitalization of our economy.

Research from McKinsey (Manyika et al., 2017) assessed the jobs lost and jobs gained under different scenarios through 2030 with the results revealing a rich mosaic of potential shifts in occupations in the years ahead, with important implications for workforce skills and wages. Their key finding is that while there may be enough work to maintain full employment by 2030 under most scenarios, the transitions will be very challenging—matching or even exceeding the scale of shifts out of agriculture and manufacturing we have seen in the past.

Their key finding should be your crucial takeaway here...due to automation and artificial intelligence, there will be a seismic increase in workers entering the service industry.

The report shares that about half the activities people are paid to do globally could theoretically be automated using currently demonstrated technologies. Very few occupations—less than 5 percent —consist of activities that can be fully automated.

However, in about 60 percent of occupations, at least one-third of the constituent activities could be automated, implying substantial workplace transformations and changes for all workers.

The predicted growth for the service industry which includes healthcare professionals, childcare workers, and community and social workers is due to grow from 30% in the U.S. to 242% in India by 2030.

The social sector has many unique pressures. Time doesn't mean money; in this sector it means lives. Being on the frontlines is often underestimated, underappreciated, and often underpaid, and that's why shaving off an hour a day for those that give their lives in service of their communities should be a no-brainer for a more comprehensive national trial of a reduced work week in the U.S.

Workplace innovation doesn't have to be the sole greenfield for courageous start-up founders and CEOs. The key here isn't to be on the front cover of Forbes, it is to ensure your staff is happy, productive, and feel safe and secure both at home and at the office (whatever that looks like moving forward).

The nonprofit sector has a huge role to play in the next chapter of this country's history as industries continue to change and evolve. It is a dynamic and willing partner in advancing society with many displaced and reskilled workers flocking to the sector as the demand for service jobs increases due to automation.

At the end of the day, how can we find new ways of solving a very old problem: just how can we work to live and prevent our lives from being all about work? It's a question posed to us by COVID and one where 35-hour weeks, 9/75s, and remote working options might be the key to unlocking a new era of pride and productivity for the nation.

INNOVATION BY SUBTRACTION

Innovation in a nonprofit organization can mean a variety of things. It can mean something new – a process, a service, or a project, it can be something new to you – an approach, a tech add-on, or a partnership, but one thing we fail to realize is that it can also be the simple act of taking something out of our day to day.

Innovation should drive better outcomes and that's where the disconnect lies, we often prioritize outputs instead, looking at quick ways to hit our annual goals rather than take the time and care to make a long-term difference in our society.

When I worked at a small nonprofit in the U.S. the outcomes were paramount, our organization had made a 12-year commitment to the students we worked with, and this commitment was based on trust and the promise of better outcomes for their kids and ultimately their families. Thinking big in this instance was having them be the first of their family to go to college, not from a standpoint of how we scale our success. Scale for this organization grew when time allowed and with compounding progress, hitting our annual goals quickly and using this 'bonus time' to innovate around the edges.

My Executive Director at the time astutely drilled into me the difference between budget relief and budget enhancement, that it was easy for fundraisers to go out and talk about what 'could be' rather than basing these conversations on the immediate needs of the organization. The goal was to effectively 'make budget' and find ways to grow from the surplus.

For those playing at home, budget relief is receiving new funding sources to free up those budgeted funds to be deployed elsewhere effectively. Budget enhancement is securing funding for new projects not planned for that year.

As I have said on many occasions, success in nonprofits does not scale like other businesses, you can't take advantage of economies of scale and effectively need to raise additional funds and hire more staff to keep up with new demands (whether internal or external). There are also issues with budget enhancement approaches because of the way grantmaking is structured, funding is usually cyclical and puts organizations in longer-term predicaments if that newly funded project fails to launch as it were.

Innovation by subtraction was one of the only tools I had at my disposal in that job. Soon after I started my role there, we had jettisoned the annual golf day and effectively 'sold' the rights to the ongoing (and quite successful) 'San Diego Beer Run' which ultimately didn't align with the organization's values. These two moves alone saved countless hours of staff time for the organization which were reallocated to fundraising efforts. Another significant move was to remove the 'get' from the 'give or get' obligation of the board.

So how might a nonprofit organization apply 'innovation by subtraction' approaches?

Development/Fundraising:

- Not being afraid to disqualify prospects from a portfolio – moving from quantity to quality.
- Starting the year by focusing on budget relief rather than enhancement – ensure financial stability before growing impact.
- Fewer touches – can a prospect be asked for a gift ahead of previously predicted timelines?
- Grant writing – focusing on more considerable funding opportunities rather than spending 10+ hours on grant applications of say $5,000.

Processes:

- Fewer meetings – the most liberating of choices.
- Automation – are there apps or programs that can free up more fundraiser time? Can we finally do away with the 'many hats' moniker?

- Event audit – do all of our events have a positive ROI if we include the staff hours and asks associated with them?
- To-do lists – there is no way you achieve 15 tasks in one day regardless of how optimistic you were when you wrote it down.

Communications:

- Fewer emails – can a monthly email become a quarterly one?
- Less time checking emails – stop pulling that slot machine arm.
- Website pages – all you need is a give now button and details on contacting the development team. The website is a shop window, not a major gift portal.

Ok, we have a couple of examples, but how might we go about workshopping change? I'm definitely not advocating for throwing the baby out with the bath water, we are more intelligent than that. Over a set period of time, the following steps can help you make informed decisions about what a subtraction strategy might deliver for your organization.

List all of the critical parts of what services you offer: This isn't your case for support, it's what your organization effectively offers those you seek to serve.

Pick one and imagine eliminating it: Don't think in terms of scarcity, think in terms of freeing up your time.

Visualize the service without that essential part elimi-nated: Would folks notice or are we failing to apply the duck-on-water test (when people see you gliding across the water, they don't notice you frantically paddle beneath the surface)?

Identify the pros and cons: This step informs a decision.

Trial the replacement: If it doesn't work, you can always revert to the norm.

Conversion: Time to bake the new streamlined approach into your day-to-day (with the bonus of creating new metrics to support its ongoing evaluation).

As you can see, this is a simple, yet practical approach if we add it to our ongoing evaluation framework. Innovation by subtraction has the potential to save staff hours, provide a reason to wind up old approaches that have become burdensome over time, free up budgets, and most importantly free up dollars to continue driving impact in our communities. I would encourage folks to add this approach to their annual planning retreats not just because it's a worthwhile exercise but because the status quo stifles the impact we so desperately seek. It's a simple equation in the end.

Facilities

Facilities for professional sports teams typically include the physical spaces and structures where the team practices, trains, and competes. These facilities can include:

Stadium or arena: This is where the team plays their home games. It includes the field or court, seating areas for fans, and other amenities such as concession stands, restrooms, and VIP suites.

Practice facilities: This is where the team practices and trains. It includes locker rooms, weight rooms, training rooms, practice fields or courts, and meeting rooms.

Front office: This is the administrative and business operations headquarters for the team. It includes offices for team executives, sales and marketing departments, human resources, and finance.

Player development facilities: These are specialized training and rehabilitation centers for the players. They include areas for strength and conditioning training, sports medicine and injury treatment, and recovery and rehabilitation.

Parking and transportation: This includes parking lots for fans and staff and transportation services for the team such as buses or planes for away games.

Overall, facilities play an essential role in the success of a professional sports team by providing a comfortable and efficient environment for players, coaches, and staff, as well as creating a memorable experience for fans. But that's the backdrop for what is in essence an anchor institution.

ARE WE HEADING FOR A NEW VIRTUAL REALITY FOR NONPROFITS?

For many people during the COVID-19 pandemic, the immediate question was, when should we expect to return to work? The question they should have been asking was, do we need to go back to work?

We aren't talking about the actual work. That will continue in earnest. And no, we are not here to expound on the wonders of Zoom or flexible working arrangements (which we already know are great and much needed, thanks for asking). We are actually talking about the bricks-and-mortar component of work, which is under a little more scrutiny— and which might not make sense for nonprofits anymore.

Nonprofit budgets are no doubt being reviewed amid the current reality, and the continuing concerns of lower revenues will bring into focus the more significant fiscal outlays, of which rent is often the second largest expense after personnel.

Organizations are now realizing that some services can be delivered virtually, including in the areas of education, training, and healthcare. While essential services are arguably best still delivered in person, improvements in delivery methods through technological advancements like computational health, AI, chatbots, online communications, and education platforms are accelerating the quality and accessibility of viable alternatives.

What effect are these potentially profound realizations having on executives whose current office for the past year was more likely their kitchen table than an overpriced electric standing desk? The answer must be these questions: What is in the organization's best interests moving forward? Is there an ability to modernize and deliver comparative or better services all while reducing expenditures and delivering on the core mission?

That answer should be a resounding yes. If anything, the COVID-19 pandemic pushed us to use technology that, in hindsight, our sector probably should have already adopted. It's high time that boards and organizational leadership had an honest discussion about what is critical.

moving forward, because folks are quick to cut staff and freeze travel and other expenditures that slow down cash flow issues without confronting them head-on.

Why don't we seriously consider how much we pay in rent and ask what the alternatives are?

Why is it that physical space has become a symbol of success or a necessity for a business?

What is the point of a boardroom if it's only used once a month anyway?

The reality is this problem has been bubbling under the surface for a long time because of a one-dimensional viewpoint of how nonprofits do business. Real estate has been forcing the hand of nonprofits for the past decade, with escalating rents pricing organizations out of the very areas they serve. Gentrification is a very real issue for communities, and while it's more acute at the individual and family level, the impact isn't lost on nonprofits.

This issue hasn't been lost on funders, either, with examples such as the Status of Bay Area Nonprofit Space and Facilities report (Harder+Company Community Research, 2014), commissioned by Northern California Grantmakers and the San Francisco Foundation, which were concerned that the cost of office space in the region had increased every quarter since mid-2010 and five years later sat at 122 percent higher than when those increases began. This report showed the vast majority (82 percent) of the 497 nonprofits that responded to the report's initial survey were concerned about the negative impact of the real estate market on their long-term sustainability. Sixty-eight percent of respondents also thought they would have to make a decision about moving in the next five years. Furthermore, 38 percent had moved at least once in the last half-decade.

With many metropolitan areas suffering from similar pressures, nonprofits should be using this critical insight as the impetus for some honest conversations when formulating new strategic plans. It's not like there isn't a wide variety of options to consider, either, including the following:

Roles and Responsibilities: Is it absolutely essential that all staff be on-site? Could development and marketing staff predominantly work from home? Could project management platforms such as Monday, Wrike, or Asana be used as a way to drive workflow and accountability? Can meetings be held via Zoom?

Service Delivery: Do all "workshops" need to be in person? Can savings be made by moving classes online or by shifting to a hybrid model that captures a significant amount of detail from clients before meeting in person (or ascertaining whether the need to meet in person is even needed)?

Rent or Buy: Is renting your best option for long-term stability? With options including New Markets Tax Credits, Community Development Block Grants, and other capital campaign approaches, organizations can seek to invest in their communities or look to partner with other organizations to create nonprofit hubs. Manchester Bidwell Corporation is a good template for what can be achieved with that approach, weaving itself into the very fabric of the community and addressing gentrification ahead of it taking hold.

Consolidation: Many nonprofits have grown exponentially over time because of demand, but nonprofits are not like consumer products. The greater the need, the higher the cost. There just isn't any economy of scale to be had here with tangible offerings and in-person services. Some organizations have expansive reach because they have several satellite offices. Could organizations consolidate into one larger headquarters and have regional staff work remotely? The National University System, which included at its height, universities such as JFK University, National University, Northcentral University, and the University of Seattle, had more than thirty campuses across the West Coast of the United States. With most of their courses becoming more flexible through online offerings, they consolidated to one primary campus and kept other prominent sites where feasible or out of geographic necessity. It's a more intelligent model and reflective of the evolving nature of a hyper-connected community.

Mergers and Acquisitions: With many nonprofits at risk of closing down their services for good (much like many for-profit businesses are forced to do), there may be opportunities for organizations to merge so they can financially strengthen each other and move to one shared address. Alternatively, boards may reach out to organizations that are rumored to be struggling to acquire or absorb some of their programming, assets, or staff to come out of this crisis with a new energy in tackling issues of commonality such as homelessness, education, or food access.

Funders should also come together to discuss this issue more broadly as a way to facilitate a difficult conversation about sustainability and the more prevailing question of how many nonprofits are too many in a given locale. Funding surveys or strategies like those mentioned in the Status of Bay Area Nonprofit Space and Facilities report (which evolved into a broader campaign by the Northern California Grantmakers called the Nonprofit Displacement Project) could provide a benchmark for tackling this issue head-on. The following steps would then be a blend of the following:

Policy and Legislation: Rental caps, rezoning, and government support.

Communications: Sharing results more broadly to highlight the impact of potential displacement.

Technical Assistance: Providing funds to facilitate moves, space planning, negotiating leases, underwriting and guaranteeing loans, and other legal matters.

If anything, the coronavirus pandemic has shone a light on our most entrenched operational issues and provided space for the conversations we have long been dreading (or avoided due to the "busyness" of how we used to work in the past). We should welcome those conversations and work better to break out of this nonprofit deficit mentality.

You can do the math too.

First, forget about the office space being donated. That's just counterintuitive. Next, multiply 250 square feet per staff member or those who regularly use your services on any given day, then multiply it by the per-square-foot rate for Class B office space. (Check out CBRE or an equivalent for real estate market reports in your region.) Once you have worked out that initial cost and added utilities and other associated costs, review it based on alternative scenarios, many of which have been highlighted above, and see where savings can be made. Finally, imagine where those savings might be applied. You can even decrease your projected revenues as a counterweight.

As for that fancy boardroom, it might be time to say goodbye to that rich mahogany table and those leather swivel chairs and embrace the conference rooms of board members' corporate offices or rent a coworking space for a few hours. Your volunteers probably won't mind, especially if it secures your organization's future and leads to more funding for frontline services and keeping talent.

REIMAGINING DONOR WALLS AS ENGAGING STORYTELLING ARTIFACTS

Look, this piece is a dangerous one to write, because donor walls are boring, date terribly, and have one primary purpose, function, and design. In terms of technology, it's severely lacking in the wow factor, and we would be doing readers a disservice if we simply said, 'Let's just make them digital.'

Simply transferring a name etched in wood or fabricated steel onto a large screen monitor as a way of 'modernizing' the approach isn't so much an evolution but one that is fundamentally lacking imagination and an opportunity to not only steward major gift donors but also tell your story and those that gave in an engaging way.

So, without falling into the trap of putting up what in essence are just new virtual noticeboards, what options could help transform this traditional donor recognition approach and have it as a compelling reason rather than a simple byproduct of a gift proposal?

Much of that promise might just be found in permanent art installations. A focal point for an organization's lobby, atrium, or grounds. Not just a park bench with a fading gold plaque but a colorful, one-of-a-kind piece that can tell many stories from a mission, vision, donor, and beneficiary standpoint. A piece that will act as a magnet for engagement and discussion rather than a snapshot of history that remains static in perpetuity rather than have the ability to grow and adapt.

It's time to draw people to your organization's success, not just capture it in the binary.

And the great thing about art is that it can appeal in a myriad of ways depending on the storyteller. That storyteller can be the CEO, board members, development staff, or even the cleaner. When you gaze on a piece of art it evokes different things in different people. When you create a piece of art it can be interpreted differently by different people. It broadens horizons and enhances narratives.

And therein lies the main crux of this need to reimagine donor walls. It can be so much more than you imagine!

Some great examples exist already of which you should track down and marvel at:

- Centro Roberto Garza Sada, Universidad de Monterrey
- University College London
- University of Washington Foster School of Business, Seattle, Washington

Just thinking out loud, I could imagine an Engineering Department at any higher education institute 3D printing QR codes that could be displayed as a 'pulse' or 'algorithm' where the shadows that form on the wall could be scanned to share donor stories.

The artwork could also enhance your mission by the type of artist you commission to do the work. For example, an artist that identifies as queer and of color from the communities you serve would enhance your commitment to DEI, conceptualize impact through a different lens and help support local artists – a powerful message through intersectionality.

I could also see potential plays and extensions on the term perpetuity – and for organizations that might become more virtual due to COVID – through the use of non-fungible tokens (NFTs) on the blockchain. "Non-fungible" means that the item is unique and can't be replaced with something else. It's one of a kind.

A lot of the current buzz around NFTs (and how it relates to nonprofits) is seen through the evolution of fine art collecting, only with digital art (think silent auctions & donations of artwork – it's a speculative asset after all). The theory is that anyone can buy a Van Gogh print yet only one person can own the original.

Every NFT is a unique token on the blockchain and while it could be like a van Gogh, where there's only one absolutely legit actual version, it could also be like a trading card, where there are 5 or hundreds of numbered copies of the same artwork. So the original art piece could reside at the organization for which the gift supported but each donor could carry 'a piece of it' as a family heirloom.

At the end of the day, donor stewardship should be more than ticking off some traditional menu items. Nonprofit organizations have always been creative and nimble on the ground, seeking unique solutions to unique (and primarily individual) problems. So why do we revert to the most basic approaches in how we share our stories of impact, why does everything have to go 'on the wall' and why can't it be woven into the very structures of our buildings and their surroundings? I challenge you to think outside the box on this one and remember you can also try and cultivate a donor to donate or underwrite the piece (and the installation)!

Kit And Equipment Managers

Fundraisers are undoubtedly one of the most underrated and underappreciated positions in nonprofits. They are equal parts storytellers, connectors, and strategists. They also play a critical role in an organization's success, helping to empower all levels of the organization to operate in a development mindset.

My favorite story is of JFK going to NASA in Houston and asking one of the janitors what they did. Their response? "I help fly people to the moon." It's that level of connection to the mission that we should all be striving for. And it's that level of organizational investment in our development staff which could kickstart a new golden age for our sector. That is a golden age in which fundraisers lead the charge on the front lines.

The team's kit manager is probably the position in a professional sports team that resembles that NASA janitor. They are responsible for organizing, packing, and transporting the team's uniforms, equipment, and supplies to the game or event.

During games or events, the kit person is on hand to ensure the team has everything they need, from spare balls and water bottles to extra uniforms or equipment. They are also responsible for repairing or replacing any damaged or broken equipment.

After games or events, they are responsible for collecting and washing the team's uniforms, cleaning and organizing the locker room, and packing up the team's equipment and supplies for transport back to the team's base.

This person plays a crucial role in ensuring the team has everything they need to perform at their best, both on and off the field.

Talking of washing the kit and organizing the locker room, there is a fantastic story about the All Blacks success over the past few decades that I wanted to share. New Zealand's national rugby team, who are a global brand known for their iconic black uniform and intimidating pre-game Haka have won the Rugby World Cup three times and hold the world's highest lifetime winning percentage of 77%. Their success has primarily been attributed to their team culture, as described in James Kerr's book Legacy, which emphasizes the importance of "Sweeping the Shed" and putting the team before individual egos.

Dan Carter who was one of the star players of that team summed it up when he shared that "No one in New Zealand likes a big head. In the All Black environment, there's no room for it and if there's ever signs of it happening, you'll soon get brought back down to earth."

"From the very start, you learn humility. There are these structures in place, like the fact that we always leave the changing room as clean as it was when we walked in. So, you'll often see the likes of Richie McCaw (the team captain), and the coach Steve Hansen sweeping the shed."

FUNDRAISING & WASHING MACHINES - WHAT IS THE BEST CYCLE TO SET?

I was recently asked to present to my peers on the donor cultivation cycle. As I was searching Google Images for a stock image of the cycle, it occurred to me that there hasn't been much innovation in the process. While some offerings had simplified the process to a four-step approach, and some had changed the flow or pattern of the diagram to make it more visually appealing, the cycle remained dimensionally limited.

In contrast, when I looked at sales funnel diagrams, which often take the shape of a cone, I noticed that they could be shown in various ways, including 3D or dissected to show how the funnel is built on the backend. This got me thinking about whether there could be a 3-dimensional, dynamic approach to the donor cultivation cycle, beyond meeting donors in person.

While I don't believe such an approach exists yet, I wanted to reflect on whether the donor cultivation cycle is the best approach or just the most tried and tested. I'm not fundamentally against using a sales funnel approach, as it largely follows the donor cultivation cycle. Still, my main qualms with it are the insidious gamification of it in for-profit sales, where people are often duped into the funnel via various offers and then go through an automated process to mine additional dollars from them. It's not about relationships, but rather the sale.

While reflecting on the donor cultivation cycle, I started to look more at the commonalities of the cycle, including the images, the words, and the word "cycle" itself. I realized that the arrows on each stage showed what the next step in the process was, and that the point of contention for me was the speed and cadence of each step and the lack of analysis of what constitutes a time for that next step to occur.

While every donor conversation is different, what we don't see in our current cycle is depth and speed. What are the markers that move us on to the next step? What are the on and off-ramps in the process? Is this a roundabout or a washing machine?

Unfortunately, I think it's more like a washing machine, where we select the cycle time after loading it up, and there isn't much opportunity to speed it up. It must go through the process, and that's one where the clothes get bounced all around the drum in the ebb and flow of time.

For some organizations that don't have a specific plan for a prospect, they will be caught in a washing machine – a profile piece here, an invitation to lunch there, a board seat here, and some network connections over there. It's tough to watch and even tougher to wait.

So, should we be reviewing the cycle? It's difficult, but there are tools out there to help, metrics that can guide us, and best practices to inform us. While thinking about how quantum computing and washing machines intersect now, it might be easier to discuss modeling software. What can help move the cycle forward, what can move our fundraisers' next steps forward, and so on?

This will ultimately come from our CRMs – propensity modeling, automated moves management, and other reporting data, stewardship support, predictions on donor behaviors, avoiding sandbagging, and avoiding dropped balls. The list goes on.

I encourage people to talk about their fundamental practices and whether improvements in processes can be made, and most importantly, automated. At the end of the day, washing machines are a staple of most households. They get the job done and go through a cycle, but even then, we periodically upgrade them as they run faster, quieter, and more efficiently. So, with that being said, how might you upgrade your fundraising machine and its approaches?

| 7 |

League Expansion

National Associations

The national associations of professional sports leagues (think National Football League, Major League Baseball, and National Hockey League) serve as governing bodies for their respective sports, providing leadership, coordination, and oversight for the member teams and leagues. Here are some of the key functions of these associations:

Rule-making and enforcement: The national associations establish and enforce the rules and regulations that govern their respective sports, ensuring that games are played safely and fairly. Nonprofit associations set standards of ethics and best practices. Whereas the Internal Revenue Service (IRS) in the U.S. and The Australian Charities and Not-for-profits Commission (ACNC) regulate charities.

Player development: The national associations may oversee player development programs, helping to ensure that the league has a pipeline of talented players who can contribute to the sport over the long term. For nonprofit and funder associations and organizations such as the Association of Fundraising Professionals (AFP) and Fundraising Institute of Australia (FIA), this comes in the form of training and conferences.

League expansion and contraction: The national associations may oversee the expansion or contraction of member leagues, helping to ensure that the league is operating at an optimal size and structure.

Some great examples of this have been at the United Philanthropy Forum, which has led to somewhat of a renaissance for Regional Associations of Grantmakers.

The community was calling for a more dynamic civic partnership in tackling some of the most critical issues of our time, and for a period of time, our community foundations were leaning into those calls by listening and beginning to build the internal infrastructure needed from a participatory community leader, diversifying their staff, public programming offerings, and grantmaking. For whatever reason this stalled for a time (even though I note many have picked up the ball once more and are showing a great deal of innovation).

During that time (approx. 2015 - 2020) it actually opened the door for other players in the ecosystem, such as Regional Associations of Grantmakers, to blaze a trail in that gap in the philanthropic sector. Regional associations are membership groups for organized philanthropy to learn, lead, and invest in their communities. They traditionally serve and represent local philanthropists, family foundations, corporate funders, and public charities by connecting funders to knowledge and resources and increasing awareness about philanthropy's role and potential for impact in its communities.

NONPROFIT MONEYBALL - 143

These associations have been around for about fifty years and were slowly losing impact through the rise of national affinity groups that support more focused donor intent and collective impact around single issues. In addition, larger foundations didn't see themselves needing their services, and community foundations sought to shield their growing donor-advised fund (DAF) base from perceived competitors, which was a flawed perception.

There was even a disconnect with their name and role within the community, with many associations calling themselves "[insert city/region here] Grantmakers," when in fact many of these organizations were not granting funds. So, what changed? And why are these groups growing when they arguably have a limited membership base to work with?

To be frank, it was probably just that. For example, a regional association on the West Coast that had around 120 members researched the potential for growth based on all the region's foundations and found that if every single foundation joined as a member, based on current fees, they would only net approximately another $250,000 in revenues. Ultimately, if they wanted to reach the potential, they saw in themselves, they would have to diversify their business model beyond dues. This was not just a strong leader ensuring the future viability of just one organization. This story formed part of a nationwide shift in the association model that has now resulted in these types of membership organizations becoming some of the most dynamic across all of the traditional actors in philanthropy. Many organizations that are members of the United Philanthropy Forum are redefining what is meant by organized philanthropy because:

- They were making big bets on new forms of philanthropy such as giving circles and impact investing by acting as fiscal sponsors in some instances and building up the ecosystem and running demonstration projects and deal flow where needed and appropriate.

- They were driving new conversations on equity, race, and real systems change, undeterred by the political leanings of some of their members and forging a new path. They believe that tackling these deep-rooted issues through the voice and resources of philanthropy is a way of improving the communities they serve through the work of their members.
- They were not only granting out their own dollars through collaborative funding mechanisms (development staff rejoice!), but they were also granting them out via the modern approaches they seek to educate their members on—full-cost, trust-based, and financial returns on their investments.
- They collaborated on a state and national scale to drive stronger outcomes.

The peak body, the United Philanthropy Forum, drove much of this potential by simply expanding its membership to include affinity groups, leading to a larger, more comprehensive network of funders that are learning from each other and understanding the intersectionality of our communities through a funder's lens.

In California, the three associations serving the three biggest regions in the state—Los Angeles, San Diego, and San Francisco—formed an alliance named Philanthropy California to collaborate on joint programming, coordinate communications and policy, and fundraise for new projects. The majority of these organizations are also changing their names with the times, with identifiable monikers such as Philanthropy Massachusetts (previously Associated Grantmakers), Catalyst of San Diego & Imperial Counties (previously San Diego Grantmakers), and the Maryland Philanthropy Network (formerly the Association of Baltimore Grantmakers) aligning with their new narratives and work.

And let's not forget about the communities they serve, communities that need their support now more than ever, and who will reap the rewards, support, and funding from a more intentional form of collaborative action.

MORE THAN JUST A TAX DESIGNATION: FIXING THE ISSUE OF OUR NONPROFIT FACTORY

Face it, everyone in our sector has had this ugly conversation: Are there too many nonprofits?

According to the PNP Staffing Group, the nonprofit sector has grown more than 20 percent over the past decade. In contrast, the for-profit sector has grown by approximately 2 to 3 percent. Independent Sector also recently released some current key facts on the sector, highlighting that there are currently 1.8 million nonprofits registered with the IRS. Most nonprofits are relatively small, with 75 percent having annual revenues of under $100,000.

Is this question one of finances? Or one of service delivery? Of investment or impact?

Saying that we should have fewer nonprofits because of the size of the pie available is an opinion that truly comes from a deficit mindset and uninformed assumptions. You see, according to the National Center for Charitable Statistics, 72 percent of revenues come from program services, which highlights a strong demand for services that have become a byproduct of government cuts and underinvestment in social services. Also, 18 percent of all nonprofits received a grant from a grantmaker, which indicates from another angle that most nonprofits are indeed needed and most importantly are financially viable, piecing together their budgets from various sources.

So, where's the breakdown? Why do we continue to hang such negativity on the size and scope of nonprofits? It's funny, but what I see is that most of these conversations emanate from urban centers when it's the smallest states in our union that have the largest per capita of nonprofits for every ten thousand residents. Think Connecticut more than California here.

My take is that the truth has to be found somewhere in the impact of our organizations. But where is the data? What defines impact? Who defines that impact?

This would need a major review and ultimately a resetting of the table, starting with a redefinition of what a nonprofit organization actually is. Because the harshest truth is that it is seen by the IRS as nothing more than a tax designation. However, the harshest truth doesn't necessarily have to mean that this is a depiction of the sector's future.

Nonprofit organizations are the backbone of our society. They are the threads that keep the nation's social fabric together in this most surreal moment in time. And due to their importance to our communities and for our national workforce (being the third largest employer in the country), we would be wise in looking strategically at their future to ensure they remain vibrant and relevant well into the next century.

What could the next steps possibly be?

Well, it has to start with a new (or reconfigured) Federal Department. This could come in the form of a Department for Communities that could finally set a strategic direction for developing solutions based on the needs and aspirations of our citizens—neighborhood by neighborhood. The first step would need to be a national review of whatever would fall under this department's purview. This would be a behemoth undertaking. But with a comprehensive and multisector-supported approach, we might be able to see the foundations of comprehensive reform that would set our nonprofits up for success rather than setting the majority up for failure, including the following:

- Clearly identifying lanes for organizations, such as identifying and eliminating duplication.
- Establishing new quality standards.
- Creating clear pathways for nonprofits to understand available funding options.
- Identifying which nonprofits should remain, merge, or cease operations (controversy alert!).
- Completely overhauling nonprofit registration.

This is ultimately the crux of my argument and the core of my angst. You know the harsh truth I mentioned earlier? Well, the fact that an organization is registered in a mostly binary fashion, reviewed solely through an application form with no nuance or localized lens, is mindboggling in this day and age. It's so basic that it was only in January 2020 that prospective nonprofit organizations could submit the 1023 paperwork online. ONLINE.

If we are to truly end this question of how many nonprofits are too many, we not only need to reframe it to how many nonprofits are needed, but completely overhaul how the IRS Tax Exempt and Government Entities Division registers a nonprofit.

Now with paperwork being submitted online (and critically the nomination of National Taxonomy of Exempt Entity codes), a fair bit of automation can occur. This will not only decrease human error and speed up the application process but will also provide comprehensive reports based on numerous data sets that will provide a more thorough understanding of a nonprofit's suitability (noting that suitability is very much different from eligibility).

Eligibility should be a baseline for reviews, not the only requirement. Currently, the only prospective organizations whose registrations are rejected have done one or more of the following:

- They sought reinstatement from an initial revocation of status for not filing for three consecutive years.
- They didn't pay the correct registration fee.
- They provided an invalid Employer Identification Number (EIN).

So how can we add more nuance to the process that will ultimately result in a stronger sector?

An Automated Solution. This is a simple process in theory. The IRS has the most comprehensive data set of the nonprofit sector. An appropriate algorithm should be able to digest the information provided by a prospective entity, run it through the system, and identify any of the following:

- Similar organizations already operating in that locale.
- The entity's need based on other data sets such as Census reporting.
- Data that highlights alternative revenue ceilings beyond program services.

And the list can go on and on, highlighting the need for established benchmarks for registration and reregistration (which should be automatically processed by tabling your 990s). Many local reports from county governments, chambers of commerce, city councils, community foundations, and other relevant nonprofits and sector associations can also really drill down on the need and demand of a new organization.

Ultimately an IRS officer would need to make a final call. But they would finally be making an informed decision, contributing to rebuilding trust in the sector and government. (I also recommend that all board members of this prospective organization go through some sort of governance training before full acceptance.) If a prospective organization had been rejected based on these new sets of criteria, a formal response could be provided to the applicant, including details of other local organizations operating in that space and encouraging them to volunteer or support their causes in other ways, ensuring we aren't losing a potential civic asset. If they went to the lengths of creating a nonprofit, then this obvious passion to make a difference in their communities must be channeled positively.

WE MUST FUND REPLICATION EFFORTS IF WE ARE TO SCALE PROMISING SOCIAL PROGRAMS IN OUR SOCIETY

The sector doesn't talk enough about scale, and when it does it truly doesn't understand it.

My opinion on this has always been one borne out of frustration. One where successful business can produce their products at a cheaper cost when they sell more, yet one where nonprofits are ultimately punished for their successful programs because they have to hire more staff and seek more funds to support their work.

But evidently, these frustrations lacked the nuance to hold up in the face of basic econometrics (which I am beginning to learn, understand, and appreciate). You see, I was looking at economies of scale and not scaling true social sector innovation. As you know nonprofits are not that simple, not that binary, and definitely not structured in a way where the average costs per unit of output decrease with the increase in the scale or magnitude of the output being produced.

The Voltage Effect.

I recently spent some time with John List, the current Chief Economist of Walmart, The Kenneth C. Griffin Distinguished Service Professor in Economics at the University of Chicago and formerly at the White House and as Chief Economist at Uber and Lyft. John was in town as the closing plenary speaker for the Society for the Advancement of Economic Theory (SEAT) 2022 conference and on the back of his new book *The Voltage Effect: How To Make Good Ideas Great And Great Ideas Scale*.

John also looks into the ways people make decisions regarding charity. Charitable giving is an important component of each country's national economy, yet few organizations understand how to promote their cause. Over the years John has conducted multiple field experiments to examine the factors that influence people's charitable decision-making which makes for fascinating reading.

John's speech had my mind buzzing for the full 90 minutes and contained threads of economic theory in which many lessons and opportunities could be observed for nonprofit organizations. Our work too often rests on hunches and intention and not on a careful examination of data and the science of using science to identify and implement promising ideas – the science of the economics of philanthropy as it were.

A good review of the book I found online by Yael Levin Hunger-ford succinctly summed up the key lessons found within its pages –

the "Five Vital Signs" – and why desirable results don't replicate when a policy scales: false positives; failure to know one's audience; scarce ingredients; spillover effects; and cost of sustaining at scale. Once an idea passes the Vital Signs test, The Voltage Effect offers insights from the field of economics to ensure its success at scale: from experimenting on the margins to setting up the right kind of incentives (hint: we are loss averse) to creating a healthy culture.

Scaling Promising Social Programs.

At the end of the day not all great ideas scale and that's ok, but we have to identify whether that is because of the chef or the ingredients as John would say. For example, a restaurant can be wildly successful in one location but not work in others which is largely down to the chef. If it does take off in multiple locations and is franchised, then that's attributable to the ingredients and systems. From a nonprofit standpoint that could also be linked to local leadership versus a common social issue such as cancer or homelessness.

The key here is in testing a program's ability to scale and this is where we apply our philanthropic lens.

John shared his opinions on A/B testing, sharing that in the academic world, the petri dish that forms the outcomes of that research is largely in a controlled state which is bolstered by the best inputs available (e.g., we do all we can to ensure our hypotheses are correct). There is a great article by Oliver Palmer on his personal website that shares the angst around A/B testing:

"People tend to have unrealistic expectations about A/B testing. Vendors and agencies alike would have you believe that experimentation platforms are magical money machines that turn button colors and copy tweaks into double-digit conversion rate increases. One highly resourced program I know of built its business case on a strike rate of 50%. Every second experiment they ran, they proposed, would generate a revenue uplift! That's complete and utter madness."

"The vast majority of experiments will not impact your tracked metrics one way or another."

A meta-analysis of 20,000 anonymized experiments by over a thousand Optimizely customers conducted by Stefan Thomke and Sourobh Ghosh gives a more realistic view. Just 10% of experiments had a statistically significant uplift for their primary metric. Airbnb, Booking.com, and Google all report a similar rate of success:

At Google and Bing, only about 10% to 20% of experiments generate positive results. At Microsoft as a whole, one-third prove effective, one-third have neutral results, and one-third have negative results. All this goes to show that companies need to kiss a lot of frogs (that is, perform a massive number of experiments) to find a prince.

The vast majority of experiments will not impact your tracked metrics in one way or another. Many optimization programs struggle to acknowledge this fact. They plod along in obscurity, not wondering why they're not getting the same results as 'everyone else'. They sheepishly sweep their 'failures' under the rug which ensures that they will never learn from them, stagnating at level 1."

Funding Replication To Replicate Successful Innovations.

What is missing from this process and what in fact shows the potential for scale is in the replication. Replication in its simplest terms is being able to copy the original experiment to see if you can produce those outputs with some degree of fidelity.

For John, replication is option c for scaling (following the A/B component). It is where several critical scale features are added to the process and important learning innovation can occur. List out all your concerns and opportunities to scale and add them to the study, taking into account quality, capacity, access, finances, geography, you name it.

It was mentioned at this point that not many replication studies were posted in science journals (which I found interesting), a fact that John ended up addressing by creating his own journal. He also found in his own research (Maniadis, Tufano, & List, 2017) that, "The sciences are in an era of an alleged 'credibility crisis' (...) By combining theory and empirical evidence, we discuss the import of replication studies and whether they improve our confidence in novel findings. The theory sheds light on the importance of replications, even when replications are subject to bias. We then present a pilot meta-study of replication in experimental economics, a subfield serving as a positive benchmark for investigating the credibility of economics. Our meta-study highlights certain difficulties when applying meta-research to systematize the economics literature.

After doing a bit more reading, something rang true for me in regard to scaling. If innovation doesn't have to be new, just new to you (and potentially in a localized context) then why do we not fund (and fundraise for) replication efforts?

We fundraise for loan loss reserves in impact investing, we fundraise for organizational capacity building, and we fundraise for flexible capital options, so why are we not investing in scaling solutions to the most critical social issues of our time? Is it time to publish a new cookbook for our local nonprofit chefs?

Social Replication Toolkit.

The great news is that cookbook exists and was developed by Spring Impact (formerly The International Centre for Social

Franchising), a non-profit that helps social organizations systematically replicate to scale.

As I mentioned, hunger, poverty, and disease: societies globally face various perverse problems. Spring Impact captures this by stating 'Though promising solutions exist; the frustration is that we can't seem to scale their social impact to match the true size of those problems.'

Their Social Replication Toolkit tests for 'replication readiness' and helps you assess your readiness for replication and help you to better prepare to replicate your solution.

Successes In The Field.

Since moving back to Australia, I have been impressed by the work, direction, and innovation of Social Ventures Australia (SVA). A systems-focused organization that learns in their communities and supports scale predominantly through impact investing, SVA recently reviewed 7 initiatives that have replicated their model to increase social impact.

The review is definitely worth reading regardless of the localized content as it helps readers understand the process, methodology, and definitions (which you will know from my book are important in demystifying much of the new tech and trends out there in the sector).

Using the Spring Impact replication toolkit to guide their findings, SVA concluded with seven lessons and observations around replicating successful programs with the following summary takeaways:

"The experience of ventures that have succeeded in replicating for scale in Australia in recent years offers emerging lessons for aspiring founders, organizations, supporters, and the social sector more broadly. The 'how' is important – identify and maintain a convincing value proposition, maintain some measure of control over design and delivery, and measure and track just the essentials.

However, these lessons have largely been learned by private sector license and franchise businesses and applied by the social sector. The 'why' is more interesting. Not only is there a good reminder never to forget to deliver on your purpose but that, even as a small organization, you can aspire to contribute to broader social change. A number of the success cases reviewed demonstrate the potential for relatively small-scale ventures to influence the underlying conditions of the social sector in which they operate."

Testing Out Tired Funder Tropes and Baked-In Biases.

Funding replication efforts also support breaking down a few structural issues associated with grantmaking, all of which we tackled in *Future Philanthropy* with our feature on Laura Tomasko from the Urban Institute.

Many funders use data to inform grantmaking decisions and evaluate the effectiveness of a particular program or organization. But do they think critically about where those data come from and what purpose they serve?

Laura recognizes how current funding practices compound historical and current inequities, privilege, and power dynamics in the sector.

"There's a lot of focus in the sector on achieving scale and supporting evidence-backed interventions," she said. "I think it's important to pair that goal with critical thinking about how systemic racism and bias might have created conditions that enable some organizations to grow and build evidence of success and others to stay afloat with few resources. Did the larger organizations have leaders who gained expertise through academic training and professional experience, with strong networks in philanthropy that enabled them to secure grants for evaluations? If given the same access to funding and evaluation, would the programs at less well-resourced organizations demonstrate similar or greater effectiveness?"

She said this: "When making grantmaking decisions, funders who want to support organizations likely to achieve programmatic objectives would be wise to consider organizations that might have fewer resources and little to no formal evaluations, but whose leaders come from the community they serve. These leaders know what might work from lived experience and have the knowledge and trust of the community to bring about change. Funding within established networks can perpetuate inequities by overlooking community leaders and solutions derived from that lived experience."

Funding replication efforts here should start by (in the words of Professor List) 'imagining what success would look like at scale, applied to the entire population with their varying situations, over a long period of time. That said, funders should think less about data as a tool for compliance and punitive action against organizations that have not achieved certain projections, and more as a tool for evaluating and supporting an organization's learning, growth, and storytelling capacity.

"We want grantmakers to recognize the ways that data can empower their grantees to thrive while also acknowledging the flaws and limits of data," Laura said. "When gathering data to evaluate effectiveness, think about who pays for the assessment, who determines the research questions, and what information is available and collected and by whom.

All of these factors influence the data that ultimately help determine the effectiveness of a program or grant. And who benefits from the data? Do the data collection efforts burden grantees and ultimately not benefit the organization? Or do they empower organizations to evaluate and improve programs, as well as equip them with information to tell their story to their stakeholders?"

Scaling New Ideas.

Not every social program needs to scale. Some people are not scalable, and some products or services are purposely not designed to scale. In other words, scalability isn't for everyone. But we must approach the results of each program in a way that captures the issues of power, race, and privilege (amongst other factors) and give the programs every chance of success especially if they have shown early promise.

This may result in multi-year grants and the opportunity to discuss the end-of-year results rather than be judged on them. So often it is seen that a funder will walk away from supporting a new partner due to limited success in year one, where it would be much more constructive to perform some self-reflection and perhaps provide capacity-building support or increase funding to help them achieve their vision.

This is something that would be a hallmark of funding replication efforts and something that should merit more attention in our sector. A first step of course would be to get yourself a copy of The Voltage Effect which *is essentially a guide on how to get rid of bad ideas and make good ones better. So, whether you choose to scale or not to scale, understanding the techniques behind scalability will help you in all aspects of your work.*

From my perspective, that work begins now by building awareness around the need and impact of funding replication in our sector. Scaling a narrative of impact after all is another part of our journey to be more effective in our outcomes.

ORGANIZATIONS NEED TO COMMIT TO EXPANDING PHILANTHROPIC KNOWLEDGE AS THE MAIN COURSE OF ACTION NOT JUST PROVIDING A SAMPLE PLATE OF WHAT COULD BE

National associations, foundations, and consultants for all of their members, clients, funds, scope, influence, and potential have a penchant for sticking their logo on almost anything, getting that dopamine hit of organizational relevance from their community, and sending out an accompanying media release (or social post) to prove that they are at the forefront of all civic trends.

It could be oh-so-different. Imagine instead of capturing that trending moment that instead they were patient and understood their ability to forge consensus–based and collaborative long-term change through playing what is a long-term game.

Imagine a foundation instead of creating a snapshot in time, used its reports as a catalyst for a one to three-year conversation around the issue they highlighted and helped educate, create awareness for, and were laser focused on executing its findings and recommendations.

You see, many reports, although well-intentioned and helpful in fostering debate, mainly gather dust in cupboards as they have run their immediate course instead of their actual course. The ROI of surveys and reports is never fully exhausted across the spectrum of the social sector. Nor do they form part of any strategic plan where any element of accountability for its success was present.

It would be great to see the establishment of a philanthropic watchdog or an entity that grades the effectiveness of reports across many metrics, such as the extent to which they are disseminated, and the leveraged impact of its findings from the community. Qualitative and quantitative examples of this include whether they are cited in media and academic papers, whether core data sets are highlighted in grant applications, or if their findings were the basis for a policy change in government. Hey, it's a metric in higher education after all.

Reports aren't helping anyone by sitting on a shelf. So, if organizations are serious about data, we need to have an honest sector-wide discussion about it. Access to, and the adoption of research and data are some of the most underused assets a nonprofit organization can have at its disposal.

If you invest the time and resources into creating research reports that address critical civic needs, you should fully exhaust that content in a variety of ways:

Distribution: Don't just have copies of the report sitting on a card table at your events as a prop. Send copies to local elected officials and organizations that are tackling the issues head-on. This includes both businesses and nonprofit organizations.

Engage: Create a monthly or quarterly "Solution Series" that convenes leaders and the community to discuss the issues and recommendations contained within the report in an intentional way. Build momentum that can lead to commitments of action.

Accessibility: Include a downloadable copy (that isn't protected by passwords or restricted by membership levels) in a prominent and easily locatable space on your website. Include print-on-demand options too!

Content Creation: A hundred-page report can generate so much content that it could easily pump-prime your social media channels for a year. Cut it up into blog posts, coauthor them for a new viewpoint, create videos, and build a six-episode-themed podcast—the choices are endless.

Issue Lab, which is part of the Candid umbrella, is a good example of this. It collects, collates, and makes available for free through its website close to 30,000 publications and reports from more than 7,500 organizations. This is all through a simple search bar and was supported by its Open for Good campaign, a concerted push for foundations to share their reports, findings, and ultimately their knowledge for the benefit of both the field and the communities they serve. This was to drive a learning tool first and foremost, because—as Issue Lab aptly puts it — "we can all learn from each other, especially the inputs and outputs associated with more than $5 billion in grants going out the door each and every year."

At the conclusion of this campaign, Candid created a compendium that captured the wisdom shared by the many authors who contributed to this work between 2017-2019. This collection of voices, representing "knowledge-sharing champions" from across the field, explored tools, practices, and examples showing how foundations are opening up about what they are learning for the benefit of the philanthropic sector, and the greater good. Definitely worth checking out.

While philanthropy can and should be leading from the front on this one by making all its reports and evaluations public, the sector should also be seeking opportunities to partner with cities that ultimately possess the mother lode of data for folks to utilize for the common good. Some larger cities are tackling this issue with open data portals to spark innovation and better inform decision-making. However, the Sunlight Foundation, an organization that fights for transparency through the utilization of civic tech and open data to "enable more complete, equitable, and effective democratic participation," finds that out of the more than one hundred cities, countries, and states that now have open data policies across twenty key areas, only around three dozen of those governments' efforts have resulted in wins for their communities.

It would be good to see a broader discussion around this from key players with the goal of moving beyond the token hackathons and student app-building initiatives. Granted, these initiatives are cute and engaging, but they are not tackling the biggest issues head-on or building solutions that the community can use beyond being packaged commercially by some local start-up.

Matthew Taylor, CEO of the Royal Society for the Arts in London and former chief advisor on political strategy to Prime Minister Tony Blair sums it up perfectly when he mentions that "cities must think like a system and act like an entrepreneur."

This quote became a cornerstone of The New Localism, a book by Bruce Katz and Jeremy Nowak, which looks into how cities can thrive in the age of populism. Ultimately, we shouldn't just make the data available, because that is just the most basic of baseline metrics. Instead, we must actively dive into it through research and development teams on the council payroll, actively seeking research grants to support these efforts, and have that dedicated team build new efficiencies that make our cities better. It's that simple.

From The Clubhouse: Advance Your Organization's Tech With The Tools You Didn't Know You Already Had

A deeper understanding and realization that social change in the digital era requires an investment in technology and that tech infrastructure helps leverage impact—indirectly helping serve more clients by identifying data trends that make programming more efficient, and automating processes to enable staff to tackle bigger vision projects —should make funding tech a no-brainer.

Tech also helps craft a narrative by helping us visualize data, use natural language processing to identify keywords that drive empathy, and also help us produce content faster and more efficiently. This segment will walk you through a few quick ways to amplify your organization's outreach in both communications and member engagement (on a budget) which will give you some vital test data to help demystify the tech we have available to us now and help build confidence in pitching new solutions to those that have the ability to say 'yes' to broader adoption.

Communications

The future of nonprofit communications teams is likely to continue to be shaped by the rapidly evolving landscape of digital communications and technology. Nonprofits must adapt to new platforms, trends, and strategies to reach and engage their audiences effectively.

One trend likely to continue is the increasing importance of social media and digital marketing. Nonprofits must have a strong presence on social media platforms and effectively use tools like email marketing, search engine optimization (SEO), and digital advertising to reach their target audiences.

Another key trend is the growing importance of data and analytics. Non-profits will need to be able to collect and analyze data on their communications efforts to understand what is working and what is not, and to make informed decisions about future strategies and campaigns.

In addition, there will likely be a continued focus on diversity, equity, and inclusion (DEI) in nonprofit communications. Nonprofits must ensure that their communications are inclusive and representative of the diverse communities they serve and that they are using their communications platforms to advance social justice and equity.

Overall, the future of nonprofit communications teams will require agility, flexibility, and a willingness to adapt to new technologies and trends, while staying true to their mission and values.

The statistics that warrant our attention:

- For every 1,000 fundraising emails sent to subscribers, nonprofits raised an average of $42
- Fundraising email response rates have seen a 9% decline, and click-through rates fell to .42%
- Only 13% of nonprofits currently use text-to-give in their fundraising strategy.

The tools that can move the needle:

ClickSend: Use this free trial to send text messages to donors at $0.06* - go beyond email. I once secured a $100,000 scholarship via a text message, text is such an underrated medium for fundraisers. Just look at the stats around trust and you'll understand why.

Hunter: You've found a prospect you would like to contact but only have their funky-sounding high school Hotmail account. Reverse engineer their work email addresses.

Calendly: Save the back-and-forth emails to arrange a time to meet. Secure that qualification coffee with a quick link and inform your strategy by what time they click (15/30/60-minute slots).

Marketing and content creation

There are several advances we can expect to see in the next few years in regard to content creation in nonprofits. The goal here will be to create more effective and engaging stories. Here are some possibilities:

Increased use of video: Video is an incredibly powerful tool for non-profits to tell their stories and engage with their supporters. With technological advances and lower production costs, we can expect to see more nonprofits incorporating video into their content strategies.

Personalization: Nonprofits will increasingly use data and technology to personalize their content for donors and supporters. This could include customized email newsletters, tailored social media messaging, and personalized video messages.

Interactive content: Interactive content such as quizzes, surveys, and polls can help nonprofits engage with their audiences and gather valuable information. Nonprofits can use this data to inform their content strategies and improve their fundraising efforts.

Collaborative content creation: Nonprofits may increasingly collaborate with other organizations and influencers to create content that reaches new audiences and amplifies their message.

Overall, we can expect to see nonprofits embracing new technologies and data-driven approaches to create more engaging and effective content.

The statistics that warrant our attention:

- Self-reported "effective" marketing strategies created roughly 9.4 short-form blog articles, 2.1 mid-form articles, and 1 long-form article per month; nonprofits dissatisfied with their own marketing results typically produced fewer pieces of digital content overall.
- For every 1,000 email addresses, the average organization has 474 Face-book fans, 186 Twitter followers, and 41 Instagram followers.
- 22% of nonprofits have a LinkedIn group.
- The value of just one blog post lasts far beyond the website traffic it drives the day, week, and month it's released. While "72% of impressions are generated in the first month...28% of a post's impressions are not counted in industry-standard metrics."

The tools that can move the needle:

Anchor: Turn your blog posts into a podcast
Canva: Design all your marketing collateral with a free not-for-profit pro account. Utilize brand kits, templates, and controls.
Lumen 5: Have AI turn your blog post into a summary video by utilizing natural language processing to determine keywords and themes derived from your original article.
OpenAI: Generate text via ChatGPT and images through their DALL-E platforms.

Impact

Nonprofits over the coming years will need to create more engaging and impactful stories about their work and to better measure and communicate the outcomes of their efforts. While I still see a role for organized philanthropy to advance this work in partnership with the social sector, that's not to say you can't take control of your data by accessing a wide range of technologies to showcase your impact in the coming years. Here are a few examples of what you should be focusing on or at least aware of its capabilities:

Data visualization tools: Nonprofits can leverage them to create interactive dashboards and infographics that communicate their impact more engagingly. These tools will help nonprofits better track and analyze their impact data, as well as communicate it to stakeholders in a more effective manner.

Social Media Analytics: Nonprofits can use social media analytics tools to measure the impact of their social media campaigns, and track engagement with their audience. By monitoring social media conversations, nonprofits can better understand their supporters' needs and interests, and adjust their messaging and strategy accordingly. I also build Twitter lists for donors and have everyone on my portfolio listed in Google Alerts so I can see opportunities to engage in real-time.

Augmented Reality (AR) and Virtual Reality (VR): AR and VR technologies can be used to create immersive experiences that showcase the impact of a nonprofit's work. For example, a nonprofit that provides clean water to communities in developing countries could use AR/VR to show donors the impact of their donations by virtually transporting them to a water well in the field.

The statistics that warrant our attention:

- Nonprofit organizations who communicated their mission and impact with outcome metrics (e.g. cost per meal served) were 82% more likely to have higher donations
- 76% of nonprofits said they still need to develop a data strategy for their organization

The tools that can move the needle:

Impactasaurus: This free platform will help you demonstrate your impact in 4 easy steps. It's the definition of easy impact reporting - something y'all all have to do to attract more funding.

Dataro: Use AI to yield better fundraising results. Fundraising Intelligence (Free version) includes fundraising-specific reports, live benchmarking, and real-time analytics with one click, for free.

I love presenting this quick session at conferences and it is targeted to what I call scrappy fundraisers. The term "scrappy fundraiser" generally refers to someone resourceful, resilient, and determined in their fundraising efforts. It is pretty much how I survived (and ultimately thrived) in fundraising and ended up raising $12 million for an education center back in 2015. I discuss this story at length in Future Philanthropy.

A scrappy fundraiser is willing to think creatively and try unconventional approaches to meet their goals. This type of fundraiser can often accomplish a lot with limited resources and is not easily deterred by setbacks or obstacles. In general, being called a scrappy fundraiser is a compliment and suggests that the individual is effective, hardworking, and passionate about their cause.

So get scrappy with the ten tools I just outlined and be equipped with stats to spark the conversations for adoption. You'll be able to communicate more effectively in half the time and yield the rewards. Moneyball was about using data to get an edge for smaller budget teams, and these platforms, along with a bit of tenacity (and luck!) will have you looking in good shape for finals!

3

ADVANCING IMPACT

Billy Beane: I know these guys. I know the way they think, and they will erase us. And everything we've done here, none of it'll matter. Any other team wins the World Series, good for them. They're drinking champagne, they get a ring. But if we win, on our budget, with this team... we'll have changed the game. And that's what I want. I want it to mean something.

| 8 |

Nonprofit R&D

So much has changed in the short span of time since *Future Philanthropy* was written. Much of the predicted advances I shared are starting to occur in the field (albeit in the largest organizations with substantial budgets and staff expertise), including substantive gifts that have been in part successful through AI models and algorithms, crypto donations in the billions, more data translated research on social sector ROI, the automation of traditional vehicles such as wills and bequests, and further democratization of donor advised funds to name but a few.

We have also seen the introduction of ChatGPT which is an artificial-intelligence chatbot that allows you to have human-like conversations and much more. The fact that this natural language processing tool exploded onto the scene without any prolonged hype meant that the nonprofit sector was again caught napping in its adoption and now struggles ethically with what to do with it when the opportunities for its use and impact should warrant its rapid adoption across all facets of our work.

The nonprofit world needs a base-level education on what AI is and what it can do for them. ChatGPT has put AI in front of the masses which has fueled a lot of speculation around the future of AI – particularly some of the dangers that have been identified with some of the darker use cases - and I fear that certain nonprofit folks will use some of the recent news to validate their hesitancy to any use of AI/ML.

The broader future is bright for the social sector though, which there is no denying, but whereas in Future Philanthropy I talked about what the next decade might look like, in Nonprofit Money-ball it was important to talk about technology in the present and the ensuing few years because if we build the team and all they have is the traditional tools which have become mired in the mediocrity of some small to medium nonprofit fundraising shops then this book would have been for nothing. Again, I want you to win, and if it means moving forward with a scrappy first few steps into the tech that will support our frontline fundraisers' success then that is the strategy we will employ.

So take a look at what exists now, demystify the tech that can support more efficiencies and effectiveness in our work, and see what's actionable not solely what is aspirational.

All businesses have some sort of research and development function. It keeps them in front of their competitors and in many instances relevant, in a rapidly evolving world. This is no different for professional sports, with the following advances over the past decade being of note.

Sports science: The use of data analytics and sports science has become increasingly prevalent in professional sports. Coaches and trainers now have access to vast amounts of data on athlete performance, which they can use to optimize training and improve performance.

Video technology: With the use of high-speed cameras and video analysis software, coaches can now analyze every aspect of an athlete's technique and make improvements accordingly. This has led to significant improvements in technique across a variety of sports.

Nutrition and recovery: Professional athletes can now access advanced nutritional supplements and recovery techniques, such as cryotherapy and hyperbaric oxygen therapy. This has helped athletes recover faster from injuries and perform at their best for longer periods of time.

Fan engagement: With the rise of social media, professional sports leagues have been able to engage with fans in new and exciting ways. From live-streaming games to interactive fan experiences, sports leagues are finding innovative ways to keep fans engaged and connected to their favorite teams and players.

Wearable technology: Athletes now use wearable technology to track various aspects of their performance, including heart rate, sleep patterns, and even brain activity. This data is then analyzed by coaches and trainers to optimize training and improve performance.

Virtual and augmented reality: Athletes and coaches now use virtual and augmented reality to simulate game scenarios and improve decision-making skills. This technology is also used to enhance the fan experience, allowing them to feel more immersed in the action.

Another key advance has been the moves into Esports with Egaming players becoming increasingly prominent in professional sports teams in recent years. Esports, or competitive video gaming, has seen a surge in popularity and has become a billion-dollar industry. Many professional sports teams, such as the NBA, NHL, and

MLS, have launched their own esports leagues or partnered with existing leagues to expand their reach and engage with younger audiences.

Some professional sports teams have also signed e-gaming players to represent them in esports tournaments and competitions. The eMLS Cup (in which I have an interest through being a fan and former season ticket holder of Austin FC) is an esports tournament held by Major League Soccer in conjunction with the EA Sports FIFA franchise. These players may compete in games and tournaments and have become ambassadors for their respective teams playing in live settings such as SXSW to crowds of thousands and reaching a peak online viewing of 29,431 people.

Overall, e-gaming players have emerged as a significant part of the professional sports landscape, and their presence is likely to continue growing in the years ahead.

Egaming is actually a great segue into examples of the trends and opportunities that exist and are available to fundraisers moving forward.

E-FUNDRAISING, IS IT TIME TO GET IN THE GAME?

The gaming and esports fundraising sector has seen significant growth in recent years. According to Statista, the global gaming market is expected to generate over $396.2 billion in revenue in 2023, with esports contributing a significant portion of that revenue.

Regarding fundraising, esports organizations, and teams have raised millions of dollars in investment over the past decade. In 2020 alone, esports companies raised over $1 billion in funding. Some of the largest esports fundraising rounds include:

Cloud9. Raised $50 million in Series B funding in 2018.

FaZe Clan. Raised $40 million in Series A funding in 2019.

G2 Esports. Raised $17.3 million in Series A funding in 2018.

There has also been a trend of traditional sports teams and investors getting involved in esports. For example, the Philadelphia 76ers and the Miami Heat have acquired esports teams, while professional athletes such as Michael Jordan and Shaquille O'Neal have invested in esports organizations.

The COVID-19 pandemic has also had a significant impact on the gaming and esports industry. With traditional sports leagues shutting down or limiting their activities, esports saw a surge in popularity and investment. The industry also adapted quickly to the pandemic, with many tournaments and events moving online.

In terms of trends, the gaming and esports industry is expected to continue growing in the coming years. Mobile gaming and esports are expected to grow significantly, with the increasing popularity of smartphones and tablets. Additionally, virtual and augmented reality technology is expected to become more prevalent in gaming and esports, providing new opportunities for innovation and growth.

Livestreaming platforms: Platforms like Twitch and YouTube Gaming allow gamers to live stream their gameplay and interact with viewers in real-time. Gamers can use these platforms to raise funds for charity by setting up a donation page or encouraging viewers to donate directly to a charity of their choice.

Gaming events: Gaming events, such as tournaments or marathons, can also be used to fundraise for charity. Participants can collect pledges from friends and family or encourage viewers to donate during the event.

In-game purchases: Many games allow players to purchase virtual items, such as skins or weapons. Some games donate a portion of the proceeds from these purchases to charity, allowing gamers to support a cause while playing their favorite game.

Crowdfunding platforms: Platforms like Kickstarter and Go-FundMe can also be used to fundraise for gaming-related projects, such as game development or hardware production.

Sponsorship and advertising: Gamers with a large following may be able to secure sponsorships or advertising deals with companies, allowing them to monetize their content and raise funds for charity.

I have been fascinated by the promise of this medium ever since I was invited to join a stream on Twitch that was being hosted by one of the students from the organization Access Youth Academy for which I worked at the time. I found it inclusive, accessible, and quite fun to participate in. Donating through the platform was easy and the host makes you feel welcome while all the while educating you about the organization they are fundraising for. While it has taken a bit longer than I envisioned to permeate our sector, there now lies a real opportunity to engage younger donors and provide a platform to empower younger volunteers to help give back.

Developing a gaming strategy for your nonprofit can be a great way to engage with this new audience and raise funds for your cause. Here are some steps to help you get moving and devise a strategy that works:

Determine your goals: What do you hope to achieve through gaming? Are you looking to raise funds for a specific program, raise awareness for your cause, or engage with a new audience? Defining your goals will help you determine the most effective gaming strategy for your nonprofit.

Research gaming platforms: There are many gaming platforms available, including Twitch, YouTube Gaming, and Facebook Gaming. Research each platform to determine which one is the best fit for your nonprofit and your goals.

Identify potential gaming partners: Reach out to gamers and streamers who may be interested in supporting your nonprofit. Look for gamers who are passionate about your cause and have a strong following on social media.

Develop a fundraising plan: Determine how you will raise funds through gaming. Will you ask gamers to make donations, set up a crowdfunding campaign, or encourage viewers to make in-game purchases?

Create content: Develop content that will resonate with gamers and align with your nonprofit's mission. Consider creating videos, graphics, or other visual content that can be shared on social media.

Promote your gaming strategy: Use social media and other marketing channels to promote your gaming strategy and engage with gamers. Encourage supporters to share your content and participate in gaming events.

Measure your results: Track your progress and measure the impact of your gaming strategy. Use analytics tools to determine which gaming platforms and strategies are most effective, and adjust your approach as needed.

The WWF-Australia Livestream program is a great example here of scaling this medium. This fundraising initiative leverages the popularity of live streaming and gaming to raise funds for wildlife conservation efforts by encouraging folks to participate in fundraising challenges.

Highlighting the program's success was the "Stream to Save a Species" challenge, which took place in 2020. The challenge involved 15 Australian Twitch streamers, who competed to see who could raise the most funds for WWF-Australia's Koala conservation program. The streamers collectively raised over AUD$45,000, with the winner, Streamlabs, raising over AUD$13,000.

Another successful initiative was the "Save the Reef" livestream event, which took place the following year. The event grew to feature over 40 Australian streamers, who played games and participated in challenges to raise funds for WWF-Australia's Great Barrier Reef conservation program. The event raised over AUD$120,000, exceeding its fundraising goal.

The WWF-Australia Livestream program has been successful in engaging a new audience of supporters and raising funds for important conservation programs. By tapping into the popularity of live streaming and gaming, WWF-Australia has been able to reach a younger demographic and inspire them to take action for wildlife conservation.

But where do you start? Well, before scanning your network for enthusiastic gamers I would recommend you seek more information on how to make it work. The Donor Participation Program has been at the forefront of educating nonprofit organizations about the opportunities around gaming for a cause and actually has a 4-week course where you can learn to leverage gaming as a powerful engagement, community-building, and fundraising tool for your nonprofit. Check out https://joindpp.org/levelupgaming/ for more information on that one!

We will also help demystify much of the fundraising tech that is out there and hopefully seed potential solutions for your organizations that may seem outside of the box right now but will soon become commonplace in our toolbox moving forward. Those seeds will also come in the form of a quick top ten of free tools available to you now to ultimately sow that success in the future that I'll drop at the end of the book.

AI/ChatGPT

ChatGPT burst onto the scene at the end of November 2022, yet its impact on society has been seismic, to say the least. At the time of writing, the site welcomes over 25 million users which might lead you to think that AI will eventually take your job. The answer in short is no, but the reality is that someone who fully knows how to leverage AI will.

The sector for most of its reluctance to be an early adopter of technology has been pretty quick on the uptake here and that's primarily because it's easy to use and tackles some of those rudimentary administrative tasks that we all push to the bottom of our to-do lists. That means getting work done in minutes rather than hours and during the day that means more time getting out and meeting with donors.

This isn't to say we are leaning into the platform too quickly or naively. We all understand both the promise and perils surrounding its introduction to the world, but without real case studies let's not wait for the sector to decide its best use case, let's get out there and start experimenting.

As you would have seen from this book and also in Future Philanthropy, I have talked quite a bit about chatbots and no/low code AI but I'll be honest and say that I have seen nothing quite as promising at this moment than ChatGPT.

Given there are no real case studies right now on its impact on fundraising beyond saving fundraisers countless hours in administrative tasks, I spent a few weeks playing around with the platform and wanted to share some of the potential benefits of it for our nonprofit community.

For those new to this, ChatGPT is a natural language processor that could be seen as a text generator based on user prompts. Think of Google search, but instead of ranking links, indexing answers, and providing tagged templates to the question posed, it provides a nuanced answer beyond the binary nature of inputs and outputs we have been using for the past decade.

It is capable of understanding natural human language and generating thoughtful human-like prose. So in short, you can just type in a command and the AI will create something based on those parameters. Think donor thank you letters, newsletters, social media content, even fundraising campaign plans. One of the best applications I saw for it recently was the CEO of Empowered Fundraising, Anne Murphy who used prompts and reprompts to map out the most efficient way to travel for meeting multiple donors across the Bay Area.

Exciting stuff right? Well, not to the levels we should be thinking of because that's just scratching the surface and our sector would be wise to dig deeper into the platform to discover its real potential.

Yes, it has the potential to automate some of the copywriting that consumes much of our time, which can include cases for support, grant writing, and the day-to-day email correspondence with our members, and yes, that should be applauded, but I wanted to share some of the more substantive applications.

The first thing I realized is that if you just use it as a text generator you will just get text as a response. This is no fun and if you use ChatGPT to draw down data to help build out a case for support then it will tell you that it is unable to browse the internet. But I found it is quick to eat up new data including direct html links to search terms and .csv docs which opened quite a few doors (and provided me with the code to unlock them). Just remember not to feed the machines with sensitive data about donors, funders, and the like.

Prospect research: You can basically scrape LinkedIn for the name, companies, roles, and URL profiles of folks that went to a particular college or work at a company that has a corporate matching program, layering it with other keywords.

Other data sets: Pull countless lists including search options like grantmaking foundations from 990s using name, IRS taxonomy codes, and location in relation to you in miles.

Dashboards: A great thing about ChatGPT is that you can also utilize other apps within the commands. This includes dashboards and data visualization which you know can tell your stories of impact better through quality and aesthetic tweaks. It can also build good UX dashboards to build out 3 years prospect pipelines etc.

These are just a couple of options that have been explored. There are many, many more and that's the beauty of the platform and why it's best to leave this chapter as a primer, not as a blueprint. The next phase of growth for ChatGPT will no doubt be those of plug-ins and apps which will nestle seamlessly into programs such as Microsoft Word and Excel and enhance the AI functions of things that already exist, such as the following two examples;

Support complete marketing campaigns: Design taglines, hooks, campaign summaries, and using image generators like Midjourney and Canva you can add that all-important visual element too.

Send thousands of unique emails: Using the google sheets extension Cargo, you can draft thousands of unique outreach and thank you emails using and running (quality) prompts.

Is the revolution in AI now here? Not quite, but it's fun to have a true usable insight into what it might do for our sector and we would be wise to engage with it now, not only to learn what's possible, not only to potentially make our jobs easier today but to ideate and provide feedback for its improvement. The better it gets, the better the outcomes. After all, it's a platform that is optimized for dialogue and we would be remiss to be a silent bystander while the tech continues to evolve at speed.

The Club Shop

The club shop at a professional sports team's stadium is a retail store that sells merchandise related to the team. This can include items such as jerseys, hats, scarves, flags, and other accessories with the team's logo or colors. Fans often visit the club shop before or after games to purchase souvenirs or gear to show their support for the team. The club shop may be located inside the stadium, in a nearby retail area, or online. It is a way for fans to connect with the team and show their loyalty, while also generating revenue for the team through merchandise sales.

Have you ever been on a sales or demo call for a tech platform and felt a strange disconnect with its narrative, stats, lingo, and insights? Like it doesn't understand your services or impact and feels it necessary to "techsplain" all of your digital deficiencies? Well, you're not alone.

According to NetChange's survey of technology use by nonprofits, only 11 percent of organizations feel their digital strategies are highly effective, highlighting the current digital divide between the adoption and use of tech solutions for both the for-profit and not-for-profit sectors.

Those in the private sector will have you believe that the question is actually whether nonprofits take their systems and services seriously when it comes to digital adoption. That my friends, is just an example of tech arrogance, where outside entities ride into the sector saying "we can fix it". The real question, however, should be whether the products being offered are in fact real solutions to the needs of nonprofits based on cost, capacity, and support.

"Tech for good" in this instance is a misnomer when the product is built by a for-profit entity, with solutions needing to be specifically built with an understanding of—not an assumption or interpretation of—the structure and needs of nonprofit clients front and center. An alarming number of tech companies have strong solutions for business but believe that, with just a couple of tweaks, the addition of a nonprofit sales department and the promise of a silver bullet can solve numerous issues for your organization.

Nonprofits need to stop being seen as an additional vertical through this lens for several reasons:

- Scaling operations are polar opposites in the business and nonprofit worlds. If you sell more products, you can drive lower margins and increase revenues. If you are successful in the nonprofit world, you drive up demand for your services, resulting in an increase in your operational costs and then needing to find more revenue streams (namely grants and donations) to meet this new budget reality.
- Nonprofit donors are not the same as venture capitalists (VCs).
- Donors are not the nonprofit's customers

- Applying a nonprofit discount to an enterprise pricing model is not being charitable. It is still just a tool to drive sales.
- The for-profit sales model is arguably a predatory approach when applied to organizations with revenues of less than $500,000 (which is approximately 88 percent of the 1.5 million nonprofits nationwide, according to the National Council of Nonprofits). These organizations are understaffed and vulnerable to professional pitches centered on a mission and impact ROI and are probably unaware of when they have entered into sophisticated sales funnels when downloading "freemium" content.

Much of my work revolves around demystifying tech in the nonprofit sector. That can ultimately be achieved if the sector chooses to help build a more sustainable tech ecosystem that will ensure progressive social change organizations are equipped with the best digital tools to build power and drive tangible outcomes on behalf of their clients regardless of their own capacity constraints.

This tech for good utopian practice however is easy to ideate but not as easy to curate, especially as we will need to support both the supply and demand sides of the house. Then we have the aforementioned misalignment around inputs and outputs, expectations, and support.

I have always seen the potential answer to these problems coming through an online marketplace that curates campaign tech packages for the benefit of grassroots organizations while delivering them at largely discounted prices. Aggregating existing platforms that solve the need and gaps in our digital toolboxes and cultivating larger adoption of those products.

While nonprofit tech companies are building innovative solutions to help organizations tackle today's most critical issues - organizations such as Fast Forward, Code for America, NTEN (the

Nonprofit Technology Network), and TechSoup - they are predominantly cultivating talent, creating real solutions that help some of our most underserved communities, and acting as a bridge for the digital divide.

However, we should advocate for something much more intentional. Something big and bold. Something that has the potential to help build the capacity of our nonprofit sector sustainably. That marketplace option.

In 2021 I stumbled across Pond. Pond was a small tech startup focused on alleviating two of the biggest stressors for nonprofit leaders: how to find the right tools and how to pay for them. Pond tried to turn the traditional seller-focused marketplace upside down by centering nonprofit needs, taking work off their plate, and then (this is the best part) paying nonprofit leaders for their time ($100 for each new connection with a provider).

As you might have noticed I am talking about it in the past tense because unfortunately, Pond wound up its services at the end of 2022. I am still optimistic that this premise can work hence why I wanted to share their story in the hope we might learn from it and that it might help guide a solution that sticks.

I spoke a few times with Pond's CEO Mitch Stein, who is definitely one of those leaders in our space that is going to reshape its impact and effectiveness. A self-diagnosed fanatic about impact with a strong belief in the scalable value of social entrepreneurship, he is on a similar mission to those that are excited about the future of our field, wanting to empower every nonprofit leader and organization by "harnessing the economic engine of the sector with shared digital infrastructure."

My conversations with Mitch had me feeling hopeful for the future of philanthropy. He was acutely aware of the issues at hand and deftly articulated the moment our field found itself. "I feel a real reckoning and transition from philanthropy and charity from one that is done to make one feel good, to focusing on the impact and outcomes. That requires looking more deeply at systems and root causes instead of just addressing the surface-level problem with a more immediate feel-good effect.

"I view one of those root causes as a system that supports and perpetuates the status quo in the nonprofit sector. My work with Pond was taking an economic model (not a philanthropic one) to centralize the tremendous economic power of the sector into a marketplace so that the entire sector can harness it and benefit. Pond's model created a pathway for vendors of products or services that nonprofits consume to put the dollars they'd spend on marketing directly into those potential customers' pockets. By valuing every nonprofit leader's time equally in this system, we created tremendous equity for nonprofits of all sizes to have streamlined access to better tools and services, but also a more universal way to afford them - without philanthropy."

Without philanthropy. That's not as strange as it sounds. As you know, one of my go-to lines in the field is that a 501 c 3 is just a tax designation, not a business model and Mitch's thinking and approach is not exactly born out of the sector. However, contrary to many folks that have brought forward solutions into our orbit, Mitch gets it, because at the end of the day, he is not selling, he is providing - tools, partnerships, and solutions.

Mitch spent 7 years as an investment banker at Goldman Sachs, but during his start-up journey, he began to appreciate that the business world has way more to learn from nonprofit work than the other way around. "There is so much finger-wagging at the sector about how to behave more like businesses or decrying all the things nonprofits are doing wrong. The innovation at Pond was all about looking inward at the sector and the value it brings and then charging people for access to it! It was not about applying outside business theory, it was about rethinking traditional business theory through the nonprofit lens. I would love to see more of that."

When you talk to Mitch you don't get the impression that he was a 'Wall Street guy', far from it. He is refreshingly open and honest about who he is, regularly sharing his experience as an impact tech startup founder on LinkedIn and through weekly email updates. And the good thing is hasn't disappeared from this place of thought leadership since Pond closed, far from it.

"The most important thing I try to hold onto is to value those moments. I am a beginner and a learner and I appreciate the knowledge or experience I bring to the situation from prior experiences. I think so often we rely on an industry veteran or expert to come up with solutions to that industry's problems, but actually an informed "outsider" will likely be able to think far enough outside of the box that the industry has put itself in."

It's an extremely delicate balance to have confidence in your prior experience, but not arrogance that causes you to miss the nuances of the new situation you're in. Mitch candidly shared that he struggled mightily with that during his time leading Pond - listening more deeply to people is definitely how his vision evolved into a far more innovative and effective solution to the original iteration, a simple, traditional marketplace.

"I think bringing a markets and economics perspective to introduce a platform that harnesses the marketplace of nonprofit spending was a fantastic example of my experiences. The technology of Pond was not our innovation. It's the economic model and the convening of such disparate and fragmented demand & supply. I brought an understanding of market making plus an appreciation of the power of ubiquitous consumer-oriented marketplaces plus a pretty insane appetite for risk that is very uncommon in the sector because everyone has convinced themselves (investors and philanthropists included) that the nonprofit sector is a bad market and it requires philanthropy to solve all of its problems. I'd argue philanthropy more often perpetuates those problems, but finding market solutions accelerates solutions."

"Philanthropy's role in our community is to fix the last mile problems and issues that our prevailing economic or government models and systems leave behind. I would like to see philanthropy reframe that role to be more situated on systems change to solve those last-mile problems instead of surface level. A big part of that is investing in innovation - I hate the tendency of the nonprofit sector being the last recipient of new tech - they get the hand-me-downs, discounts, and giveaways. The best tech isn't built for them but falls down to them over time.

"I believe philanthropy has the power to drive innovation in nonprofits first, which could even benefit other sectors after the fact instead of the reverse. It will take a letting go of control - particularly of narrative - which is incredibly challenging for philanthropists who often need to center themselves in the story. Systems change and developing new infrastructure is rarely as sexy as your name emblazoned on a new building."

This is where our conversation became a bit more philosophical. We talked about what philanthropy could be, what it should be, and why so. What systems were holding back meaningful change and how might philanthropy help accelerate possible solutions? Importantly, we discussed racial justice at the core of all these problems.

"It intersects every element of our society in ways I'm still grappling to better understand daily. I think the funding of the status quo in the nonprofit sector perpetuates a lack of progress on the racial justice front - I hear from so many nonprofits that waste countless hours trying to secure grant funding, or not qualifying for grant funding because they are too young or the worst - not having robust data systems in place.

"By keeping the process to secure funding complex, we are limiting the number of BIPOC folks leading organizations solving these issues on a grassroots level - where they must be solved. By keeping the time horizon on grant funding short, we are limiting innovation and equity because there's no room for risk!"

Mitch discusses risk openly. And to be honest, it's something that should be more widely discussed in our field, as ultimately it's a trait of the bold and courageous leadership we so desperately need in our society right now.

"I think we should be pouring philanthropic dollars into new organizations and leaders of color at the grassroots level - wealth hoarding is a primary symptom of white dominant culture and I think we should raise the minimum annual distribution from tax-protected foundations - Could it go up to 10%? 20%? Philanthropy should exist to courageously solve today's problems, not hoard wealth into perpetuity."

Philanthropy means different things to different people, to Mitch Stein it is pretty clear cut. "If you have money today, you benefited from a system that left others behind. Philanthropy is taking what one has gained from that broken system to both help those negatively affected and address root causes of that inequity."

"While there are so many ways that the ultra-wealthy could practice better philanthropy, I think a much bigger portion of the population could also participate in charitable giving. Simple things like recurring giving, round-up apps, all kinds of passive forms of giving that imbed it into our daily lives are the most exciting to me to activate a larger segment of the population to be engaged with impact."

Fundamentally Pond attempted to challenge the economic efficacy of advertising (what if you could spend your ad dollars talking to the customer who says directly they have the problem your product solves and the majority of the money goes into their pocket, increasing their ability to pay?), but I think they ultimately contributed to something much larger.

Civic engagement, civil discourse, trust in government, and voter participation are at historic lows and our communities suffer as a result. With the increased levels of societal isolation (exacerbated by COVID) and constantly growing inequities - in what is the most technologically connected age in our history - it's no wonder people feel the system is rigged and are calling for circuit breakers rather than fighting for systemic change. We must embolden and equip our progressive organizations and their staff with the tools to support campaigns and self-organize.

I believe technology will be able to bridge these gaps and that organizations such as Pond can play a generational role in building a reinvigorated civil society by helping them be more effective and where people through the collective strength of nonprofits, clubs, and membership associations can build both power and influence the majority for better, more inclusive outcomes on behalf of our communities.

I was definitely a big fan of Pond and am still an advocate for nonprofit tech marketplaces as it creates a more human-centered non-profit sales environment. I'm also a fan of Mitch and what his team achieved. You see, a better philanthropy, heck, a better society is an all-hands-on-deck approach and one where we must bring together key players and assets and unify these where possible.

From The Clubhouse: Fundraisers Relationships With Tech - Why It Matters And Why It Should Still Remain Personal

A digital-first shift is changing how nonprofits operate but we are struggling to keep pace.

Technology is a critical tool enabling nonprofit organizations to reach a wider audience, improve effectiveness, streamline operations, and ultimately achieve their missions. However, there is often hesitation among nonprofits to adopt new technology due to the perceived complexity and cost. Technology is constantly evolving, and organizations that are slow to adopt new systems and tools may struggle to keep up with the impact of similar organizations.

A great article from Yale Insights (from the Yale School of Management) provides some real nuance to the hypothesis that nonprofits don't get it yet. It features a robust Q&A with members from Compass (a group that inspires business professionals to engage with their local communities) that discusses the transformative value of technology and what the future might look like with a more strategic direction. The question frames the article: Do nonprofits take the digital world seriously? This is troubling for many reasons, and the reality is that this will forever be the disconnect if nonprofits are viewed as a business model in dire need of support (or saving) from the business community.

So what's the go? Is it a simple case of literacy or more demystifying the tech? I tend to go for the latter in these cases except for data. We sit on troves of it but don't even come close to utilizing it in a way that informs new decision-making or approaches to tackling prevailing social issues in our society. We either cherry-pick data that supports our own organizational vanity metrics (have you ever seen an impact report that says we aren't moving the needle on this issue) or ignore them either because we don't know how to use it or that we can't see what's hiding in plain sight - another case for machine learning to be fast-tracked in our field.

There is no sector-wide agreement on what it means to be data literate, and conversations on data literacy skills range from a basic understanding of the value of data to advanced topics of Artificial Intelligence. This skills gap is also generally lacking across employees and recent college graduates, which may be surprising considering that Gen X and Millennials have grown up with technology.

We need to be aware of the critical distinction between being comfortable with technology and being data literate. The lack of a clear definition of data literacy poses a key stumbling block, making it difficult to measure and teach. Many conversations about data focus on technology, which can be misdirected. For nonprofit organizations, it is important to focus on how data can support their mission, and the critical skills and abilities needed for success. By focusing on data literacy and the specific skills and abilities needed for success, nonprofit organizations can become more confident in their ability to use data analytics effectively and achieve their missions.

Demystifying something is to make it easier to understand, but to be frank, I think that our field tries to oversell it, when encouraging adoption and sharing successful campaigns and client stories should be the immediate focus. I believe we need tech solutions onboarded quickly so our nonprofit organizations can stay focused on outcomes and not outputs, and remain relevant in an ever-changing landscape where we are realizing lots of our societal ills are intersectional in nature. Tackling the issues is going to all we have in the toolbox and tools that can help us see the myriad of options available.

Since Future Philanthropy was published, the door to the nonprofit tech world swung wide open for me and I was lucky enough to meet with some people doing amazing work in our field. Meeting those making my predictions of impact ring true not only helped me understand the space in a much more nuanced way but also set the table for a conversation around what next, and how we might fast-track the solutions of tomorrow.

One of those conversations was with the company Pilytix and its founder Jim Dries. Pilytix is an AI company dedicated to solutions that essentially lower costs, saves time, and increases profitability for universities, and sports & entertainment organizations. So as you can see, we had mutual interests.

Our first conversation was over at his office in Austin, Texas, where we spoke for a few hours about the state of advancement analytics, AI, and what fundraisers need now and could do down the track. It was a refreshingly candid conversation that drew a pretty easy conclusion, that if we can find a way to demystify the tech, we might see it rise to prominence far more quickly.

That means more gifts, larger gifts, identifying new partners, driving new efficiencies in fundraising practice and process, informing fundraisers of donor patterns leading them to smarter asks, etc. Pretty much the simple description of his company that I just mentioned.

I jumped at the chance to build on our conversation and share our thoughts for *Nonprofit Moneyball*.

Nonprofit Moneyball is something Jim instantly connected with especially given his company started out in sports sales and then expanded into fundraising. But was this a natural evolution or simply an opportunity to pivot given the relationship with one of the biggest fundraising machines in the world, the University of Texas at Austin?

Jim explained that their expansion from sports sales to fundraising was completely natural – though not intentional – and only made possible by smart, creative, and patient leaders in the University of Texas' fundraising operation.

They began working with UT-Austin's Athletics department in 2017 with their tools deployed to support a small sales staff selling ticket packages for their ticketed sporting events – Football, Basketball, Baseball, Volleyball, and Soccer. Data and Analytics personnel at UT who supported both the sales team and the fundraising team encouraged them to attempt making slight modifications to their tool sets built for high-volume sales environments – and then apply those toolsets to fundraising. In other words, they were convinced of the applicability before Jim and his team even considered expanding into fundraising.

"That experience has been indicative of what we found in philanthropic organizations – and why we are so optimistic about our future in fundraising. In addition to working with smart and capable business leaders in this space, there is a warmth and a collaborative ethos that seems to run in the DNA of the people who have committed their lives to philanthropy. Serving and supporting good people following noble passions and making the world a better place has been the most gratifying part of my entrepreneurial journey." Jim said.

Jim agreed that the best tech solutions are those built in partnership with the end user especially in niche markets like fundraising. He noted that their ability to build a strong and growing business serving fundraising organizations has been a direct function of the generosity and patience of their 'early adopters.'

"When we got into fundraising, we knew there were enough parallels to our legacy business which supports large sales organizations that our platform could be adapted to fundraising. The early adopters convinced us of the parallels. That said, we were unfamiliar with many of their data-producing systems and we needed to be educated on the process differences – sometimes very subtle – between sales and fundraising."

"To provide reliably transformative insights we need to model behavioral patterns of donors and gift officers. We need to understand the nuanced processes of the organization that we are serving. We need to understand their goals and we help them define their needs. The early adopters, remarkably, saw enough in our vision to take the time to get us up to speed. We spent almost a full year implementing our first university fundraising client and there were dozens of conversations and modifications over that span." Jim shared.

Understanding was one thing but educating the clients was a two-way street. Speaking more broadly about the sector beyond the more mature fundraising shops we see at universities, Jim accepted that there is a growing gap in data and tech literacy in nonprofits ranging from a distorted showcase of social media engagement to understand what an algorithm is. This got to the crux of our conversation of demystifying it all. So how can organizations become better informed to understand, use and benefit from tech options?

Jim was quick to point out his take on it. "I think there are two broad categories of learning that everyone can – and probably should – take advantage of."

Proactive learning: Carving time from your schedule to seek information.

Reactive learning: Engaging with vendors coming to you in a way that compels them to teach.

"Proactive learning would involve seeking out a few thought leaders. Follow their social media, subscribe to their podcasts, and add yourself to their email lists. The data and tech world is evolving so rapidly, that this is time well spent – whether you are trying to stay ahead of the curve – or just want to avoid looking lost when team discussions inevitably take a technical or data-focused turn."

"The key to reactive learning is asking vendors lots of questions – and choking back any compulsion to preface any question with "this might be a dumb question." If you don't know the answer, it's a smart question. It's not your job to connect the dots. That's the technical salesperson's job – and most of them are very well compensated to educate you."

Fundraising has always been – and always will be – driven by relationships, particularly at the major gift end of the giving spectrum. Many fundraising organizations have convinced themselves that technology undermines relationship building and consequently have been slow to adopt technologies that are commonplace in other industries. Indeed, some technologies were developed for highly transactional industries where relationships aren't as important. But, it's a big mistake to group all technical tools under that umbrella. Tech companies can accelerate success. Companies like Pilytix can support decision-making. They can create efficiencies that allow teams to accomplish more. However, technology cannot replace the humanity that lies at the core of each donor relationship. Worthy tech companies with good products recognize this and position their products accordingly.

Jim interjected and also called out a high degree of tech arrogance too. This awareness makes Jim such a great champion of his field and he hasn't gotten drunk off his own Kool-Aid. "Companies in this space build good products, but then position themselves as the answer to everyone's challenges - always. Many philanthropic organizations – particularly those organizations that don't have the in-house technical resources to vet new technical purchases have been burned by over-promising and under-delivering vendors."

"How do we change? Unfortunately, I don't think we will ever live in a world without unscrupulous vendors, so the industry needs to take ownership of its technical future. I think there are basic steps that philanthropic organizations can take to minimize the risk of making bad technical purchases. Ultimately, though, there are a lot of good, value-driving vendors. I think for the industry to accelerate its digital and technical transformation, there have to be more fundraising leaders willing to experiment with technology and demand experimentation from their top deputies – knowing that not all experiments will succeed. Still, failure is sometimes the most powerful teacher and a necessary step toward greater success." Jim professed.

Jim clarified what he meant by experimentation too. "try new tools and accept going in that they may not work. Run small but significant trials and give them enough time to succeed or fail. If the experiment is a bust, keeping it small will prevent damage to the organization."

There was an invitation here to the field to preach it if it is a success too. And he is right, we ultimately need to start using real data to educate our peers. This industry needs to hear about it. We also need to talk candidly about the "value" that tech companies bring in very binary terms and in fundraising that has to be their ability to make money or their ability to save money. And this is how nonprofits need to evaluate technical purchases. And when implementing any new technology, nonprofits need to clearly understand what metrics are going to be impacted by the purchase – and how those impacts are going to contribute to the bottom line.

We then shifted to the future, which we joked was already here, but set our sights on going back and forth on the fundraising areas that seem like obvious candidates for a tech revolution over the next few years.

The first was 'Donor Identification Technology' which we noted had to be fast-tracked given the number of large-scale campaigns becoming the norm. "Whenever I hear from an organization prepping for a campaign launch, there is almost always a fully baked plan already in place to hire lots of new fundraisers – but there has been little attention paid to the size and quality of their prospect universe. Jim shared.

"The first question I ask is "do you have enough qualified prospects to hit the campaign goal." The answer is almost always "no" – though it sometimes takes some back and forth to arrive at this inevitable conclusion."

Without enough qualified prospects, an organization can double or triple the size of its fundraising team and will likely come up short. Intuitively, most organizations know that likely donors share two characteristics: they have the financial means to donate and interest in donating. The most progressive organizations are now including interest levels in their definitions of "qualified prospects" and beginning to harness the huge volumes of untapped behavioral data that correlates with interest – event attendance, web visits, email opens, social media engagement, and more. Success rates are significantly higher when fundraisers engage prospective donors who are both capable of and interested in donating.

Jim added, "Even marginal increases in win rates translate to a huge financial impact over the life of a campaign. However, interest levels ebb and flow which means the qualified prospect pool is a constantly moving target. This is where technology comes in; a basic manually populated spreadsheet approach can't keep up with the huge volumes of constantly changing data – nor interpret the impact of each change."

The second conversational thread was around the "Donor / Customer Journey. "The For-profit tech industry has been tinkering with the "customer journey" for decades. That is, figuring out the levers that they can pull to accelerate the journey from "brand awareness" to "purchase" to "repeat purchase" to "lifelong customer." I think this is an area with obvious parallels to fundraising. Every organization has a contact database that includes prospects who have never given, prospects who have repeatedly written large checks – and everything in between. Technology that empowers fundraising teams to integrate disparate data sources, efficiently segment their contacts, and then deliver relevant messaging via various communications channels is just beginning to see disciplined adoption in fundraising."

We ended on a back and-forth around empowering gift officers to make smart decisions and scale themselves, which sounds like a novel idea until we weaved in the fact that as a sector we have seen unprecedented turnover in fundraising personnel in the past few years. The recent turnover – likely caused by several factors – comes with a silver lining: this turnover crisis is compelling many organizations to invest in the success of their fundraisers, knowing that they can't afford to lose any more talent.

"They know working harder is not a sustainable long-term strategy for a smaller team. The key activity metrics they historically used to drive aggregate team success can't continue with a smaller team – revving any engine too hard for an extended period will break it. But they also realize it will be an uphill climb to hit larger fundraising numbers with a significantly less experienced team. So, many organizations are also looking more skeptically at hiring their way to increased revenue goals."

"Every day of the week, I hear from organizations saying that they want to empower their teams to work smarter. This means different things to different organizations – but the general strategic approach is absolutely necessary. Other industries have adopted "work smarter strategies" and are finding they can improve financial results while providing a better work-life balance for their employees. I think that fundraising organizations who fail to adopt these principles will have a difficult time attracting and retaining good fundraising talent." Perfectly stated Jim, perfectly stated.

And so, we finish where we started, with an agreement that while there was a long way to go and education was a critical part of the broader adoption of AI in fundraising, it is driven by people and their relationships, just not always with donors, their relationship with technology too.

| 9 |

Marketing And Modelling

Personal Branding

Sponsorship deals in professional sports are agreements between a player and a company, in which the player agrees to endorse or promote the company's products or services in exchange for compensation. These deals are a common way for professional athletes to supplement their income. They can involve a wide range of products and services, from sports equipment and apparel to automobiles, food and beverage, and financial services.

The specific terms of a sponsorship deal can vary widely depending on the athlete, the company, and the sport, but typically involve some combination of the following:

Endorsement: The player agrees to endorse the company's products or services, often through advertising campaigns, social media posts, or other promotional activities.

Appearance: The player agrees to make appearances on behalf of the company, such as attending events, speaking engagements, or participating in product launches.

Exclusivity: In some cases, the player may agree to an exclusive sponsorship deal, which prevents them from endorsing or promoting products or services from competing companies.

Compensation: The player is typically compensated for their endorsement or promotional activities, either through a flat fee, a percentage of sales, or a combination of the two.

Sponsorship deals can be highly lucrative for professional athletes, particularly those who are highly visible and have a strong following among fans. They can also be beneficial for companies, as they provide a powerful endorsement from a respected and influential figure, and can help to build brand awareness and credibility.

However, sponsorship deals can also be controversial, particularly if they involve products or services that are seen as unhealthy or unethical. In some cases, players may face criticism or backlash from fans or the media if they are seen as promoting products inconsistent with their image or values.

So how might you go about branding yourself in today's market? The first step is to highlight your skills in a way that complements your resume and enhances your personal brand. A personal website allows you to build a portfolio of your work and refine your personal narrative, values, and goals in ways resumes just can't. Immediately after you finish this chapter, go to a domain marketplace and buy your name or a close derivative. Set up your personal email and link it to your networking bios and cover letters—it looks professional and gives you more content control.

Blog to Your Heart's Content: Think of it as a way to develop your voice and a complement to your professional growth. Over time, it could also lead to speaking and consulting gigs if leveraged correctly. Refining your voice on social media is all well and good, but according to Maria Peagler, the founder of the now defunct socialmediaonlineclasses.com and now her own digital marketing consultancy, resonance, and relevance are earned only for minutes, hours, or days on social media channels, while blog post content lasts around two years. Play the long game by building quality over quantity in terms of content, regardless of what fly-by-night influencers say. Trust me, they don't know our sector if they are trying to make a quick buck.

Engage Online: There has never been a more accessible way to connect with leaders in the field. Build lists of leaders whose work and values you admire or aspire to and interact with their posts. Develop your own voice and cultivate your own audience by using hashtags such as #Causes, #Philanthropy, #DoGood, #Charity, #SocialGood, and #Change. Another great use of time is periodically hosting a Twitter chat, which lets you moderate a conversation and connect with individuals intentionally. Promote the chat beforehand, and ask my favorite question: "Who is doing great work in X?" Then write a summary and tag all those who participated to continue the conversation and build rapport with like-minded individuals.

I will show you a couple of trickle-down strategies that will establish yourself, your knowledge, and your experience as a leading voice in the field, one of which is craving new content as we push for continued professionalism in our work and inspire a new generation of fundraisers.

If you know your stuff and have been in fundraising for a few years then trust me, you are an authority on the subject matter whether it be annual giving, major gift fundraising, or stewardship. Many influential consultants have considerably less frontline fundraising experience, so you don't need to have a famous name, big title, or fancy degree—but you do need to be well-positioned to speak on your topic and able to convey it. Know what you are an expert in and why, then write about your experiences, thoughts, and results. Don't forget that case studies are highly popular, so if you are one of the small numbers of folks in our field that have raised eight-figure gifts, then share how you did it.

Writing is the obvious starting point and while blogging is a solid option, you will probably want to reach an audience quickly and thus need to pitch your articles. Map out websites and publications that align with your work and might be looking for unique hooks.

Don't restrict your outreach to sector-specific outlets: I often write about nonprofit technology which has opened doors into broader tech publications that have been looking for insight on how to engage with and understand, the social sector better.

My favorite resource on how to write, pitch, and everything in between is the Op-Ed Project website. It is run by a group with a mission to increase the range of voices and quality of ideas we hear in the world.

After your pitch is accepted, get down to writing. Once your first article is published, continue exploring that topic by expanding its reach. Many articles from top thought leaders in our field are the same themes but from multiple angles. After a while, you will see which gain traction from your peers. You'll gain a clearer understanding of what resonates with readers, making it easier to get new articles accepted for publication.

Here are some approaches to building out your writing:

Write one article: Identify something you are interested in and pitch the topic to an editor. Once it is accepted, write a 500-word article on it. Write it for yourself, not for the clicks. Let your genuine expertise shine.

Expand that article: Cut the article up into conversational pieces. Share on social media channels to keep the conversation going.

Partner With Someone from Another Site: Write an article with a peer to enhance the viewpoint and gain exposure to new networks.

Investing in your writing is a win-win: Not only can you articulate your successes (which will be helpful for interviews down the track), but it's also a way to develop your voice in the field and is a true complement to your professional growth. Over time, it could also lead to speaking and consulting gigs, if leveraged correctly. This could even trigger other points-earning opportunities in the Education category. And who knows? If you write enough content, you might be looking at an award-winning fundraising book in the future!

THE RETURN ON IMMERSION - A NEW METRIC FOR CHARITIES & THEIR VIRTUAL NARRATIVES

Much of the nonprofit tech that is discussed in our sector revolves around software – state-of-the-art platforms that help lift up our fundraising, new CRM plugins that automate & personalize our unique processes, and other operational offerings that help us deliver our work more effectively and efficiently for both internal and external clients.

What we haven't seen in the industry are robust discussions around hardware. You know, the ones that excite us about what is coming, and how we might adopt it.

The Return on Immersion (a term I originally coined in 2017 at the PRSA International Conference) is a proposed performance measure used to evaluate the impact, empathy, and investment of a user exposed to virtual, mixed-use, and augmented realities.

Much of my thoughts on this in relation to fundraising has been through the research of Paul J. Zak who is a Professor of Economic Sciences, Psychology & Management and the Director for the Center for Neuroeconomics Studies.

While many nonprofits already understand the power of storytelling and how compelling a well-constructed narrative can be, Zak's recent scientific work is putting a much finer point on just how stories change our attitudes, beliefs, and behaviors.

"A decade ago, my lab discovered that a neurochemical called oxytocin is a key "it's safe to approach others" signal in the brain. Oxytocin is produced when we are trusted or shown a kindness, and it motivates cooperation with others. It does this by enhancing the sense of empathy, our ability to experience others' emotions. Empathy is important for social creatures because it allows us to understand how others are likely to react to a situation, including those with whom we work.

More recently my lab wondered if we could "hack" the oxytocin system to motivate people to engage in cooperative behaviors. To do this, we tested if narratives shot on video, rather than face-to-face interactions, would cause the brain to make oxytocin. By taking blood draws before and after the narrative, we found that character-driven stories do consistently cause oxytocin synthesis. Further, the amount of oxytocin released by the brain predicted how much people were willing to help others; for example, donating money to a charity associated with the narrative.

In subsequent studies we have been able to deepen our understanding of why stories motivate voluntary cooperation. (This research was given a boost when, with funding from the U.S. Department of Defense, we developed ways to measure oxytocin release noninvasively at up to one thousand times per second.) We discovered that, in order to motivate a desire to help others, a story must first sustain attention – a scarce resource in the brain – by developing tension during the narrative. If the story is able to create that tension, then it is likely that attentive viewers/ listeners will come to share the emotions of the characters in it, and after it ends, likely to continue mimicking the feelings and behaviors of those characters."

Zak's research lends itself to my thoughts that VR can be a straight-up empathy machine, that if harnessed correctly can help drive deeper connections with donors, generate more meaningful and transformative gifts to your organization, and also capture the unique nature of what the nonprofit sector does and how it serves and supports society.

Zak's lab discovered in 2004 that the brain chemical oxytocin allows us to determine who to trust and trust is a big barrier to tech adoption. So to advance this new ROI into the mainstream we ultimately need a deeper understanding of empathy and what motivates folk to give.

People trust science, right?

Well, people have been trying to capture empathy through testing for decades, the empathy quotient is, and one that is intended to measure how easily you pick up on other people's feelings and how strongly you are affected by other people's feelings, another is situational empathy which is measured either by asking subjects about their experiences immediately after they were exposed to a particular situation, by studying the "facial, gestural, and vocal indices of empathy-related responding".

All interesting, but hardly going to be captured in a post-VR session survey, regardless of whether it's delivered on an iPad or not.

I have been excited to see the development of wearables to assist in building the scaffolding for a new ROI. Neurosensors will also play a role too. That's why I have been following its development and roll-out in the entertainment industry.

There currently exists a 'return on experience' platform and wearable neurosensor that captures what audiences care about in real-time. Using this tech, we are seeing corporate event planning professionals tracking moments of peak immersion, when people become frustrated, and identifying those who are extraordinarily immersed in your program. You can see where I'm going with this, yes, when a person is probably at a point where they should be asked to make a gift.

So, if neurosensors are how to capture a return on experience, how do we spin it towards immersion? Again, going back to Zak's research around narrative will provide the clues, and perhaps being supported through data modeling to show comparative data sets based on past engagements, contact reports, and giving could do the trick.

To the issue of the former, it is one thing to read and contextualize impact, but quite another when you can see the real difference it makes to a person's life — and see it from their eyes. Feeling an emotional connection to a foundation's work in Kenya and Tanzania for example and appreciating the reality of these everyday problems that are so often looked over in favor of more dramatic conflict is a start.

And while I'm buoyed by the trajectory of fundraising AI to provide that undercurrent of predicting a quantitative outcome, I still think we are ways away from the ethical elements of calculating immersion. I would have issues asking someone for a major gift knowing that we have potentially elevated their emotions and taken advantage of it in the moment.

So, to sum up, we have ways to go, but we are not moving blindly in this space with both academic research and innovative tech ensuring that this will be more a case of when and not if.

With many nonprofits desperate to break through the clutter of a sector clamoring for new funding sources, virtual reality may be the key to increasing the amount of donations. It can give stakeholders a unique vantage point to understand and be emotionally moved by what you do and the communities you benefit from.

This new ROI once understood and quantifiable will help justify its adoption and investment. My gut still tells me that the future of virtual reality (VR) does not lie in the hands of Hollywood production houses or video game enthusiasts, but in those of documentarians and storytellers worldwide, but we will need a bit of sector-wide help.

Reporters

Reporters who cover professional sports teams are responsible for providing news, analysis, and commentary on the team's performance, as well as covering the broader landscape of the sport as a whole. They may work for various media outlets, including newspapers, magazines, websites, and television or radio stations.

Specifically, reporters may attend games, practices, and press conferences, interviewing players, coaches, and other team personnel to gather information for their stories. They may also research, watch game film, and analyze statistics to provide insight into the team's performance.

In addition to reporting on the team's games and events, sports reporters may also cover off-field issues, such as contract negotiations, trades, and other news related to the team and the sport. They may also write feature stories and opinion pieces that provide a deeper look into the team's culture, history, and impact on the community.

Overall, reporters who cover professional sports teams play a critical role in providing fans with the information and analysis they need to understand and appreciate the team's performance, as well as the broader landscape of the sport.

Ticket Sales

Ticket salespeople at professional sports teams are responsible for selling tickets for various events hosted by the team, such as games, matches, and tournaments. Their primary goal is to generate revenue by selling as many tickets as possible.

Ticket salespeople typically work closely with the team's marketing department to develop sales strategies and promotional campaigns to drive ticket sales. They may also work with external partners, such as ticket brokers or other ticketing agencies, to help sell tickets to a broader audience.

In addition to selling tickets, ticket salespeople may also be responsible for managing customer relationships and addressing customer concerns. They may work with fans to resolve issues related to ticketing, such as lost or stolen tickets, seating preferences, or refunds. They may also be responsible for managing ticket inventory, tracking sales metrics, and forecasting future sales. They may use data analysis and other tools to identify trends and opportunities for improvement, such as identifying new target audiences or developing new sales channels.

That's quite a bit more than simply selling tickets at a counter. Sales teams exist to maximize your profitability. In an age of spam blockers, reduced budgets, and workforce reductions, teams need an edge to stay motivated and ensure the most motivated and at-risk customers don't get lost in an unprioritized pile of leads.

Your best sales prospects are constantly moving targets – their interest levels vacillate based on team performance, life circumstances, and financial priorities. Sounds like our donors, right?

Once a lead is engaged, it becomes an open opportunity. Traditional follow-ups on open opportunities are driven by random distribution and often result in surprise losses or unexpected wins – but almost always in wasted time.

So how might we provide our fundraisers with actionable, data-generated insight into their open opportunities, allowing them to move opportunities of higher quality through the pipeline quickly – and close more gifts by winning or losing faster? Perhaps bringing in the support machines?

CAN MACHINE LEARNING THAW OUT THE RETURNS OF COLD CALLING IN FUNDRAISING?

How many cold calls to prospects have you had to make during your fundraising career? How many do you still have to make? Do you still find a reason not to make them, letting them fall off your to-do list despite your best intentions?

When you make the call are you super prepared should they pick up the phone or do you just wing it on some loose research, past engagement, and knowledge of your organization's needs?

Look, we are all friends here. I know it's a little bit of everything because the reality is that cold calling is rough. It's awkward. It can be a nightmare for those going in under-prepared and compounded even more so if you are new to the fundraising game and have simply been handed a call list by a delegation happy Director of Development saying, "Can you go through this list in the next 48 hours?"

A harrowing part of structuring this piece was trawling through countless cold call statistics. I'll pick 5 to make my point and move swiftly along...

- 87% of prospects say salespeople don't understand their needs. (TOPO)
- 63% of sales representatives identify cold calls as the worst part of the job, according to sales agent stats. (No More Cold Calling)
- 58% of prospects say they currently find cold calls useless. (RAIN Group)
- 60% of cold calls go to voicemail. (XANT)

A reasonable cold call success rate is 1-2%, according to sales statistics on cold calling (Cognism, 2021). This might lead to the conclusion that cold calling is dead, but the truth is that this technique is still valid in an overall marketing strategy.

So, if it's still a valid strategy and still sneaks itself into fundraising plans worldwide, how do we find the right language, make it authentic, and make it more effective? How do we build confidence in our frontline fundraisers and understand that emailing is not the substitute here, it is just throwing our requests to meet with potential donors into the abyss where everyone is a/b testing subject headings to break through the clutter. Here's one more stat for you. Over 80% of cold emails stay unopened forever (Campaign Monitor).

It's enough to bring a tear to the most optimistic gift officer's eye.

One of the last in-person events I went to before COVID took hold, I saw Babylon Health CEO, Dr. Ali Parsa discuss computational health and in particular how artificial intelligence is revolutionizing the health sector. Dr. Parsa shared a video of how the AI of Babylon Health can help detect your disease. I have watched it countless times since considering its application across several sectors. Take a quick look at their video on YouTube and rejoin me in the next paragraph...I have an idea.

Welcome back...cool platform, right? So where are we trending here? It's not like a donor will call up your organization, press '7' to talk to an automated bot, and then systematically fall on a gift based on a predictive model of what you might be passionate about. This isn't about organizations bombarding donors with robocalls either.

Donor conversations will always require building trust, active listening, and authenticity. However, that's not to say you can't weave in some automated support.

There are some great companies out there for campaigns and advocacy that build out scripts and forward them via email, calls, letters to the editor, etc. Many with just one click, but many with an accompanying 'coldness' of its own in the form of its delivery.

A great blog post that talks about the need for authenticity when working with fundraising scripts (albeit from the angle of political fundraising) comes from Calltime.ai which state that "fundraising should be relational, rather than transactional. This is why a conversation guide is far preferable to a script. Most of us can tell when you're reading off a script, and it instantly feels impersonal and disconnected. Those are not the feelings you want someone to have before asking them to give you money. It's important to stay present in the conversation, really listening to the person on the other side of the phone so you can offer a genuine response and let the conversation have a natural flow to it. A script often gets in the way of this."

What if there were platforms that existed that were, in essence, fundraising scripts, but instead of being static, had more of a conversational tone, could still help move qualification to cultivation and eventually to a gift? What if this platform tailored the ebbs and flows of donor meetings in a more intentional and relational way and simultaneously ascertain with higher degrees of certainty what that prospect might be interested in?

I could see a platform that syncs with your CRM that builds individual scripts in real-time, dynamically pulling previous data points. Imaging talking to a recurring donor who has been giving unrestricted gifts for many years and during a call suggesting possible named scholarships that might be of interest and then scouring college databases to see what matching gifts are available, ultimately presenting proposals with the donor math calculated and spelled out in easily understandable terms.

Imagine having a conversation with a donor who shares information about their spouse that you didn't have, sharing that they do their philanthropy through her IRA. The system could then in real time identify her biographical data, see that she is over 70 & ½ and that the IRA Charitable Rollover exists. Within the next 5 minutes, you might be able to walk them through a Charitable Gift Annuity, the benefits, and what returns they might receive across a sliding gift scale.

Couple this high touch, highly personalized approach with automatic thank you emails and text messages, syncing back to your CRM with a recommended follow-up that will ping you when an algorithmic model has pinged you to do so, then you have all the hallmarks of what could be deemed fundraising optimization.

But let's not get ahead of ourselves here. This would be restricted to calls and emails and not in-person meetings. It could provide a briefing pack that would recommend certain points you might want to cover.

The tech to make this happen exists and could be optimized by uploading countless scripts from nonprofits nationwide, together with conversion rates across a range of different qualitative and quantitative data points. The numbers to make this effective certainly exist with about 2,610,000 results being shown via a simple Google search for fundraising script templates.

Making this work would be a mix of text mining and analytics to derive qualitative insights from unstructured text and identifying patterns or trends from it. What words work, what words evoke stronger levels of empathy, what words move a prospect closer to a gift, and which words whether through a direct ask or proposal converts a prospect to an actual donor.

Building out 'conversation guides' using predictive scripts will never be perfect but with a mix of both reinforcement and supervised learning as an ongoing process (and commitment) we will make the modeling stronger and help build out more effective scripts across a wide range of disciplines not just 'hey here is a good generic fundraising script I wanted to share'.

Supervised learning (SL): This is the machine learning task of learning a function that maps an input to an output based on example input-output pairs for example if they say this, then this desired outcome is the more likely next step. It can also map out new examples.

Reinforcement learning (RL): This is an area of machine learning concerned with how intelligent agents ought to take action. This means rewarding the machine for the 'correct' answer.

The main difference here is around exploration (suggesting patterns) and exploitation (widely understood & accepted knowledge). You won't have to worry too much about what is happening in the background as I believe most of the AI modeling used commercially in the social sector will largely have explainable functions. For example, predictive scripts will show the rationale for choosing those words and why in that order. The models will also update daily at a minimum which will mean stronger lead generation and identification.

My only concern is that predictive text might see a renaissance in headsets to ensure hands-free calling. So, if you are happy to look ridiculous on the other end of the phone, we might be able to confine cold calling to being a simple descriptor and not a critical assumption of a result.

| 10 |

Democratizing Tech For Good

Data

Advanced analytics has become an integral part of sports strategy with teams using data to gain a competitive edge. This includes everything from player tracking to performance analysis to predictive modeling. But for all the talk of big data, how many nonprofits, foundations, and national associations genuinely have the capacity to use it in a way that could find innovative new ways to tackle some of the most critical issues of our time? This might be the case for larger foundations sitting on billion-dollar endowments. But even then, they are focused on more significant ROI in developing countries or newer industries where they can move the needle.

As we continue to see rapid growth in this digital age, small to medium organizations continue to double down on the status quo with limited capacity software supporting a glut of program managers, mar-com staff, and grant officers with visualization tools that simply highlight the problem through a more focused lens.

This is a missed opportunity given that tech exists now that can identify new patterns that could determine a different approach to solving the issues people have dedicated their careers to within these organizations.

The origins of explaining big data were not initially applied as a term as they are today, but more of an adjective for tackling a problem. This drift in interpretation has ultimately affected the social sector's approach, with folks selectively using data sets to reaffirm their own symbolic reasoning and process in solving a particular problem.

Philanthropy is changing. The vehicles through which funds are being invested are changing. Philanthropy is transitioning from funding as a charitable transaction to one with a social justice lens at its core. To adapt to this paradigm shift, the sector is going to need new voices, experiences, education, training, and expertise when it comes to executing these dynamic new takes on how we support programs and projects looking to deliver real impact for those they serve. And it's not just the type of staff that must change. It's also the jobs that support the work.

The accumulation, sorting, analysis, and reporting is one area that will help drive this change. A mind-shift from outputs to outcomes and an understanding of your work beyond the narrative you have crafted. But there is a trap waiting for those looking for a quick fix.

You can invest in data technologies and collect all the data you can possibly imagine. Still, it's worthless if it's not analyzed or communicated to decision-makers so that action can be taken from the insights. Some organizations attempt to communicate data findings across departments of an organization. Still, something typically gets lost in translation as it makes its way from the data scientists to the executive decision-makers. This issue is so prevalent that only 18% of companies believe they can gather and use data insights effectively, according to a McKinsey survey. Due to this, some organizations have opted to add a data translator to help bridge the gap.

The above excerpt was very much business focused but has many lessons for the charitable sector and that's in the translation of data to help inform better and more impactful decision-making.

Looking again at business applications for an insight into market shifts, did you know that Kmart Australia recently hired a team of 10 'data translators' that sit embedded within its top three operational areas to improve traction and take-up of analytics?

CIO Brad Blyth showcased the retailer's efforts to build its data analytics maturity internally by sharing that Kmart is in a constant "three-phase development cycle" for its analytics capabilities – "trying to understand the problems and establish solutions; scaling that up; and then really trying to drive the value out of whatever we've built there."

The following excerpts from Blyth at a recent AI Summit shared some insights that could be relevant for the social sector moving forward.

"Like all good tech organizations, the minute we got our access to some funding, we went off and started building things, and we had a very much 'build it and they'll come' mentality that we tried to push through," Blyth said.

But the business was often indifferent to what was being presented to them.

"In the early days, we really didn't get a lot of traction," Blyth said.

"We started thinking about what we are missing here, and really there was a communication problem.

"*The people who had access and could build the solutions didn't really understand the problems, and the people that had the problems didn't really understand what was possible.*"

The solution was to hire and embed "data translators" into key parts of Kmart – people whose job it was to understand the problems and articulate them in a way that made them understandable as data problems.

"*We've seeded data translators in our top three operational areas – online, stores and merchandise,*" *Blyth said.*

"*They understand that area of the organization. They're close to the P&L and close to the problem spaces, and they have the necessary skills to articulate it in a way where we can start solutioning and coming up with a hypothesis of how we could potentially problem-solve for this.*"

Blyth said there are now 10 data translators. He said their impact was immediate.

"*The minute we put them in, something amazing happened. There was an unlock,*" *he said.*

"*We had a 400 percent growth in three months in our backlog – this is all the ideas that we collected, potential things that we could chase and generate value with.*

"*For each single one of those we noticed a dramatic increase in the amount of benefit that we thought we could go after. This really helped drive that establishment piece.*"

So, what are data translators and how might they be helpful to the for-purpose sector in addressing some of the defining social issues of our time?

The most straightforward definition I found as to what exactly is a data translator and what are the critical skills required to be one came from an article written by Louise Maynard-Atem and Ben Ludford who shared that:

A data translator is someone who can bridge the gap in expertise between technical teams, made up of data scientists, data engineers and software developers, and business stakeholders.

From a nonprofit perspective, those groups will be less technical and more programmatic but will help inform leadership to make better decisions.

And that's what we need. Someone to make sense of the data objectively, stating what it shows, what it means, and what it means for the organization. There are some organizations I know that do try and interpret the data. Still, the stats are cherry-picked to reaffirm the current strategy and on many occasions layered with nothing more than assumptions with a heavy dose of bias.

These roles don't have to be that explicit in the non-profit realm either. A program manager that has the following qualities could be charged with translating data from its IT/Tech functions through to the relevant decision-makers.

- A desire to ask questions and get a deeper understanding of issues (mission and data/outputs and outcomes)
- The confidence and authority to challenge perceptions and biases of individuals at every level of the organization
- A solid understanding of sector-wide requirements and vernacular
- Analytics knowledge or desire to acquire it to be effective in communicating with data scientists
- A passion to give others on the team an advantage of understanding the work and outcomes by using accessible language

A fantastic primer for data translators and what they might do for your organization can be found here – Forget Data Scientists And Hire A Data Translator Instead? By Bernard Marr for Forbes.

Data translators in the future are people I see based within the programmatic areas of for-purpose organizations. They will also form a critical partnership with fundraisers who you all might have heard me call knowledge brokers. They share similar skills and traits but have vastly different outcomes.

Knowledge brokering is a role that acts as a connector and interpreter of new and emerging concepts, acting as a bridge for people seeking answers to questions on one side and those with the answers on the other. The defining traits include translating technical info or complex numbers into something more accessible and understandable and providing links to knowledge, market insights, and research evidence while helping to convert that into practical tools, actions, and narratives. This role is becoming increasingly important because knowledge is a precious commodity these days, especially with the rapid advances in technology and the way we do, understand, and interact with things.

Whether we're discussing data translators or knowledge brokers, the sector would benefit from some professional self-definition of these kinds of actors moving forward.

Data, when defined, has the ability to help guide our decision-making in tackling some of the most significant issues of our time. And over the next few years, it will become more readily digestible and available for future-focused groups that genuinely want to solve these existential problems. Philanthropy has a significant role to play in bringing data into the mainstream, whether that be through direct funding, advocating for or supporting public philanthropic partnerships that use it to inform and de-risk large-scale invest-ment, or simply by being a trusted vehicle for its reporting (think community foundations, economic development corporations, and industry groups).

So, let's not be afraid of investing in things that may challenge our thinking and approach, and let's reinvent the missions of our organizations so that they can be more successful and profitable for decades to come.

THE CASE TO UNLOCK (& DIGITIZE) THE REAL POTENTIAL OF DONOR-ADVISED FUNDS

I just had to write about a recent Senate bill introduced by Senators Angus King (I-Maine) and Chuck Grassley (R-Iowa) which, if passed would reform the tax laws that cover charitable donations, and in particular, those made to, and by Donor Advised Funds (DAFs), with the goal of this new legislation being for philanthropic funds to be 'made available to working charities within a reasonable time period.' The Accelerating Charitable Efforts (ACE) Act would establish a timeline for donations to working charities from donor-advised funds (DAFs), which currently have more than $140 billion set aside for future charitable gifts, but no requirement to distribute these funds.

As per Senator Grassley's media release:

Donor-advised funds currently have more than $140 billion set aside for future charitable gifts – but under current tax laws, the funds have no requirement to ever distribute these resources to working charities. Accordingly, DAFs can accept and hold charitable donations that have generated a federal income tax deduction, but never devote the resources to charitable *work. The ACE Act will address this problem and speed the provision of money to working charities by replacing existing DAF rules with two new types of DAFs:*

*   **15-year DAFs:** The bill will create a new form of DAF under which a donor would get upfront tax benefits (as under current law), but only if DAF funds are distributed (or advisory privileges are released) within 15 years of the donation. To avoid overvaluations, the income tax deduction for complex assets – such as closely-held or restricted stock – would be the amount of cash made available in DAF accounts as a result of the sale of the asset (instead of the appraised value).*

*   **50-Year DAFs:** As an alternative, donors who want more than 15 years to distribute their DAF funds will be allowed to elect an "aligned benefit rule." Under this rule, a DAF donor would continue to receive capital gains and estate tax benefits upon donation, but would not receive the income tax deduction until the donated funds are distributed to the charitable recipient. All funds would be required to be distributed outright to charities no later than 50 years after their donation.*

Look, this is a step in the right direction, but doesn't it feel like if this gets passed we are simply deferring a decision on the real issues surrounding DAFs for fifty years? I'm talking about the $140bn still sitting in DAFs, the barriers to entry to establish DAFs, and the fact that regardless of what this bill establishes, funds are not getting into the community in a timeframe that will help our communities now. 50 years? 50 years? 50 years of funds sitting there, benefitting no one but those that house the funds. It's not a bequest, it's not a pledge, so what's the point?

According to an Associated Press article that took a look at the broader national debate around DAFs when this legislation was introduced, John Arnold, a Texas-based billionaire who made his fortune in hedge funds and now co-chairs Arnold Ventures, joined with a group of scholars and philanthropies to propose a set of reforms under a coalition they called The Initiative to Accelerate Charitable Giving. Members of the group met with lawmakers to advocate for the reforms, which have largely been incorporated into the Senate bill.

What sparked Arnold's interest was seeing rich people with philanthropic intent funneling money into DAFs yet distributing very little of it to charities.

"The money was just sitting there growing," Arnold said. "There wasn't any intent of abuse of the system. But the money was just building up because there was no forcing mechanism."

I agree with that last line. What I disagree with is what was shared in the ensuing paragraphs stating that Opponents of the bill counter that tighter restrictions on DAFs are unnecessary because the average annual payout rates for DAFs hover around 20% — much higher than the 5% minimum required of private foundations. Richard Graber, who leads the conservative Bradley Foundation, calls the legislation "a solution in search of a problem." (The foundation is affiliated with Bradley Impact Fund, a DAF sponsor).

Pretty sure we have a problem folks. A $140 billion problem and the litany of social ills and injustices which continue to plague our society and ultimately are symbolic of this whole argument – that the status quo benefits a certain few.

This legislation feels like all the times government builds 4 lane highways in growing regions, only to build a further four lanes once the original construction has been completed and then has to pay double what it would've cost if they had just built 8 lanes in the first place. Again, the intent is sound but the execution lacks foresight.

So how could they perhaps do this right?

Define the gift: Philanthropy and giving ultimately means different things to different people. So instead of the 15-year and 50-year options, why don't they get defined as charitable or philanthropic donations where the differences are that charity is focused on providing immediate relief to people and philanthropy is focused on helping people and solving their problems over the long-term.

Set bold parameters: Charitable gifts might have a window of 3 years to be disbursed. Philanthropic dollars should be no more than 10 which could include a yearly payout component to a nominated cause or nonprofit.

Apply sunset provisions: After the disbursement window has passed the funds should be moved to a discretionary fund at the institution that the DAF is housed at. Given that a gift to a DAF is effectively a donation to that entity. It shows that they believe in the mission & values of that organization, and they should in turn be able to steward that trust into essential donations to the community.

But they will not do that, so how can we do it better? Well, before we move forward I wanted to share a little disclaimer.

Look, I'm a big fan of DAFs, I have one. It was free to set up when I worked at a community foundation and I was grandfathered into a no-fee arrangement on that fund. For the past ten years, I have made small unrestricted grants to organizations that help our next generation of leaders reach their potential, support our most vulnerable communities and help build a better civil discourse.

Grantees have included: Teach for America, Youth Will, Civic Leadership Fund, San Diego Diplomacy Council, Equity

& Innovation Fund, San Diego Leadership Alliance, Partnerships With Industry, Voice of San Diego, World Affairs Council, United Nations Association, and Travelling Stories.

I would set up a payroll deduction and every time it got to $250 and above, I would make a grant. It was like a charitable bank account for me which helped me be more intentional in my giving and more connected to my community. I ended up saving funds and putting them up as a matching gift for a Giving Circle I helped establish with 15 other people when I was Chair of the San Diego Chapter of Emerging Leaders in Philanthropy (EPIP).

For every book sold of *Future Philanthropy*, I also reinvested 10% of the sale price into the fund, intending to help to lift up new voices in the social sector. Since the book launched, we have been able to support Girls Who Code, The Nancy Jamison Fund for Social Justice housed at Catalyst of San Diego & Imperial Counties, Austin Urban Technology Movement, Code.org, and Access Youth Academy.

DAFs have the potential to revolutionize giving but first, there is an urgent need to democratize this form of philanthropy to make it accessible to everyone that wants one.

Many eyebrows were raised when the Fidelity Charitable Gift Fund (FCGF) took the top spot in the annual rankings of the nation's largest grantmaking charities a few years back, surpassing United Way Worldwide in private contributions. Fidelity's private contributions had been surging up to 20 percent year over year, according to the Washington Post when they first reported it. Still, as we know, the FCGF is not your traditional charity.

Fueled by donor-advised funds (DAFs), these giving vehicles signaled a shift in how the wealthy approach their philanthropy.

But we aren't here to discuss current trends. We are here to anticipate new ones. And regarding DAFs, the future is through automated online platforms.

Why this direction? Because of three things:

1. The insatiable thirst of the sector to engage young donors & take advantage of the upcoming $60trillion generational wealth transfer
2. The reality is that the fees associated with opening and administering DAFs are over-inflated.
3. The sector's ripeness for disruption.

When I say disruption, I mean further disruption. You see, Fidelity, Schwab Charitable Fund, and the Vanguard Charitable Endowment program were the first to disrupt the sector twenty-five years ago. All spin-offs of established investment companies turned these flexible charitable accounts into a multibillion-dollar-a-year funding vehicle that has seen more than a 500 percent increase from 2010.

Why is it that these companies - sorry, I mean charities - were able to outpace other more established institutions, such as community foundations that offered the same options with arguably better outcomes? In short, it was cost. Community foundations charged up until recently an average $25,000 to open an account. Fidelity, on the other hand, charged $5,000 until recently decreasing the barriers to entry even further, supporting households that annually donate $2,600 to charity (and word is they are looking at cutting this even further).

DAFs have been among the most popular philanthropic vehicles for around thirty years. Yet once applied through that elusive millennial lens, they have been traditionally out of reach for younger or limited-capacity donors due to the costs of opening a fund. In the coming years, though, we should see yet another seismic shift in giving, and the catalyst will be mobile apps. DAFs will become commonplace when hybrid corporations understand the marketplace and can open these accounts at substantially lower rates because their software won't need physical locations or bloated numbers of financial, charitable giving, and administrative staff.

With millennials coming of age professionally, DAFs and charitable banking will become more common and accessible, especially when grant recommendations can be made instantly.

And in the not-too-distant future, they will surely be combined with the following:

- AI that will identify compatible charities and trends for users.
- More robust dashboards that will show the impact of donors' dollars.
- Blockchain technology that will track dollars from donation to implementation, increasing trust, transparency, and accountability within the sector.

With 84 percent of millennials donating each year according to Nonprofit Source, it's time that the traditional actors within the sector anticipate these future trends (not only DAFs but also the technology that supports round-up spending options, administering giving circles, and pooled funds for collective impact) and look at providing flexible alternatives for their charitable giving. Otherwise, they risk becoming stagnant institutions of yesteryear.

NO (OR LOW) CODE NONPROFIT AI - LEVERAGING A TRANSCENDENT OPPORTUNITY

No programming required, just plug and play. Is that wishful thinking for nonprofits or the only way they can take ownership of AI processes in the future?

Will social sector organizations be able to harness the potential of AI and machine learning to help solve the defining issues of our time with localized solutions or will they continue to look at expensive third-party vendors or consultants, looking towards innovative foundations, donors, and investors to help fund it all?

Look, it's not too wild a notion to think that no code solutions (or low code options) will be readily available and more affordable in the coming years, especially if we realize that many vehicles currently exist if we are willing to look for them, adopt them and ultimately utilize them to their utmost capabilities.

It's not too wild a notion as we readily utilize 'no code' options for a variety of our work. White-label companies are out there for you to build your own apps and crowdfunding platforms too. Simply building out and personalizing on top of their templates with a simple drag and drop and suddenly you look like one of the top 10% of cutting-edge nonprofits in the country.

For $50 a month, you can take donations, set up chatbots, send push notifications, and other custom content to engage your clients, donors, and volunteers.

Other traditional nonprofit disciplines will soon be turned on their head soon too including:

Fundraising: Companies such as Fundmetric, Dataro, and DonorSearch are already building out algorithmic modeling that is helping organizations identify, build and review donor pipelines.

Communications: Canva (a graphic design platform) and Wix (a website builder) utilize ADI (Artificial Design Intelligence).

Operations: Multiple companies are already out there supporting enhanced business operations and workflows.

Many of these groups will also begin to identify more as AI companies rather than software companies. All you have to do is look at the jobs at Canva currently being advertised, machine learning engineers, data analysts, and computer scientists.

But your quintessential nonprofit isn't going to have data scientists and the like on staff, heck 40% of for-profit companies (according to a Deloitte survey), state AI technologies and expertise are too expensive. So how can AI be democratized to be widely available at a low cost?

The answer lies in no or low-code AI.

No Code AI: Platforms with visual, code-free, and in most cases a drag-and-drop interface to deploy AI and machine learning models. This option supports non-technical users to classify and analyze data to build effective prediction-making models quickly.

Low Code AI: Perfect for IT folks on staff with development skills. These platforms require technical knowledge but allow them to work faster (like an IKEA for building algorithms).

The inherent benefits of these options include:

Usability: It allows anyone in your organization to find an AI solution. No code platforms are designed with non-developers/non-tech-savvy folks in mind.

Speed: Building off templates with drag-and-drop options allows for rapid ideation and real-time changes (based on both the data, UX/UI issues, and of course, typos).

Risk: No-code tools are built on top of proven scaffolding thus mitigating the risk of building something from scratch and having it not work.

Scalability: AI gets better with more data. Fuel the machine and don't pay a dime extra for each piece of metadata uploaded or how many users upload said data.

Cost: It's a much lower investment than bringing on new staff or consultants.

Potential: Template-centered platforms can justify the more extensive adoption and use of AI in the future.

The social sector is probably leaning more on no-code AI offerings especially given some key stats that loom large over the sector including:

Awareness & Trust (stats here via 'The State of AI in the Nonprofit Sector' was conducted by PwrdBy')

Nonprofit practitioners are aware of AI, but have reservations:

- 59% of nonprofits hear about AI from their CRM provider. (nooooooo!)
- 83% of nonprofits believe an ethical framework needs to be defined before the full adoption of AI in the sector. They also

found that the decision-making process for adopting AI is still very mixed.

- Most people believe they need more time with AI before feeling comfortable (63% of respondents) and 83% believe an ethical framework should be implemented before full AI adoption occurs.
- 52% of respondents also reported being scared of AI advancements.

In addition to how they hear about AI, this largely falls at the feet of organizational technology champions (55% of respondents), their boss (47%), and their board (44%).

Internal Infrastructure (stats here are derived from both the 2020 State of Philanthropy Tech from the Technology Association of Grantmakers and the Salesforce Nonprofit Trends Report)

Lack of IT staff is hindering understanding, adoption, and opportunities:

- 93% of respondents state a lack of IT or technical staff is a challenge to their organization's adaptation of new technologies (remember that 55% of the use of technology is actually championed by IT).
- 17:1 continues to be the average ratio of staff to IT staff
- 40% of IT departments do not have any DEI programs (compounding issues of trust)
- 51% of respondents expected to see their IT budget increase in 2021 (and that's with COVID exposing the limited effectiveness of our service delivery models).

Coupled with a demand shortfall of around 1 million computer scientists in the US alone, we see that engineering talent is scarce, so no code options might be the best chance of onboarding this generational tech to the social sector en masse. It's just whether the industry has enough verve to see their calls for AI democratization through.

Ok, that's a lot of stats, we get it. But what are the substantive benefits? Well before we get to those we should put this all in context with some actual examples otherwise this just becomes a ton of unrelatable jargon to those that just want to take advantage of AI to improve inputs, outputs, and solutions where the cost and accessibility barriers are stripped away. How do nonprofits and small to mid-sized foundations create A.I. systems using simple visual interfaces or drag-and-drop menus?

Well, much of its early uses will be made for binary/rudimentary uses that tackle unstructured data such as:

HR: Analyzing all new employees onboarding documents in real-time and being notified when files are complete.

Grantmaking: Find out if nonprofits qualify for funding based on your criteria by analyzing public data (possibly identifying other organizations and inviting them to apply).

Grant Reports: If you're going to make nonprofits write lengthy reports (something tech solutions could end up eliminating altogether), then run the reports through a model segmenting the data and uncovering underlying patterns.

A good visualization here from the for-profit sector can be seen on the Levity site (which is referenced in the notes at the back of this book - #97).

AI ultimately is something that works in the background and is dynamic, not static, running its models daily and feeding off the inputs of new data from wherever it pulls it from (mainly your CRM – hence why they want more data, and for it to be better categorized and labeled, and why they are pushing new advances!)

As you know AI stands for Artificial Intelligence, but we need to see it as automation if we are to have our sector lean into it and not be – as the above report stated – scared of it. So, if we are scared of automation how will we fully grasp or understand the power of AI moving forward?

Firstly, there is ultimately potential in power, it's just how we conceptualize it. Do we want systems that automate the most mundane administrative tasks to allow staff space to think, learn, ideate, and grow (not backfilling that time with additional rudimentary tasks)? Do we want to run models that review our donor prospect pipelines to see if they are ready for an ask? Do we want an independent review of our data to identify trends and patterns that we might not necessarily see, especially if it helps us identify clients needing urgent help or throws up ideas that might recommend a new approach to solving some of the most critical social issues of our time?

And that's just on the nonprofit side.

For organized philanthropy, imagine purchasing several data sets that help inform grant cycles rather than create them based on potentially biased assumptions about trending issues. Imagine modeling that identifies successes (or issues) with a funded project and triggers additional funding to ensure success. Imagine models that review projects and build out their own independent reviews that are then distributed to similar organizations with the same NTEE codes to effectively help everyone 'level up'.

Now imagine you can build these yourselves. And that tech for good advocates are building them and making them available to the sector at a reasonable cost. While it would still need a broader sector dialogue, it's a conversation worth having. The conversations around ethics in ai are already occurring across all industries and are driven mainly by some of our leading higher education institutions. Still, we need to talk more concurrently about the possibilities of ai for the social sector and how as many people as possible can benefit from it before the power we mentioned earlier becomes entrenched once more at the top. That potential is another opportunity missed to level the playing field and advance society.

At the end of the day, no-code AI is still an emerging market. It hasn't even begun to turn its eyes towards the social sector (beyond government) yet, nor has it even trended towards use case management options (classification problems, CRM, web-builders, business apps) as it focuses on building out its core technologies in vision & speech recognition, etc. But it will come, and nonprofits will be seen as a potential revenue stream.

The point is that we should be thinking about it, its applications, and reaching out to those building out the technology – to partner, inform and volunteer to beta test its applications. Companies should also be proactive in reaching out to nonprofits and philanthropy too to help understand how to make their models and templates more dynamic, robust, and practical too. For far too long it has been a top-down approach with tech companies 'bringing our sector the solution' and making us pay a premium for it when all it has done is simply rebadge their for-profit enterprise model. Let's get the tools into the hands of those that can make a difference and let us all reap the rewards but with the novel idea of a shared focus on lifting up those most vulnerable in our society.

| 11 |

The Future Is Now If
You Want It

INFORMING YOUR FUTURE. A CRYSTAL BALL INTO TOMORROW'S FUNDRAISING OPPORTUNITIES (OR A MAGIC 8 BALL INTO CHOOSING WHAT TO ADOPT NOW)

Several off-the-shelf tech offerings exist now that nonprofits could benefit from if they felt it could move the needle for them. However, it takes a sound strategy, courage, and vision from leadership, and a risk appetite second to none to pull it off. So, what's available and how might you take advantage of it?

Over the past couple of years, I've begun to change my tune on the impact of Bitcoin and other cryptocurrency donations as a transformative source of charity over the short- to mid-term, from negligible to fathomable, meaning there may be some depth to it.

Look, I'm intrigued by the proposition of digital currency that is highly transparent with additional layers of security in a globalized economy especially given the impact it could have in philanthropy, but I see parallels with that of virtual reality, where it seems to have been around for a while now, is part of our lexicon but still hasn't hit the heights we expected at this point in its evolution.

I would tend to agree with the following statement from Nils Smith, the Chief Strategist for social media & Innovation over at Dunham+Company who recently shared his thoughts on where crypto donations currently are:

"I believe that we're in a similar moment as to when non-profit organizations began to accept credit card gifts. We were used to cash and checks and knew how to process them and what to do with them. Credit cards had a stigma and we were confused on what to do with them. So most non-profit organizations avoided them for seemingly as long as they could. And they missed out on many potential gifts because of it.

Cryptocurrency is different from credit cards and it's unlikely that the majority of your giving will be via cryptocurrency anytime soon, but don't miss out on the potential gifts that individuals do want to make to your organization.

Unlike the transition to credit card giving years ago, cryptocurrency giving is much easier to integrate. Utilizing a platform like Engiven allows you to accept crypto, receipt donors and instantly liquidate cryptocurrency into USD or the fiat currency of your choosing. It really is that easy."

The fact is that it isn't a mainstream proposition for the sector as yet. I'm bullish however on some real advances for the technology more broadly over the coming years and am excited to see some new trends breakthrough or garner more attention.

Donations. Expansion continues to gather momentum:

This is an easy prediction to make. Donations will continue to increase based on current trends:

- 45% of the cryptocurrency holders donated $1,000 or more to charities in 2020 compared to 33% of other investors, according to a recent report by Fidelity.
- At the time of writing CNBC reported that cryptocurrency now represents more than $3 trillion in value
- Engiven shared that the average cryptocurrency donation on their platform is over $7,500 in value.
- The Giving Block led #CryptoGivingTuesday which was the year's biggest one-day celebration for crypto fundraising and giving. Around 1,000 nonprofit organizations participated in 2021, almost 10x more than in 2020 – $2.4M was raised with an average gift size of $12,600.

At the end of the day, non-profits will need to be prepared to accept cryptocurrency donations moving forward and that will require a couple of things organizationally – so, get informed through resources that can be found on The Giving Block, get yourself a wallet, but don't invest a ton of time or capacity into actively chasing it – we aren't quite there yet.

Experimentation: I think we will see a lot of experimentation in the space and that's the beauty of this emerging technology. There is no way to predict which of its applications will revolutionize the nonprofit sector. I can see a new and defined cryptocurrency with a real charitable bent rather than a meme spin-off.

A new cryptocurrency for the sole purpose of donating could be on the cards. And that's something we could all get behind. Much like the Australian 'donation dollar' which became the world's first legal tender designed to be donated. The Royal Australian Mint created a Donation Dollar for every Australian, creating twenty-five million reminders to donate.

We will also see a lot of the buzz around non-fungible tokens (NFTs) and how they relate to/can be used by nonprofits. I discussed this more broadly in Chapter 6 but note that NFTs will expand beyond art, at least regarding conversations about its future. A terrific article on The Conversation set the stage for what that might entail for society:

"NFTs goes much further because they completely change the rules of ownership. Transactions in which ownership of something changes hands have usually depended on layers of middlemen to establish trust in the transaction, exchange contracts and ensure that money changes hands.

This has the potential to completely transform markets like property and vehicles, for instance. NFTs could also be part of the solution in resolving issues with land ownership. Only 30% of the global population has legally registered rights to their land and property. Those without clearly defined rights find it much harder to access finance and credit. Also, if more of our lives are spent in virtual worlds in future, the things that we buy there will probably be bought and sold as NFTs too.

There will be many other developments in this decentralized economy that have yet to be imagined. What we can say is that it will be a much more transparent and direct type of market than what we are used to. Those who think they are seeing a flash in the pan are unlikely to be prepared when it arrives."

I could also see potential plays and extensions on the term perpetuity – and for organizations that might become more virtual due to COVID. As you might know, "non-fungible" means that the item is unique and can't be replaced with something else. It's one of a kind. This could come in the form of gala prizes, donor recognition pieces, and ultimately the replacement of that traditional 'donor wall' we have all been grandfathered into.

Gamification to drive insight into new habits: Arguably, many folks have already made their mind up about crypto and it's very much based on their gut and/or risk tolerance and the who and where they receive their information. Are they genuinely curious about its potential or do they just see it as a 'get rich quick' strategy?

Either way, there are organizations out there that understand the need to educate consumers about it, and I predict that this will ramp up over the coming year through gamification. By creating a 'gamified user journey' the major players in the sector will be seen to leverage game mechanics to influence desired behaviors and promote ongoing engagement.

Examples I have already seen nudging the field towards greater understanding and adoption of crypto (by rewarding behaviors with the biggest impact on their business goals) come from Tokens for Humanity and Coinbase.

Coinbase is using gamification in a variety of ways. Firstly, they are driving engagement and understanding by having potential new customers take part in a quick quiz to understand how it works and then give them some free Bitcoin for their time. They also recently gave users the ability to link their accounts to the League of Traders which means that Coinbase users can link portfolios from different exchanges and partake in real-time competitions, check out leader boards, and, get a view of the platform's top-rated traders' port-folios – in the form of an asset distribution chart, risk and volatility assessment, positions currently open, and a growth chart.

TokenSpin is far simpler and comes from the Australian Tokens for Humanity team. It's effectively a lottery for nonprofits to win

Ether with its premise built around making charity lotteries enjoyable, straightforward, and, well, charitable. It is developed to enable greater efficiency and transparency in the charitable fundraising industry.

According to their website they "were inspired to create a product that would appeal to a new market of socially minded players. TokenSpin is the first blockchain raffle to be offered in the Australian market and is subjected to high standards of compliance (external financial audits annually, charitable regulatory compliance, et cetera) ...empowering crypto users to make a difference and have fun."

The next few years are going to be important to getting the sector comfortable with crypto and blockchain and the reality here is that you will need to speculate (give bitcoin et al) to accumulate (users for your product). And with increased users and outcomes, we can drive more insights and research.

Research: We can't truly talk about the potential impact of the blockchain in the social sector without the research, and the reality is that there simply isn't enough of it out there. And I'm talking substantive research, not the vanity/pump-primed statistics that show an 850% increase in participation just because the number of folks that used your product went from 100 to 1000 people over a year.

In an article for the Harvard Business Review, associate professor of business administration at Tufts University, Alnoor Ebrahim, says there is a discernible trend in the social sector: "Claims about making a difference are no longer sufficient; evidence of how much difference you're making is now required."

Recently there have been some investments in this space with $3 million to Cornell; the University of California, Berkeley; and the University of Maryland by the National Science Foundation to conduct wide-ranging research into the pain points of the current ecosystem. There is no doubt that considerably more investments will be made both publicly and privately over the course of the year.

Giving – New Applications: Giving is the act, the intention, and the culture around being charitable. The blockchain can play a role here, just as long as it can inspire a more meaningful narrative around the tech rather than the allure of the potential gains of cryptocurrency.

We will see new applications for this tech in the nonprofit space soon and the start of 'what could be' rather than 'what if' discussions.

Giving cryptocurrency as mentioned above is, "easy" in the greater scheme of things, there is a real necessity here to ensure the blockchain and its boundless opportunities aren't lost in the shadow of its more widely known application.

We might be entering the time of the 'token' and an understanding of the notable difference between tokens and coins and what they represent. While crypto coins are essentially digital versions of money, tokens can stand for assets or deeds. You can buy tokens with coins, but some tokens can carry more value than any of them. For example, a company's share.

Expect a few more years of positive growth for cryptocurrency and blockchain technology from an impact, narrative, and adoption standpoint. Let's not be naïve and realize it has a long way to go. But to that point, I wanted to acknowledge that organizations such as Silicon Valley Community Foundation, Square, and UNICEF are advancing grant programs in this space.

I've never used fruit as my final analogy for a segment before, but the question is are we close to seeing a new wave of philanthropic giving where gifts are more like the Pineapple Fund, which in 2018 saw an anonymous donor gift of $55 million to sixty nonprofit groups via Reddit. Gifts ranged from $50,000 all the way to

$5 million and included the ACLU, charity: water, and Pencils of Promise, to name but a few.

Or will we just be disappointed by stories such as the Banana Fund, which was found to be a crypto-crowdfunding Ponzi scheme? Ok, that last reference wasn't fair, but it just goes to show what can happen if the sector doesn't truly understand the tech and is looking at raising funds over building lasting donor relationships that will deliver real long-term impact.

VR: Nonprofits and associations within the sector are beginning to use virtual reality, augmented reality, 360 video, and other innovative storytelling vehicles to help advance their missions with some encouraging (if not, exceptional) results. So how far away is the charitable sector from using VR as a legitimate communications and fundraising tool and what's in store for this medium in the next few years? Here are 5 bold predictions for its usage as it seeks to become more mainstream in our industry.

The use of VR in the nonprofit sector is still in its infancy and is predominantly used right now by large international charities and higher education institutions due to the costs, skills, and capacity required in creating original content. These costs have come down considerably in the past 5 years from (in some cases) six figures down to $5-10k, so I'm optimistic that it might be more viable now as we can see both a return on investment and the magic that comes from a return on immersion.

However, for it to permeate the sector, it will require the foresight (and goodwill) of first movers in this space to continue to increase awareness of VR in marketing and fundraising, and ultimately share its results to help more organizations become more comfortable in utilizing these lived experiences for the common good.

So, with increased awareness of VR still top of our list, here are my top 5 nonprofit VR predictions for the short-medium term;

Conferences: With the continuing return of conferences to an in-person model, at least half of all large nonprofit conferences (250+ attendees) will have some form of VR component for use by attendees. This will range from simple VR booths for people to be exposed to these computer-simulated realities or breakout sessions discussing the possibilities of its future use amongst other new technologies. The content shown will be largely replicated (not original) yet will drive important conversations around the medium's potential and also see attendees begin to purchase VR hardware for their own private use.

Gala Events/One-Off Fundraising Events: Given that VR is still relatively new, creating special events around these unique virtual experiences allows charities to reap rewards in real-time and drive new levels of empathy to highlight stories of impact and combat major donor fatigue. Event managers that can successfully execute the use of VR and weave it into the experience rather than simply adding it on because it's a cool trend will be the ones see their organizations reap significant benefits.

The leading example of this experiential approach is Pencils of Promise who created a 16ft replica of a Ghanaian classroom to set the scene for one of their Wall St Gala's. They raised $1.9m at this star-studded event with just a 90-second video. I predict several events this year will become even more innovative with their use of VR with the possibility of a single event or multi-day conference raising $5m+.

Major Gifts: Examples of major gift projections surpassed by up to 70% have been reported by UN-backed conferences using VR for refugee donors to highlight the devastation in Syria. It was also found that 1 in 6 people pledged donations after participating in that same experience, double the normal rate. Higher education is also beginning to use it too with the University of San Francisco's facilities department currently providing VR resources to new capital campaigns, which includes their new basketball gym. The VR content is currently being used to showcase interactive architectural renderings of the completed new gym.

One of the best stories I have read was when a donor visited Charity:Water's office. He had already committed to giving $60,000, yet watched a VR film on their work in Africa and was so moved by the story that he gave $400,000 instead. This example is in many ways an outlier for the moment but should also be seen as an example of its unbridled potential with VR revenue predicted to grow to $12.19 billion in 2024.

I would also not be surprised if the sector or academia embark on significant research projects to help fundraisers understand the empathy triggers, motivations, and power of immersive experiences of major donors.

Activism: With the 2024 Presidential Election starting to heat up, we can imagine a VR campaign video will be released to highlight key policy issues and drive donations toward engagement efforts. While you're probably thinking of parties and/or specific campaigns, it's just as likely that advocacy groups like the International Rescue Committee and Amnesty International will continue linking virtual content that communicates their missions and current work both locally and globally.

It's already being taken to the streets through innovative grassroots engagement tactics. A great example of this was Amnesty International which launched its 'Virtual Reality Aleppo' campaign in three major UK cities to amplify the effectiveness of their traditional street fundraisers' messages. This campaign used refurbished smartphones and basic VR headgear and took viewers on a tour of the war-ravaged Syrian city of Aleppo, 100 kilometers south of the Turkish border to highlight the impact caused by barrel-bombs.

Industry & Foundational Support: There are huge equity disparities within nonprofits exacerbated by access to this technology. The top 10% of charities have large teams of communications and fundraising staff and also the budgets to execute. Smaller nonprofits that often do the hard work on the ground and have truly inspiring stories to share are more concerned with raising enough money to keep the lights on, let alone taking on the risk and costs associated with creating a VR experience for its limited donor base.

To help close this gap I believe some major national foundations will either expand or create grant opportunities that will allow for smaller organizations to create VR content. This may also come in the form of partnerships with major companies and platforms such as Oculus VR to help partner VR production companies with impactful nonprofits.

'Telling your story' has always been at the forefront of advice given to nonprofits and now the sector has a new tool to add to its fundraising arsenal and assist in their ongoing narrative. It is one thing to read and contextualize impact but quite another when you can see the real difference your donation makes to a person's life, through their eyes and devoid of the harsh realities of which it's all too easy to ignore. The VR industry understands that adoption and conversion will be driven from the outside-in and that VR won't flourish in this sector without its intervention and ongoing commitment.

Look, I want VR to take off but understand that we are still in the exploration stage and awareness in the nonprofit world is on-going. Progress has a compounding effect though and with some truly impactful and innovative uses of the medium sure to dominate some of the sector's online conversations when they happen, I remain as excited as I did back in 2015 when I first donned a headset at the Clinton Global Initiative in New York.

BAKE SALES ARE NOT FUNDRAISERS SO LET'S MAKE THEM IN 3D

Whenever I am asked about fundraising from someone outside of the sector the question 'but aren't you all just fighting for the same resources' comes up. And like any optimist, the reply is always a sharp, confident reply of 'well, we will just expand the pie'.

That fundraising pie as you might know does indeed have the capacity to be grown but what if there were other varieties of pies that we have neglected to put on the menu?

I then started thinking of bake sales, that traditional fundraiser associated with smaller nonprofits, schools, and church groups. Many of those treats are donated by members and supporters of those organizations which lead to terrific margins and a good few hundred dollars in the coffers.

But then something clicked. Bakes sales and the like (BBQs, booths at school fetes, etc.), are not fundraisers and are another misnomer for how not-for-profits operate. The key words here are 'sales'. Yes, we know 501 c 3 is just a tax designation and not a business model but why do we restrict our revenue models to one purely based on philanthropy?

Some of the most successful nonprofits out there have additional mission-driven income streams that go beyond giving. Red Cross, Habitat for Humanity and St Vincent de Paul's have thrift stores, schools, and sporting organizations rent out their facilities, disability service providers take on commercial jobs, and I know of some organizations with dynamic leaders who raise funds for their organization through consultancy fees.

Yes, not-for-profit organizations can sell goods and services. Yes, it can drive a surplus if it is furthering its charitable purpose, in fact, it is generally considered good practice (I would encourage folks to do a deeper dive on social enterprises in Australia to see this approach in action).

And no, it's not a blurring of the lines. It's tax-exempt if it is mission-related and if financial gain occurs from unrelated activities, then it is simply taxed as business income e.g., subletting office space to other entities.

As you know, much of my writing is about the future, and it would be remiss of me not to talk about what nonprofits might offer in terms of products in 5 or 10 years. I'm pretty bullish on 3D printers not just for what they can create, but what they could also do in terms of community support.

Physical products that assist organizations in their mission and service delivery and potentially improve their bottom lines through revenue generation will become commonplace when the costs of acquiring large-scale 3D printers come down through advances in technology and of course via scale.

There are myriad uses for the tech too, from small desktop printers to industrial-sized printers that could play a role in housing affordability and the mobility of nonprofits beyond the confines of their walls.

Think arts and education as great sectors to disrupt in this instance. For example, advocates of this tech are calling 3D printers in education the "TV on the rolling stand" of our incoming generations of students. Imagine printing a skeleton, piece by piece, for biology or creating a model of each element of the periodic table during chemistry. It has the ability to revolutionize teaching and inspire careers in the jobs of tomorrow that will have some element of STEM attached to them.

Products: While 3D printing is not commonplace in the stereotypical non-profits we have probably worked for or volunteered at, there are already some truly game-changing applications for this tech.

The Hand Foundation is building free prosthetic hands for children, and the organization New Story has been working in Bolivia, Haiti, and Mexico to transform blighted favelas with the construction of six- hundred-square-foot homes for less than $4,000, with plans in the future to build an entire community of around one hundred homes in El Salvador.

It's not hard to see a future where workshops equipped with large printers tackling these kinds of issues exist in a children's hospital or at a local Habitat for Humanity, especially when printing patterns and designs will be widely available for download or purchase. It's also not beyond comprehension that whatever you can think of to assist you in your work can be "printed," which is a truly exciting proposition, especially when viewed through the lens of global scale and potential impact in emerging and remote countries. So regardless of the size or scope of your organization, you can use 3D printing in a wide range of ways (including building molds) for pens, rulers, Lego pieces, you name it.

Programs: By constructing new homes, 3D printing can help tackle homelessness and housing affordability. Leading philanthropic institutions are pushing a housing-first approach to solving the homeless crisis, with homes touted to be built within twenty-four hours and costing less than $4,000 to make. This could be the key to unlocking a new future for those who have fallen through the cracks or been victims of our system.

Austin, Texas (where I previously lived), is the home of 3D-printing company Icon, which in 2018 created a 350-square-foot tiny house that cost $10,000 to build within two days. Given that the printer wasn't running at full speed and Icon has since closed a Series A funding round of $35 million, there is no doubt they will be pioneering a new era of construction that will accelerate conversations around new solutions across the sector. All of these 3D-printed buildings will probably be LEED certified, making for an attractive proposition for something that could be commonplace by 2030.

Given the price points and the fact that companies will no doubt scale 3D printing to build bigger and better structures, we could possibly see a boom in first-home ownership, a new generation of wealth building, and a strengthening and expansion of the middle class. Not to mention the racial justice connotations it will have, as mentioned earlier in this book. In short, this technology could have various applications for programming in a nonprofit context. But for now, take some time to ideate how it might work in your own organization. This is a future where if you can dream it, then you can make it. It's wild if you truly think about it.

Community Response: With an ever-increasing spate of natural disasters, civil unrest, and a volatile economy that have only been exposed and exacerbated by the coronavirus pandemic, the need to activate people and businesses to support governments in supporting and rebuilding communities beyond a cash donation or "hopes and prayers" is driving a new focus on disaster planning, mitigation, and response.

The pandemic showed us two things. First, our systems were wildly underprepared for the virus, seeing ventilators, PPE, and even sanitizer being in short supply. The second part was more inspiring and a common effect of incidents that reach the level of emergency: Folks stepped up and helped fill an urgent need. Breweries and distilleries converted their operations to make sanitizer. Equipment manufacturers shifted their production focus to face-masks and ventilators, and tech start-ups pivoted to create new contract-tracing apps.

An example of this comes from my previous neighborhood of Scripps Ranch in San Diego, whose civic association called on residents with 3D printers to create face shield holders for first responders via a design they had on file. The simple headgear shield took six to seven hours to make, with volunteers then attaching the transparent sheets and bands. Yet they still managed to source and distribute hundreds of them to areas of urgent need. It was one of those rallying calls that restore your faith in humanity, especially with doctors, nurses, and paramedics taking photos and sharing their thanks online.

Moving forward, it would be wise for state emergency departments to create a list of organizations with 3D-printing capabilities (perhaps even providing equipment in advance to preferred partners) that could be called upon during an emergency and then provided with the digital files to begin creating items of the biggest need. This can be supported by donations that come in to be used for rapid-response grants. Also, the costs of 3D printing are lowering as the technology's processes and capabilities are being improved with each iteration.

In the future, we will see greener outcomes versus the traditional manufacturing options, including new energy efficiencies achieved across the production, distribution, and waste management processes. This will be an attractive opportunity for impact investors and major gift prospects. It is not to be ignored: 3D printing will become a mainstream technology and probably expand its capacity and capabilities, including metals, automation, and new product

development. Opportunities abound, and the sector should be proactive around it.

Organizations should apply for funding for printers, and funders should have the foresight of its potential ROI by making awards
to nonprofits seeking these tangible goods since they will directly
benefit our communities in a potentially more dynamic, affordable,
and environmentally conscious way. And with edible applications
gathering pace too, we will also be able to print all those cakes for
our future commercial endeavors!

| 12 |

Roll The Tape

In pro sports, "roll the tape" is a phrase that refers to watching game film or video footage of a previous game or practice session. Coaches and players will often review the tape to analyze their own performance and their opponents, looking for areas where they can improve or exploit weaknesses. This practice allows them to understand the game better and make strategic adjustments in future matches.

Now that we are at the end of the book, instead of a test or a set of questions to show that you did read the content, I encourage you to go and watch the movie 'Moneyball.' Not only will a few of the analogies click for you, but seeing it again through a different frame will hopefully reaffirm all that has been shared in this book, and also inspire your own innovative thinking around what could be for your organization.

There is no right way of fundraising, and every fundraiser is different. Still, with the proper knowledge, attitude, and access, you can regularly raise 7 figure gifts and truly transform the small to medium nonprofits you work for. And if they are transformed, think about what that will mean for the communities you serve. Heck, they might even make a movie about it!

So, grab a seat, open up Netflix, and follow this new complementary guide to the movie you never thought would inspire your future fundraising success...

Thesis statement: Using the principles of Moneyball, small nonprofit organizations can compete with larger organizations by identifying the right data and people to build a successful fundraising team.

Building a Winning Team. Overview of how the Oakland Athletics built their team to compete with larger, wealthier teams.

Beane's theory: that traditional ways of evaluating players were flawed, and that by focusing on overlooked data and skills, the team could find undervalued players who would perform well.

Examples from the movie: Beane and his team analyzing player statistics and identifying undervalued players like Scott Hatteberg (00:15:48).

How this theory enabled the team to identify the correct data and people: by focusing on specific skills and statistics, the team could identify undervalued players who would fit into the team's strategy and help them win.

The problem with cognitive biases. Overview of how cognitive biases can affect player evaluation and strategy in baseball.

Examples from the movie: scouts and coaches relying on traditional metrics like batting average and home runs to evaluate players, and ignoring other factors like on-base percentage (00:13:09).

How these biases can also affect nonprofit fundraising teams: by relying on traditional metrics like donor dollars raised, nonprofits can overlook other important factors like donor retention and engagement.

Generalizing tactics from Moneyball. Overview of how the principles of Moneyball can be applied to nonprofit fundraising.

Examples from the movie: focusing on specific metrics to evaluate players and building a team around those metrics (00:31:33), using data to drive decision-making and strategy (00:44:18).

How nonprofit fundraising teams can apply these tactics: by focusing on specific metrics like donor retention and engagement and using data to make informed decisions about fundraising strategy and tactics.

So there you have it, I hope that this season, you have gained a deeper understanding of the trends shaping our industry and are ready for finals! I encourage you to use this knowledge to spark discussions and explore new technologies and approaches that can drive innovation and impact in your work and community. While planning for the future is essential, taking calculated risks can help accelerate change and move us forward.

As a fundraiser in your organization, you must have the courage to lead with conviction and embrace new and innovative ways of thinking. Building a fundraising culture and 'championship winning' team requires commitment and action, not just words. Seek out challenges and opportunities to make a difference, and don't be afraid to take bold steps.

Don't limit yourself or your potential by waiting for the "right" time or someone else to ask you to take on a leadership role. Instead, reimagine what your organization and career could be and take action to make it happen. Whether securing a promotion or executing a successful campaign, don't wait to be asked - go out and get it.

This is a call to arms and a playbook for change. Let these insights inspire you to dream big and be that change you want to see in your field. Find your north star and pursue your future with passion and determination. While fundraising is a team sport, we can all look to the captain to carry us to fundraising immortality.

NOTES

Acknowledgements

1. The Hon Dr Andrew Leigh MP. (2023, February 11). Harnessing generosity, boosting philanthropy. Ministers Media Releases, Australian Federal Government, Treasury Portfolio. https://ministers.treasury.gov.au/ministers/andrew-leigh-2022/media-releases/harnessing-generosity-boosting-philanthropy

Introduction

2. Moneyball. (2011). Directed by Bennett Miller [Motion picture]. Sony Pictures Home Entertainment
3. Lewis, M. (2003). Moneyball: The Art of Winning an Unfair Game. W. W. Norton & Company
4. Three True Outcomes. (n.d.). MLB.com. Retrieved March 19, 2023, from https://www.mlb.com/glossary/idioms/three-true-outcomes
5. Sanchez, M. (2021, May 12). Nonprofit Ratios: What They Are and Why They Matter. Warren Averett. https://warrenaverett.com/insights/nonprofit-ratios/
6. Springfield United. (n.d.). Home. Retrieved April 16, 2023, from https://www.springfieldutd.com.au/wspHome.aspx
7. Simply Benefits. (2022, January 24). Employee Retention: What Is The True Cost Of Losing An Employee? https://www.simplybenefits.ca/blog/employee-retention-what-is-the-true-cost-of-losing-an-employee
8. Chronicle of Philanthropy. (2020, February 25). 51% of Fundraisers Plan to Leave Their Jobs by 2021, Says New Survey. https://www.philanthropy.com/article/51-of-fundraisers-plan-to-leave-their-jobs-by-2021-says-new-survey/

9. Philanthropy Daily. (2022, March 29). Shutting the Door on Development Turnover. https://philanthropydaily.com/shutting-door-development-turnover/

Pre-Season Training

10. Kaplan, R. S. (1994, January). The Fall and Rise of Strategic Planning. Harvard Business Review. https://hbr.org/1994/01/the-fall-and-rise-of-strategic-planning

11. Prive, T. (2016, January 7). Why 67 Percent of Strategic Plans Fail. Inc. Australia. https://www.inc-aus.com/tanya-prive/why-67-percent-of-strategic-plans-fail.html

12. Florida Statutes. (n.d.). § 876.12, Florida Statutes. LawServer. Retrieved July 31, 2021, from https://www.lawserver.com/law/state/florida/statutes/florida_statutes_876-12

13. Federal Trade Commission. (n.d.). National Do Not Call Registry. https://www.donotcall.gov/

14. Fowler, M. (2005, November 22). The Etymology of "Refactoring". Martin Fowler. https://martinfowler.com/bliki/EtymologyOfRefactoring.html

15. Fowler, M., & Beck, K. (2018). Refactoring: Improving the Design of Existing Code. Addison-Wesley Professional

16. Admiral McRaven. (2014, May 17). University of Texas at Austin 2014 Commencement Address - Admiral William H. McRaven [Video]. YouTube. https://www.youtube.com/watch?v=pxBQLFLei70

Chapter 1

17. XpertHR. (2017, July 27). Charting the Evolution of Strategic HR. https://www.xperthr.co.uk/commentary-and-insights/charting-the-evolution-of-strategic-hr/27445/

18. Schneider, M. (2018, August 2). 5 Years of Google Data Reveals the Number of Interviews It Takes to Find the Perfect Candidate. Inc. Australia. https://www.inc-aus.com/michael-schneider/5-years-of-google-data-reveals-number-of-interviews-it-takes-to-find-perfect-candidate.html

19. Perrin, A. (2017, October 4). Americans' attitudes toward hiring algorithms. Pew Research Center. https://www.pewresearch.org/internet/2017/10/04/americans-attitudes-toward-hiring-algorithms/

20. Giving USA Foundation. (2022). Giving USA 2022 [Infographic]. Giving USA Foundation. https://givingusa.org/wp-content/uploads/2022/06/GivingUSA2022_Infographic.pdf

21. Johnson Center for Philanthropy. (2022, July 26). Philanthropy 1992-2022: Giving Changed, How Much, Where To, and Who From. https://johnsoncenter.org/blog/philanthropy-1992-2022-giving-changed-how-much-where-to-and-who-from/

22. Institute of Sustainable Philanthropy & Revolutionise International. (2022). What Makes Fundraisers Tick? A Study of Identity, Motivation, and Well-being. https://static1.squarespace.com/static/62d7378f7e36475c6adf18ee/t/635c317e7c826e6c3f89339b/1666986367934/What+Makes+Fundraisers+Tick+Report+V2.pdf

Chapter 2

23. Gallup. (2018). Fixable Problem Costs U.S. Businesses $1 Trillion. https://www.gallup.com/workplace/247391/fixable-problem-costs-businesses-trillion.aspx

24. Altman, J. (2017, January 18). How Much Does Employee Turnover Really Cost? HuffPost. https://www.huffpost.com/entry/how-much-does-employee-turnover-really-cost_b_587fbaf9e4b0474ad4874fb7

25. National Skills Commission. (2021). Fundraisers. 25 Emerging Occupations. https://www.nationalskillscommission.gov.au/reports/emerging-occupations/25-emerging-occupations/refreshing-anzsco/fundraisers

26. Johns Hopkins Center for Civil Society Studies. (n.d.). COVID-19 and the state of nonprofit employment. http://ccss.jhu.edu/research-projects/nonprofit-economic-data/covid-nonprofit-employment/

27. Harris, T. (2021). FutureGood: How to Use Futurism to Save the World. Wise Ink Creative Publishing

28. Predictive Index. (2019, October 7). Nine-Time 2019 Award Winner, The Predictive Index (PI), Celebrates 30% YoY Revenue Growth Following Launch of Talent Optimization Discipline. [Press release]. https://www.predictiveindex.com/news-press/news/nine-time-2019-award-winner-the-predictive-index-pi-celebrates-30-yoy-revenue-growth-following-launch-of-talent-optimization-discipline/

29. LinkedIn. (n.d.). About LinkedIn. Retrieved April 18, 2023, from https://about.linkedin.com/

30. Feldman, J. (2021, July 22). Innovation Moves to Middle America. The Wall Street Journal. https://www.wsj.com/articles/innovation-moves-to-middle-america-11626199747

31. CNN. (2019, October 29). $10,000 for remote workers if they move to Tulsa. CNN Business. https://edition.cnn.com/2019/10/29/business/10k-for-tulsa-trnd/index.html#:~:text=Tulsa%20Remote%2C%20a%20program%20funded,the%20course%20of%20a%20year

32. Anders, G. (2021, January 20). Shelter in a job? 74% of us are on a cautious path that feels right for 2021. [Blog post]. LinkedIn. https://www.linkedin.com/pulse/shelter-job-74-us-cautious-path-feels-right-2021-george-anders/

33. Australian Government Department of Education, Skills and Employment. (2021, August 23). Golden Gurus funding for mature-age volunteers. Retrieved from https://ministers.dese.gov.au/evans/golden-gurus-funding-mature-age-volunteers

Chapter 3

34. Verywell Mind. (2021). Narrative therapy. https://www.verywellmind.com/narrative-therapy-4172956

35. Association of Fundraising Professionals. (2018). Code of ethical standards. https://afpglobal.org/ethicsmain/code-ethical-standards

Chapter 5

36. Mightycause. (n.d.). Donor Attrition: What It Is and How to Avoid It. https://blog.mightycause.com/donor-attrition/

37. Council of Better Business Bureaus. (n.d.). BBB Standards for Charity Accountability. https://give.org/donor-landing-page/bbb-standards-for-charity-accountability/

Chapter 6

38. Council for Advancement and Support of Education (CASE). (2017). The CASE competencies model. https://www.case.org/focus-future-case-competencies-model

39. Friedman, R. (2019, September 18). Here come the nonprofit unions. The Chronicle of Philanthropy. https://www.philanthropy.com/article/here-come-the-nonprofit-unions

40. Newport, F. (2021, August 17). Approval of labor unions at highest point since 1965. Gallup News. https://news.gallup.com/poll/398303/approval-labor-unions-highest-point-1965.aspx

41. Bureau of Labor Statistics. (2022, January 21). Union members – 2021. News release. https://www.bls.gov/news.release/union2.nr0.htm

42. Autonomy. (n.d.). Iceland's four-day workweek trial to be expanded. https://autonomy.work/portfolio/icelandsww/

43. Veal, A. J. (2007). Whatever happened to the leisure society? London, UK: Routledge.

44. Manyika, J., Chui, M., Miremadi, M., Bughin, J., George, K., Willmott, P., ... & Saleh, T. (2017). Jobs lost, jobs gained: What the future of work will mean for jobs, skills, and wages. McKinsey Global Institute. https://www.mckinsey.com/featured-insights/future-of-work/jobs-lost-jobs-gained-what-the-future-of-work-will-mean-for-jobs-skills-and-wages#

45. Harder+Company Community Research. (2014). Status of Bay Area nonprofit space facilities: Challenges and opportunities. https://harderco.com/sample_work/status-of-bay-area-nonprofit-space-facilities/

46. Given, M. (2018, April 30). Mark Zuckerberg's JFK quote is a master class on the art of leadership. Inc. Australia. https://www.inc-aus.com/matt-given/mark-zuckerbergs-jfk-quote-is-a-master-class-on-th.html

47. Kerr, J. (2013). Legacy: 15 lessons in leadership. Constable

Chapter 7

48. Candid. (n.d.). Open for good: Voices from the field. [Curated content]. Learning for Funders. https://learningforfunders.candid.org/content/curated-content/open-for-good-voices-from-the-field/

49. Sunlight Foundation. (n.d.). Projects & resources. Open Cities. https://sunlightfoundation.com/our-work/open-cities/projects-resources/

50. Goldsmith, S. (2018, March 22). The new localism: Think like a system, act like an entrepreneur. [Blog post]. RSA. https://www.thersa.org/comment/2018/03/the-new-localism-think-like-a-system-act-like-an-entrepreneur

51. Katz, B., & Nowak, J. (2018). The New Localism. Brookings Institution Press

52. PNP Staffing Group. (2019). Retention Report 2019. http://pnpstaffinggroup.com/wp-content/uploads/2019/06/RETEN-TION-REPORT-2019.pdf

53. Independent Sector. (2021). Health of the U.S. nonprofit sector. https://independentsector.org/resource/health-of-the-u-s-nonprofit-sector/

54. Urban Institute. (n.d.). National Center for Charitable Statistics. https://nccs.urban.org/

55. List, J. A. (n.d.). Charitable Giving. https://voices.uchicago.edu/jlist/research/charitable-giving/

56. Manzi, J. (2017, September 11). Looking for the Next Big Thing. City Journal. https://www.city-journal.org/article/looking-for-the-next-big-thing

57. Palmer, O. (2018, February 5). Why Most A/B Tests Will Fail (And That's OK). https://www.oliverpalmer.com/blog/most-ab-tests-fail/

58. Thomke, S. (2020). Experimentation Works: The Surprising Power of Business Experiments. Harvard Business Review Press

59. Maniadis, Z., Tufano, F., & List, J. A. (2017). To Replicate or Not To Replicate? Exploring Reproducibility in Economics through the Lens of a Model and a Pilot Study. Economic Journal, 127(605), F209-F235

60. Social Ventures Australia. (n.d.). Making Replication Work. SVA Quarterly. https://www.socialventures.com.au/sva-quarterly/making-replication-work/

Clubhouse #2

61. Bergstein, A. (2022, March 31). The M+R Benchmarks 2022 Are Here: Monthly Giving +24%! NonProfit Pro. https://www.nonprofitpro.com/post/the-m-r-benchmarks-2022-are-here-monthly-giving-24/

62. Kivi Leroux Miller. (2021, December 6). The Nonprofit Communications Trends Report. Nonprofit Marketing Guide. https://www.nonprofit-marketingguide.com/the-nonprofit-communications-trends-report/

63. IZEA. (2022, January 24). The Lifetime Value of a Blog Post. IZEA. https://izea.com/collabs/the-lifetime-value-of-a-blog-post/

64. Springly. (2020). The State of Nonprofit Technology Report 2020 [PDF file]. https://www.springly.org/wp-content/uploads/2020/11/Springly-State-of-Nonprofit-Technology-Report-2020.pdf

65. Salesforce.org. (2021). Nonprofit Trends Report, Fifth Edition. https://www.salesforce.org/resources/report/nonprofit-trends-report-fifth-edition/

66. NetChange Consulting. (2018). Digital Teams in 2018: The New Landscape of Digital Engagement. https://netchange.co/digital-teams-in-2018-the-new-landscape-of-digital-engagement

67. NetSuite. (n.d.). Dollars to outcomes: A nonprofit's journey to impact. https://www.netsuite.com/portal/business-benchmark-brainyard/industries/articles/nonprofit/dollars-to-outcomes.shtml

68. Sage. (2022). 2022 Nonprofit Technology Trends Report. https://www.sage.com/en-us/cp/tech-trends-nonprofit/

Chapter 8

69. ESCharts. (2023). EMLS Cup 2023. ESCharts. https://escharts.com/tournaments/fifa/emls-cup-2023

70. Statista. (2021). Games - Worldwide | Statista Market Forecast. Statista. https://www.statista.com/outlook/amo/media/games/worldwide

71. Perez, M. (2018, October 15). Esports Company Cloud9 Raises $50 Million In Series B Funding. Forbes. https://www.forbes.com/sites/mattperez/2018/10/15/esports-company-cloud9-raises-50-million-in-series-b-funding/?sh=6ac8a6f33dd3

72. Esports Insider. (2020, April 17). FaZe Clan raises $40m in Series A funding. Esports Insider. https://esportsinsider.com/2020/04/faze-clan-series-a/

73. Perez, M. (2019, February 26). G2 Esports Raises $17.3 Million In Series A Funding. Forbes. https://www.forbes.com/sites/mattperez/2019/02/26/g2-esports-raises-17-3-million-in-series-a-funding/?sh=4f3af56b7492

74. World Wide Fund for Nature (WWF) Australia. (n.d.). Wild Livestream. https://www.wwf.org.au/get-involved/wild-livestream#gs.vkdcyq

75. Donor Participation Project, Inc. (n.d.). Level Up Gaming. https://joindpp.org/levelupgaming/

76. Forbes Business Council. (2020, November 12). How Technology Can Help Nonprofits Prove Their Value To Donors. Forbes. https://www.forbes.com/sites/forbesbusinesscouncil/2020/11/12/how-technology-can-help-nonprofits-prove-their-value-to-donors/?sh=296cc9c721d8

77. National Council of Nonprofits. (n.d.). About Us. https://www.councilofnonprofits.org/about-us

Clubhouse #3

78. Yale School of Management. (2018, February 22). Can Technology Transform the Nonprofit Sector? Yale Insights. https://insights.som.yale.edu/insights/can-technology-transform-the-nonprofit-sector

Chapter 9

79. Simmons, A. (2014, October 28). Why your brain loves good storytelling. Harvard Business Review. https://hbr.org/2014/10/why-your-brain-loves-good-storytelling

80. Funraise. (2021). The State of Modern Philanthropy 2021 Tech Report. https://www.funraise.org/techreport

81. Kumar, N. (2020, January 15). The world wants big tech companies to be regulated. U.S. News & World Report. https://www.usnews.com/news/best-countries/articles/2020-01-15/the-world-wants-big-tech-companies-to-be-regulated

82. SmallBizGenius. (2021, January 12). 48 cold calling statistics that even the most experienced salespeople don't know. SmallBizGenius. https://www.smallbizgenius.net/by-the-numbers/cold-calling-statistics/

83. Cognism. (2021, March 16). Cold calling success rates: A comprehensive guide. Cognism Blog. https://www.cognism.com/blog/cold-calling-success-rates

84. Amazon Web Services. (2018, May 2). Babylon health: Revolutionizing healthcare with AI and AWS [Video file].https://www.youtube.com/watch?v=Y8NkwQLo-6o

85. Blinkoff, J. (2019, May 22). The effective call time fundraising script. Medium.https://medium.com/call-time/the-effective-call-time-fundraising-script-b3b089631428

Chapter 10

86. Manyika, J., Chui, M., Brown, B., Bughin, J., Dobbs, R., Roxburgh, C., & Byers, A. H. (2011, May). How to get the most from big data. McKinsey & Company. https://www.mckinsey.com/business-functions/mckinsey-digital/our-insights/how-to-get-the-most-from-big-data

87. Crozier, R. (2022, August 2). Kmart Australia embeds 'data translators' in its key operational areas. ITnews. https://www.itnews.com.au/news/kmart-australia-embeds-data-translators-in-its-key-operational-areas-582982

88. Marr, B. (2018, March 12). Forget Data Scientists And Hire A Data Translator Instead. Forbes. https://www.forbes.com/sites/bernardmarr/2018/03/12/forget-data-scientists-and-hire-a-data-translator-instead/?sh=7b4bb745848a

89. King, A., & Grassley, C. E. (2019, May 23). King, Grassley Introduce Legislation to Ensure Charitable Donations Reach Working Charities. Press Release. Office of Senator Angus King Jr. https://www.king.senate.gov/newsroom/press-releases/king-grassley-introduce-legislation-to-ensure-charitable-donations-reach-working-charities

90. Accelerate Charitable Giving. (n.d.). About. https://acceleratecharitable-giving.org/about/

91. Hadero, H. (2021, July 20). Accelerate Charitable Giving program hits 25,000 donations. AP News. https://apnews.com/article/business-government-and-politics-philanthropy-96d20b59013d25fd1edf504587888c2d

92. Swanson, A. (2016, October 27). America's biggest charity is no longer what most people think of as a charity. The Washington Post. https://www.washingtonpost.com/news/wonk/wp/2016/10/27/americas-biggest-charity-is-no-longer-what-most-people-think-of-as-a-charity/

93. "Online Giving Statistics You Need to Know in 2022." Nonprofits Source. Accessed on April 17, 2023. https://nonprofitssource.com/online-giving-statistics/

94. Deloitte. (2018). Cognitive technologies in the enterprise: An adoption survey. Deloitte Analytics. https://www2.deloitte.com/us/en/pages/deloitte-analytics/articles/cognitive-technology-adoption-survey.html

95. Sheehan, J. (2020). The state of artificial intelligence in the nonprofit sector. Powered by Impact. https://pwrdby.com/the-state-of-artificial-intelligence-in-the-nonprofit-sector/

96. "Philanthropy Tech 2020: Innovation, Access, and Equity." Technology Association of Grantmakers (TAG). Accessed on April 15, 2021. https://www.tagtech.org/page/philanthropytech2020

97. "Use Cases." Levity. Accessed on April 15, 2021. https://levity.ai/use-cases/

Chapter 11

98. Avery, D. (2021, September 4). In the midst of political crisis and un-certainty, affordable housing remains scarce in Haiti. Architectural Digest. https://www.architecturaldigest.com/story/in-the-midst-of-political-crisis-and-uncertainty-affordable-housing-remains-scarce-in-haiti

99. Canales, K. (2019, October 13). An Austin startup can 3D-print tiny homes in 24 hours for a fraction of the cost of traditional homebuilding — here's how Icon could revolutionize affordable housing. Business Insider. https://www.businessinsider.com/icon-3d-printer-tiny-home-austin-photos-2019-10

100. Smith, N. (2021, December 15). Blockchain Based Fundraising is Expanding. Retrieved from https://www.dunhamandcompany.com/crypto-currency/blockchain-based-fundraising-is-expanding/ (Updated: February 14, 2022)

101. Fidelity Charitable. (2018, February 26). Growing popularity of crypto-currency could fuel charitable giving. Fidelity Charitable. https://www.fideli-tycharitable.org/about-us/news/growing-popularity-of-cryptocurrency-could-fuel-charitable-giving.html

102. Locke, T. (2021, November 8). Ether hits all-time high, NFT infra-structure bill: Crypto news. CNBC. https://www.cnbc.com/2021/11/08/crypto-news-ether-hit-an-all-time-high-nftnyc-infrastructure-bill.html

103. Wright, T. (2021, November 30). Charity platform expects significantly larger crypto than fiat donations for Giving Tuesday. Coin-telegraph. https://cointelegraph.com/news/charity-platform-expects-signifi-cantly-larger-crypto-than-fiat-donations-for-giving-tuesday

104. The Giving Block. (2022, November 29). Crypto Giving Tuesday 2022: Recap. Retrieved December 21, 2022, from https://go.thegivingblock.com/crypto-giving-tuesday-2022#recap

105. Bowden, J., & Jones, E. T. (2021). NFTs are much bigger than an art fad – here's how they could change the world. The Conversation. https://the-conversation.com/nfts-are-much-bigger-than-an-art-fad-heres-how-they-could-change-the-world-159563

106. Ebrahim, A. (2013, March). Let's be realistic about measuring social impact. Harvard Business Review. https://hbr.org/2013/03/lets-be-realistic-about-measuring.html

107. The Giving Block. (2018, April 5). Pineapple Fund Bitcoin Donated to Nonprofits: Here's What Happened. Retrieved from https://thegiving-block.com/updates/news/pineapple-fund-bitcoin-donated-to-nonprofits-here-s-what-happened/

108. Nafarrete, J. (2015, November 2). How Pencils of Promise raised $1.9M with the help of VR. VRScout. https://vrscout.com/news/pencils-of-promise-virtual-reality/#

109. Shen, J. (2021). VR for social impact: Integrating virtual reality into the nonprofit space. Semantic Scholar. https://www.semanticscholar.org/paper/VR-for-Social-Impact%3A-Integrating-Virtual-Reality-Shen/c73468f362776c95b04a9c6a5418e257904fd0b2

110. Swant, M. (2016, May 31). How Virtual Reality Is Inspiring Donors to Dig Deep for Charitable Causes. Adweek. https://www.adweek.com/performance-marketing/how-virtual-reality-inspiring-donors-dig-deep-charitable-causes-171641/

111. Boland, M. (2021, February 2). New Report: VR Revenue to Reach $12.2 Billion by 2024. VR/AR Association. https://www.thevrara.com/blog2/2019/2/20/will-ars-killer-app-be-social-new-report-rwccm-g8ajl-e4sr5-b9f9r-gt64y-5e3e8-asrs2-d9xry-ymp6b-7s7bl-cbtsm-39bwj

112. Amnesty International UK. (2016, March 11). 360°Syria virtual tour website reveals devastation of Aleppo barrel bombing. Amnesty International UK. https://www.amnesty.org.uk/press-releases/360syria-virtual-tour-website-reveals-devastation-aleppo-barrel-bombing

About The Author

Ryan Ginard, CFRE, is the international award-winning author of Future Philanthropy: The Tech, Trends & Talent Defining New Civic Leadership and founder of Fundraise for Australia, a social enterprise whose mission is to identify, recruit and train over 1000 new fundraisers by 2030, leveraging an additional $120 million in charitable donations as the Government of Australia seeks to double giving by 2030.

Currently the Head of Advancement for Australia's top-ranked university, The Australian National University, Ryan's career in organized philanthropy has seen him lead dedicated efforts in civic engagement, public policy, operations, and fundraising at the University of Texas at Austin, The San Diego Foundation, and as Chief of Staff for a $185 million philanthropic program across early education and charitable giving, impacting over 11 million students and 22,000 schools across 20 countries including the top 10 school districts in the U.S.

An active writer and thinker about future directions in philanthropy, Ryan has had his work highlighted in numerous sector-leading publications and has been a speaker at internationally renowned conferences such as South By South West (SXSW), the Public Relations Society of America's International Conference (PRSA ICON), Good Tech Fest and Social Media Week, on themes focused on civic technology and immersive storytelling.

Ryan's work has leveraged over $2.5 billion in community infrastructure funding and raised over $35 million for charity and groundbreaking academic research including transformative gifts in machine learning, computational oncology, and social justice efforts.

Other available titles from the author;

Future Philanthropy
The Tech, Trends & Talent Defining New Civic Leadership.

Printed in the USA
CPSIA information can be obtained
at www.ICGtesting.com
LVHW020725290923
757852LV00035B/360